RUBY WIZARDRY

AN INTRODUCTION TO PROGRAMMING FOR KIDS

BY ERIC WEINSTEIN

no starch press

San Francisco

Printed in USA

First printing

18 17 16 15 14   1 2 3 4 5 6 7 8 9

ISBN-10: 1-59327-566-8
ISBN-13: 978-1-59327-566-2

Publisher: William Pollock
Production Editor: Riley Hoffman
Cover Illustration: Karen Teixeira
Developmental Editor: Tyler Ortman
Technical Reviewers: Peter Cooper and Pat Shaughnessy
Copyeditor: Rachel Monaghan
Compositor: Riley Hoffman
Proofreader: Paula L. Fleming
Indexer: Nancy Guenther

For information on distribution, translations, or bulk sales, please contact No Starch Press, Inc. directly:
No Starch Press, Inc.
245 8th Street, San Francisco, CA 94103
phone: 415.863.9900; info@nostarch.com
www.nostarch.com

Library of Congress Control Number: 2014953112

To my teachers

About the Author

Eric Weinstein has helped millions of people learn to program through Codecademy, where he designed and authored the Ruby curriculum and contributed courses on Python, JavaScript, HTML/CSS, and PHP. He has also taught creative writing to undergraduates and veterans of the wars in Iraq and Afghanistan at New York University, where he was a Veterans Writing Workshop Fellow. He writes Ruby for a living in New York City.

About the Technical Reviewers

Peter Cooper is the editor of *Ruby Weekly*, a chair of O'Reilly's Fluent web development conference, and the author of *Beginning Ruby* (Apress). He tweets at @peterc.

Pat Shaughnessy is the author of *Ruby Under a Microscope* (No Starch Press) and also blogs at *http://patshaughnessy.net/*. A fluent Spanish speaker, Pat frequently visits his wife's family in northern Spain. Pat lives outside of Boston with his wife and two children.

Brief Contents

Contents in detail

4
Staying in the Loop 47

5
Array of Sunshine and Hash on the Range 63

6
The (Chunky) Bacon to Ruby's Hash 91

7
The Magic of Methods and Blocks 109

8

EVERYCHINg IS an OBJECC (ALMOSC)

9

Inheriting the magic of Ruby

FOREWORD

A long time ago, I was a little kid growing up on a farm in rural Pennsylvania. My hometown is small enough that my parents' farm was just half a mile down the road from my maternal grandparents' house, my mother's childhood home.

One day, when I was seven years old, I was visiting my grandparents. It just so happened that one of my uncles also dropped by on that particular day. He wanted to give my grandparents a present: their first computer, a Mac Plus.

You see, my uncle was heavily involved in all kinds of computing shenanigans. And computers were still a new thing in those days, so not many people had them. My grandparents, caring about their son and his interests, decided it would be a good idea to check out this whole "computer" thing.

Excited by all the hubbub, my uncle called me over to the computer and explained what it was. He told me that you could do all kinds of things with computers, but that

he thought I might like this one. On the screen appeared these
immortal words:

```
                    Welcome to ADVENTURE!

            Original development by Willie Crowther
               Major features added by Don Woods
           Conversion to BDS C by J. R. Jaeger
               Unix standardization by Jerry D. Pohl
                Conversion to PHP by Matt G. S. Cox
                Adapted for AMC.com by Rick Adams

To play the game, type short phrases into the command line below.
If you type the word "look," the game gives you a description of
your surroundings.  Typing "inventory" tells you what you're
carrying.  "Get" "drop" and "throw" helps you interact with
objects.  Part of the game is trying out different commands and
seeing what happens.  Type "help" at any time for game
instructions.

Would you like more instructions? no

You are standing at the end of a road before a small brick
building.  Around you is a forest.  A small stream flows out
of the building and down a gully.

What's next?
```

Then, just a blinking cursor. By typing in simple instructions, I was able to explore a wonderful world, with an endless
cave, a sneaky pirate, and a maze of twisty little passages, all
alike. I was absolutely enthralled. My uncle told me, offhand-
edly, that some people called *programmers* had to actually
teach the computer know how to play the game. I was hooked.
I started asking to "go see Grandma" so much that my parents
started saying, "You don't want to see Grandma, you want to
play with Grandma's computer."

"No, I want to see Grandma *and* play with her computer," I
replied.

Today, computers are very different. That Mac Plus had an 8 MHz processor, which could handle 1.4 million instructions per second. It also had 1MB of RAM. An iPhone 5s, today, has a 1.3 GHz processor, which can handle 18200 million instructions per second, and has 1GB of RAM. Games today don't present you with some text; they present you with full 3D graphics.

But I still firmly believe that a computer can change a child's life.

Ruby Wizardry is a book that captures that wonder I had as a child, sitting at this thing they called a "keyboard" for the first time. Ruby is a much nicer programming language than the GW-BASIC I cut my teeth on, but the core idea is the same. Give a child a way to bring their imagination to life, and amazing things will happen.

I hope *Ruby Wizardry* brings you the same joy that computers have always brought me.

Steve Klabnik

acknowledgments

This book would not have been possible without the tireless efforts of dozens—possibly even dozens of dozens!—of people.

First, my wife, Laura, who not only tolerated my all-night writing sessions and endless requests for feedback on story ideas, but also at various times pinch hit as literary agent, proofreader, sanity checker, and stop-reading-the-Internet-and-get-back-to-work!-er. This book would never have come to be without her love and support.

My family, especially my father, who read to me almost every night for years, and my mother, who (for better or worse) taught me that I could do anything to which I stubbornly committed myself.

My teachers, to whom this book is dedicated, particularly my teachers in the Ruby community: Cole Brown, Linda Liukas, and Dean Strelau, as well as all the brilliant, dedicated facilitators and students at Hacker School.

Of course, *Ruby Wizardry* would not have been possible without Tyler Ortman, Riley Hoffman, Bill Pollock, and the amazing people at No Starch Press. I literally can't thank them enough for their insight, energy, and dedication.

Steve Klabnik, who read an early version of this book and wrote a wonderful foreword for it, as well as Peter Cooper and Pat Shaughnessy, who did the technical review and gave me much greater insight into the nitty-gritty of the Ruby language. All three are phenomenal teachers and Rubyists.

why the lucky stiff, whose book *why's (Poignant) Guide to Ruby* was one of the first Ruby books I read and who was the first to really show me the significance of and enthusiasm for art in the language and the community. I hope this book evokes some of the same feelings of excitement and wonder I felt when reading why's work.

Finally, Dave, who introduced me to Bill at No Starch Press and made this whole thing possible.

1
What This Book's About

You found this book! Okay, awesome. I was really hoping it would get to you.

Imagine someone tells you he's discovered a new way of writing. Not a new language, like French or Japanese or Elvish, but a whole new *kind* of writing that makes your stories *actually happen*. If you described a maze, people could enter—and get lost in—that maze. If you wrote about a far-away planet where robot pirates fought ninja wizards, that planet would totally exist. Not only that, but you could write dialogue like "Beep boop shiver me circuits" or cast spells like ninja_wizard.throw_flaming_ninja_stars. Crazy, right? And that's probably exactly what you'd say: that this is completely crazy and whoever thought of it has too much time on his hands. Too much imagination.

Well, it turns out there's no such thing as too much imagination. So! Imagine me this: not only is this crazy new way of writing *real*, but you can learn how to do it. You could, with a little practice, figure out how to make your own worlds with your own rules. You'd be in charge, and you could do pretty much anything you could think of. Not only that, but if you got really good at it, people would come from all over to experience the worlds you built and use all the amazing things you created.

You can stop imagining (for now, at least). I'm telling you that this is true! And this book can help you do it. The pages you now hold in your hands are a guide to a *programming language* called *Ruby* that will let you do all these things, and all you need is your brain, a computer, and Ruby.

How can this be? you might be thinking. *If something this cool and powerful existed, I definitely would have heard about it by now.*

Which brings us to our next topic.

Why Learn Programming (and Why Ruby)?

Learning to program sounded boring to me when I was younger. I thought programming and computers were all about math and logic—that there was no room to be creative or do anything interesting. All day long, people told me what to do: go to school, walk the dog, go to the dentist, do my homework. I figured programming would be more of the same, so I avoided it completely. Instead, I wrote stories about space travel, magic, and distant worlds where not only did amazing things happen, but I was in charge! I still write stories all the time, but even the best stories end when the reader turns the last page. As much as you want starships or ninja wizards to be real, writing stories about them doesn't make that happen. So I did write a lot of stories, but I also had to go to the dentist.

Then something very strange happened: I decided to give programming a try. I discovered that this thing I thought would be terribly dry and boring was exactly the opposite—it was challenging and fun. Suddenly, I was calling the shots! If I told the computer to make a puzzle game, it made a puzzle game. If I told it to make a website, it made a website. It made real things in the world that I could see, play with, and use. It was as if all the stories I had been writing for years could now come to life, and all it took was this little box and a language I could use to talk to it.

It's true that some programming languages are hard, and some are downright confusing. Ruby is different: it was designed to make you happy—to be easy for *you* to read and understand, not just the computer. Ruby was built to help you tell stories that computers and human beings can both enjoy, and so instead of weird symbols or words like static and void, you get programs that look almost like English, with words like unless, rescue, self, and even begin and end.

Just as with any programming language, learning Ruby will help you learn important skills, make cool things, and feel accomplished. But mostly, you'll just have *fun*. And among programming languages, I think Ruby is the most fun.

Let's say you wanted to program the computer to say "Howdy!" If you wanted to do this in another language—for instance, Java—you might have to write something really complicated, like this:

```
class Howdy {
  public static void main (String[] args) {
    System.out.println("Howdy!");
  }
}
```

That's a lot of code to print one word. To do the same thing in Ruby, you just type:

```
puts "Howdy!"
```

That's it! Ruby puts the word right there on the screen. Simple, right? Ruby is all about making you a happy and productive programmer (oh yeah—you're a programmer now), so it gets rid of a lot of complicated *syntax* (like { and ;) and lets you avoid writing boring things like `public static void main` all over the place. And since Ruby can do pretty much all the stuff that trickier languages like Java can do, you'll be able to build amazing things faster and with less effort.

Let's get started!

all adults on deck: Installing Ruby

All right—this is the part where you might want to grab your mom, dad, grandpa, grandma, aunt, uncle, teacher, or another local adult to help you install Ruby on your computer. Ruby is free, but you'll need an Internet connection to download it if you don't already have it.

The directions are a little different depending on which kind of computer you have, so ask your adult if you're not sure!

If you're running Windows, skip ahead to page 6.

Installing on Mac or Linux

First, let's check to see if you already have Ruby installed. If you're on a Mac or a computer running Linux, you can check to see which version of Ruby you have on the *command line*—this is where you'll be typing your Ruby programs.

The command line is probably very different from the way you usually use your computer (clicking icons and moving things with your mouse), but once you get used to it, the command line can be much faster and easier.

On a Mac or Linux computer, your command line is in an application called *Terminal*. Find your Terminal application and open it. You should see something like this:

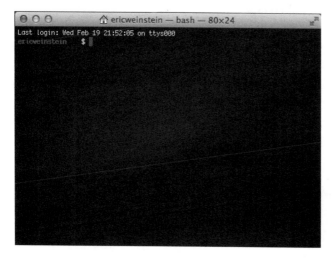

Once you've got the Terminal open, go ahead and type the following line (you don't need to type the dollar sign—just the ruby -v bit) and press ENTER:

```
$ ruby -v
```

If Ruby is installed, you'll get back something like this:

```
ruby 2.0.0p247
```

If you get this response and it includes 2.0.0, you're all set! Skip ahead to "Achievement Unlocked: Ruby Installed!" on page 8. If you get a number other than 2.0.0 (for instance,

1.9.3 or 1.8.7), we'll need to get you on version 2.0.0 (the version this book uses). If your computer is super fancy, you might already be on Ruby 2.1—the code in this book should work in Ruby 2.1, too. For maximum awesomeness and minimal errors, you should run all the examples using Ruby 2.0.0.

If your computer says something like this:

```
-bash: ruby: command not found
```

then you don't have Ruby. No worries. Grab an adult and skip to Appendix A for detailed step-by-step instructions. We'll install it there! Come back to this chapter when you're done.

Installing on Windows

If you're on a PC running Windows, you can check if Ruby is installed by opening the *command prompt*. We'll be using Windows 7 in this example. You can open the command prompt from the Start menu or by searching for *cmd.exe*; once you find it, double-click it to open the application. You should see something like this:

Your command prompt—the little bit before the >—will probably be different from mine, but that's okay! Type **ruby -v** and then press ENTER:

```
> ruby -v
```

If you get a response that includes 2.0.0, you're all set! If you see a Ruby version other than 2.0.0, or if you get this error:

```
'ruby' is not recognized as an internal or external command,
operable program or batch file.
```

then we'll need to go ahead and install Ruby. Let's get to it!

Using RubyInstaller

The easiest way to install Ruby on Windows is to go to *http://rubyinstaller.org/downloads/* and download Ruby 2.0.0-p481. (Don't worry if the number after the *p* on the installation website is a little higher than what's shown here; that just means that version is very slightly newer, but it's still Ruby 2.0 and should work great.) Once the download is finished, go to the folder where you saved the *.exe* file and double-click it to run the installer. Here's what it will ask you to do:

1. When it prompts you for the language to use during installation, choose "English" (or whichever language you know best).
2. The installer will ask you to accept its license agreement. Check "I accept the License" and then click **Next**.
3. The installer will ask you where you'd like to install Ruby, defaulting to C:\Ruby200. This is great! You'll also see a checkbox that says "Add Ruby executables to your PATH." Make sure that box is checked, then click **Install**.
4. If all goes well, you should get a "Completing the Ruby Setup Wizard" screen. Click **Finish**, and you're done!

Once the installer runs, close your command prompt, reopen it, and enter `ruby -v`; you should see your computer print a response with `ruby 2.0.0` in it. Mine looks like this (yours might be slightly different):

```
ruby 2.0.0p481 (2014-05-08) [i386-mingw32]
```

Achievement Unlocked: Ruby Installed!

Perfect! Now that you've got Ruby installed, we can start learning our way around. In the next chapter, we'll cover some Ruby basics and learn how to use Ruby interactively, meaning you'll get to see Ruby run your code just by pressing the ENTER key. In the chapters that follow, you'll learn the ins and outs of the Ruby language through a series of stories. Since Ruby programs are, after all, just stories you write for the computer to understand, and Ruby is all about writing code that's nice for people and computers to read, I figure it only makes sense to use stories to show you how it all works. They're pretty good stories, I think.

You might be tempted to just read the code in this book and say to yourself, "Yup, this makes sense! I don't need to run the code." I thought that was true when I started programming, but boy, was I wrong. The only way to learn how to write code is, well, to write code, and you're cheating yourself out of a lot of really cool knowledge if you only read these examples and never run a line of Ruby.

One more word of advice before we set out on our adventure: you might have to read something more than once or run a piece of code a few times to really get it. That's okay! Learning to program isn't just a new way of writing—it's a new way of thinking, too. It might be a little hard sometimes, but I promise that if you stick with it, you'll get it. Believe me, there are people way less smart and enthusiastic than you who have learned how to program, and if they can do it, so can you.

Putting on the Ruby Slippers

Okay, so you've got your very own copy of Ruby, and you know that Ruby is a language you can use to tell computers to do anything you want. But you're probably overflowing with questions: Where did Ruby come from? Who created it and why? What amazing things have been created with it? What *good* is Ruby?

Well, question no more: I'll give you all those answers (plus a few bonus ones).

While computers were invented about a bajillion years ago (the first devices you'd recognize as computers were created in the 1940s), Ruby was cooked up relatively recently, in 1993. You might think that 1993 was a bajillion years ago, too, and in some ways, you're right. The Internet only had about a hundred websites. Nobody had smartphones. In fact, most people's phones were *connected to their walls by wires*. These were dark times.

But in the ancient world of the mid-1990s, a man named Yukihiro Matsumoto (or just "Matz" to his friends) was busy trying to invent the future. He was frustrated by programming languages that were designed to make life easy for computers but were hard for people to understand, read, remember, and use. Why wasn't there a language that was built to be easy for *people* to use, a language that was clear, simple—and even fun?

Matz realized that his ideal programming language didn't exist, so he created it. "I hope to see Ruby help every programmer in the world to be productive, and to enjoy programming, and to be happy," Matz has said. "That is the primary purpose of the Ruby language."[*] And that's Ruby in a nutshell: a *fun* way for you to create games, websites, or anything you can imagine with just your brain and a computer. Matz has had such a positive influence on the language he created that Ruby programmers have a saying: "Matz is nice, so we are nice," or MINSWAN. Remember MINSWAN when you're learning Ruby and especially when you're teaching it to others!

Which reminds me: there are a lot of amazing things you can create with Ruby. Over the last few years, Ruby has been used to build major websites like Twitter and Hulu, iPhone apps, and even NASA simulations. That's right: you can use Ruby to explore space! People are using Ruby for more and more projects every day, and with all the cool new tools and ideas constantly coming from the Ruby community, your imagination's really the only limit when it comes to building your own programs.

---

* Google Tech Talks, Feb. 2008 (*https://www.youtube.com/watch?v=oEkJvvGEtB4*).

These programs are written in *scripts*. This means that instead of having to do a long and boring process called *compiling*, you can just write a quick Ruby program, run it, and presto!

Your website is up, your game is working, your starship is shooting lasers at a witch queen. But how do you run these Ruby scripts? For that, we'll need to learn about the ruby command and a little program called *IRB*.

Getting to Know IRB

In Ruby, you can print something to the screen just by typing the puts command. Let's say we want to print out "Ruby is awesome!" Let's give it a try—first we have to open IRB, a program for exploring Ruby.

If you're using Mac or Linux, open the terminal and type:

```
$ irb
```

You only need to type irb, not the dollar sign; the dollar sign is my way of showing you that you should type something in the terminal.

If you're using Windows, you can run IRB from the Start menu.

Once you have IRB open, you should see something like this:

```
2.0.0p247 :001 >
```

That's IRB's *prompt*, which is IRB's way of telling you it's ready for you to type something. It might look a bit different to you depending on your Ruby version, but it should end with a >.

In this book, we'll simplify that to look like this:

```
>>
```

Whenever you see >>, we'll be using IRB. If you type this after the >> (don't forget the quotation marks—they're very important!):

```
>> puts "Ruby is awesome!"
```

when you press ENTER, you should see Ruby print out:

```
Ruby is awesome!
=> nil
```

Excellent! We've written a simple program to print some text to the screen. You'll also see Ruby say something about "nil." Don't worry about this just yet; I'll explain that part in a little while. (If you can't wait: basically, this is Ruby telling you that it's all done printing and has nothing else to give you. You'll learn all about nil in Chapter 7.) The cool thing is, you've just written your very first Ruby program!

IRB will continue to prompt you and wait for you to type things until you tell it to stop, which you can do at any time by typing exit (or just quitting your terminal program).

Using a Text Editor and the Ruby Command

The other way of writing Ruby commands is as a script, which is just writing many lines and then running them all at once, instead of one at a time. To write a script, you'll need a program called a *text editor*. (This is *not* something like Microsoft Word, which is a *word processor*; a word processor is great for writing stories or reports for school, but it's terrible for writing programs.)

NOTE *You can download all the scripts that appear in this book at* http://nostarch.com/rubywizardry/. *But if you're learning to program and following along with the story, try typing things out instead of just copying and pasting! You'll learn a lot more.*

Mac

All Macs come with a text editor called TextEdit (you can find it in your *Applications* folder). It's very simple to use and works great for writing Ruby programs. If you're looking for something with a little more pizzazz, you can download a very nice free text editor called Sublime Text 2 from *http://www.sublimetext.com/2* (you'll need OS X 10.6 or later).

Linux

There are a number of good editors for Linux, but Gedit is one of my favorites. You can download it from *https://wiki.gnome.org/ Apps/Gedit*. Sublime Text 2 is also a very good editor for Linux and is available at *http://www.sublimetext.com/2*.

Windows

As I just mentioned, Microsoft Word is *not* good for writing programs. Notepad++, on the other hand, is a great free text editor for Windows that you can get from *http://notepad-plus-plus.org/ download/v6.6.7.html*. You can also use the Sublime Text 2 editor, available at *http://www.sublimetext.com/2*.

Creating Your First Script

Once you've installed a text editor, open it and type the same thing you typed in IRB:

```
puts "Ruby is awesome!"
```

Go ahead and save this file as ***awesome.rb*** in any folder you'd like (it's a good idea to create a *ruby* folder now to put all your Ruby programs in). Then, open your terminal and change into the folder where you saved *awesome.rb*. Here's how to do that with the `cd` command:

- On Mac or Linux, your prompt (the bit to the left of the $ on the command line) looks something like /Users/*username* $. If you saved *awesome.rb* in a folder called *ruby* in your home folder, you can get to that folder on the command line by entering:

```
$ cd /Users/username/ruby
```

Don't type the $ part, just everything after it. Also, don't literally type *username*; you should replace that with whatever you see in your prompt! (Mine is /Users/eweinstein/, but yours will be different.)

- On Windows, your prompt (the bit to the left of the > on the command line) looks something like C:\Users*username*. If you saved *awesome.rb* in a folder called *ruby* in your home folder, you can get to that folder on the command line by entering:

```
> cd C:\Users\username\ruby
```

Don't type the > part, just everything after it. Also, don't literally type *username*; you should replace that with whatever you see in your prompt.

Once you're in the *ruby* folder, enter:

```
$ ruby awesome.rb
```

You should see Ruby print out:

```
Ruby is awesome!
```

And that's you running your first Ruby script. Nice work!

When to Use IRB and When to Use a Text Editor

So if we type the same thing into IRB and into our script file, and we get the same output, what's the difference between the two? Basically, IRB will let you try out only one line of code at a time; every time you press the ENTER key, IRB will read, or *evaluate*, the code you wrote and spit out an answer. It's a great way to try things out and see if they work.

This means that every time you press ENTER, Ruby will interrupt you with the result of calculating each line, like this:

```
>> 2 + 5
=> 7
>> 24 * 10
=> 240
>> 'Hi ' + 'there!'
=> "Hi there!"
```

The code in bold is what you've typed; below it is the response you get from IRB when you press ENTER. We don't always need all that noise! Sometimes we just want to know the final result of all our work. To do that, we can write this same code as a script. Just open your editor from earlier (for example, TextEdit if you're on a Mac, Gedit if you're using Linux, or Notepad++ for a PC running Windows) and type the following:

```
puts 2 + 5
puts 24 * 10
puts 'Hi ' + 'there!'
```

Then save the script as *script_example.rb*, or any name you like with a *.rb* at the end (but no spaces allowed!), use cd to switch into the directory where you saved the script, and finally run the script with the ruby command:

```
$ ruby script_example.rb
```

This way, we'll just get the printed-out information we want, without having to type line by line:

```
7
240
Hi there!
```

Not only is this easier to read, but we can now run the script over and over with `ruby script_example.rb` and do our calculations without retyping all the commands each time. We can save our program forever, change it, and build on it later.

The Prompts Used in This Book

Throughout the book, we'll alternate between using IRB for small bits of code and running scripts for longer ones. Whenever you see the IRB prompt, which looks like this:

```
>>
```

that means you should be running the code using IRB; when you don't see it, it means you should type the script in your text editor and run it using the `ruby` command. Here's what an IRB example looks like:

```
>> 2 + 2
=> 4
```

Let's take a moment to talk about what each piece of this code does. The `>>` bit says, "We're in IRB, which is a program that understands Ruby commands." Remember, you don't want to type `>>`; this just lets you know we're using IRB. The `>>` in the book represents the IRB prompt on your own computer.

The bold code that reads `2 + 2` is a command for you to enter—type these lines exactly, then press ENTER. When you see several bold lines at an IRB prompt, just type them one at a time, pressing ENTER after each line.

But the second line in this code begins with `=>`. This is what IRB spits back out in response after you press ENTER. (That means you don't have to type these bits either.) If you get an error after typing a command instead of seeing the result shown in the book, make sure you've typed your Ruby commands *exactly*. Computers are very dumb: they do exactly what you *say* and not always what you *want!*

Other programs in the book are longer, so you'll want to be able to change or improve them and fix mistakes. That means you'll want to write them with a text editor. I'll remind you of what to use for each example as we go. But remember, when you don't see IRB's >>, you'll want to use a text editor.

Once we jump into the story, you'll hear about *Computing Contraptions*. These are imaginary versions of computers just like yours, and whenever you see characters in the story running Ruby on a Computing Contraption, they're really just giving IRB and Ruby a spin, so you can follow along yourself at home.

Finally, some of the scripts later in the book get pretty long. I'll break those up into multiple sections and narrate each one. You'll see numbered balls that look like this:

❶ ❷ ❸ ❹ ❺

I'll refer to those numbers in the text so you can walk through each of the examples step-by-step. You don't type these into the computer; they're just for reference!

Again, don't worry if you forget the differences between the IRB and Ruby script prompts—I'll remind you as we go along!

Into the Shiny Red Yonder

Don't worry about understanding all the code you just saw in these examples. We've only just started learning Ruby, and I promise we'll go through all of its secrets over the course of the next few chapters. We'll cover how to handle text and numbers, how to help our programs make decisions based on information they get from the people using them, how to create our own Ruby commands, how to write scripts that will connect to websites on the Internet, and much more.

I said earlier that writing Ruby is more like writing stories than writing instructions for a machine, so I'll be using stories to teach you how Ruby works. In the pages that follow, I'll introduce you to a few characters who will help explain everything you'd ever want to know about Ruby. Some will be expert Ruby programmers, and some, like you, will be brand new to the language. Many will have all sorts of problems that they think can't be solved, but with a bit of hard work and some Ruby magic, they'll find out that their troubles aren't nearly as bad as they seem. Speaking of magic, there'll be a bit of that, too—a king, a queen, a castle, an enchanted (possibly slightly haunted) forest, a wandering minstrel, some witches and wizards, a dragon or two, and a couple of kids a lot like you who have wandered into this crazy kingdom and have no choice but to explore . . .

Scarlet!

Ruben!

2
the KING
and his
STRING

a short yarn

The King was in a foul mood. I mean a *truly terrible*, scream-at-the-cat, throw-a-snowglobe-out-a-third-story-window kind of mood. If you saw him rumbling toward you down the sidewalk, you would quickly change sides of the street. If he were your dad, you would write letters to Santa year-round asking for a replacement dad. Really, it was capital-*B* Bad News Bears for everyone.

The thing is, the King had lost his favorite possession that morning, somewhere between eating his usual breakfast of parched oats and his pre-late-afternoon vigorous stroll. He had turned his palace upside-down (literally: the King had a lot of money and a lot of servants), but to no avail. When Scarlet and Ruben found him, he was weeping bitterly in his study, sitting in an overstuffed armchair of solid gold.

"What did it look like?" Scarlet asked.

"What did *what* look like?" asked the King, gargling slightly on his own salty tears as they flowed down his finely coiffed moustache and into his mouth.

"The thing you lost," said Ruben.

"Like a string!" said the King. "Because that's what it was: a string, with a knot on each end to secure my bits and trinkets. This particular string had several beads on it that spelled out 'Property of His Royal Highness, the King,' like so:

'Property of His Royal Highness, the King'

"A string of letters," said Ruben.

"More like a string of *characters*," said the King. "Each letter is really very unique. The *K*, for instance, is a crooked fellow. And don't even get me started on the *p*—"

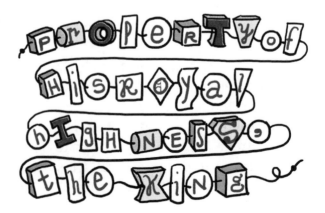

But Ruben and Scarlet weren't listening. They were already searching high and low for the King's missing string.

"Could your string have fallen into this Mysterious Pipe?" Scarlet asked, gesturing toward a sputtering black metal pipe with the words *Mysterious Pipe* written on it in white chalk.

"No," said the King. "The Mysterious Pipe is deceptively narrow at the top, and a string as long as mine could never fit into it."

"How long *is* your string?" Ruben asked.

"I'm not sure," said the King. "I suppose we could count all the characters, and then we'd know." (Take it from me: this would be super boring.)

"That would be boring," said Scarlet. "I think there's a better way." She walked to a corner of the room, blew the dust off a very old Computing Contraption, and carefully typed the following at its little green IRB prompt:

```
>> 'Property of His Royal Highness, the King'.length
=> 40
```

"Great coats!" said the King. "That's right! I remember now—my string is precisely 40 characters long. But how did you do that?"

"Ruby has lots of great tricks like this," said Scarlet. "Here's another."

```
>> 'Property of His Royal Highness, the King'.reverse
=> "gniK eht ,ssenhgiH layoR siH fo ytreporP"
```

The King nodded. "Yes, that's pretty much what my string looks like in the mirror when I hang it up to dry after a refreshing shower."

In the meantime, Ruben had been counting the number of characters in the King's string using a bit of chalk he found resting near the Mysterious Pipe. "Hang on a second," he said. "I'm counting 42 characters, including the quotation marks on each end."

The King snorted like an overweight wiener dog. "You don't count those!" he said. "Those are the little knots on each end that keep the characters contained! You only count the characters, not the quotes."

"And that's exactly what Ruby does," explained Scarlet. "But you have to put quotes around your strings, or Ruby will think you're trying to use a *variable*."

a Bit more about Variables

Believe you me, this confused the bejeepers out of the King. Since he's not nearly as bright a bulb as you are, I'll let Ruben and Scarlet spend ages explaining variables to him while I take a moment to explain them to you.

A Ruby variable is just a name (without quotes!) that you can give to a *value* (which is a piece of information, like the words that make up the King's string). One kind of value is a string; another kind is a *number*, which you already saw when Ruby told you that the length of the King's string was 40.

You make a variable like this:

```
>> kings_string = 'A string fit for a king'
>> wiener_dog_weight = 22
```

The equal sign says to Ruby, "Hey! Take this value on the right and save it with the name on the left." This means that later on, you can type the variable name and get the value right back:

```
>> wiener_dog_weight
=> 22
```

This could come in handy when you're trying to keep track of your wayward pet (let's call him Smalls) and his fluctuating weight:

```
>> smalls_weight = 22
=> 22
>> pounds_lost = 4
=> 4
>> smalls_new_weight = smalls_weight - pounds_lost
=> 18
```

Smalls.

Don't worry about the 22 and the 4 being repeated back to you; Ruby's just trying to be helpful. Ruby always expects the variable name to be on the left and the value to be on the right, so make sure not to mix up the order!

You'll also notice I used _ (called an *underscore*) instead of a space in the variable names. Ruby doesn't allow spaces in names, so it's a good practice to use _ instead.

It sounds like the King is still getting the hang of strings (imagine my ear pressed to the heavy oak door of his study), so I'll clue you in on one more bit of Ruby magic. When you see code like this:

```
>> 'Property of His Royal Highness, the King'.reverse
```

it means you're *calling* the reverse *method* on the string. When we say we're "calling a method," what we mean is we're asking Ruby to carry out a command: "Hey, Ruby! Reverse this string for me, please!" I'll go on and on about methods later, but for now, you can think of them as commands that work on particular Ruby objects. For example, strings can be reversed, but numbers can't:

```
>> "18".reverse
=> "81"
>> 18.reverse
=> NoMethodError: undefined method `reverse' for 18:Fixnum
```

NoMethodError!? That's Ruby saying, "Whoa, whoa, *whoa*. I know how to reverse a string, but I don't know how to reverse a number!" As you practice, you'll get to know which methods go with which kinds of Ruby objects. Author's honor. (I was never a scout.)

Ruby Operators

"Let me see if I've got this right," said the King. "Variables are names for Ruby values, like strings and numbers. They don't have quotes around them and can't have spaces in them. I can use the equal sign to set a variable equal to a value, and then I can use my variable's name to get that value back."

"That's exactly right," said Ruben.

"And when I see an object followed by a dot followed by a command, that means I'm using that command on that object," said the King.

"Precisely," said Scarlet.

"You mentioned that I can't reverse a number," said the King. "That makes sense. But what *can* I do to a number?"

"All sorts of things," said Ruben. He nudged Scarlet aside and typed at the Computing Contraption:

```
>> 100 + 17
=> 117
>> 50 - 20
=> 30
>> 10 * 10
=> 100
>> 40 / 20
=> 2
```

"Yes, yes," said the King. "I can add them with +, subtract them with -, multiply them with *, and divide them with /."

"You've probably seen ÷ for division," Ruben continued, "but in code we can just use /. For example, 4 ÷ 2 will be 4 / 2."

"But what can I do that's *interesting*?" the King complained.

"What about this?" asked Ruben, as he typed some more.

```
>> 22.next
=> 23
>> 22.pred
=> 21
```

"Aha!" said the King. "*Now* you're talking. next must tell Ruby to calculate the *next* number, and pred asks Ruby for its *predecessor*, which is the number that comes right before it."

"Right as rain," said Ruben.

"RAIN!" exclaimed the King, jumping up so forcefully that he knocked his solid gold armchair right over. He ran out of the room at what seemed an impossible speed for a man of his age, and Ruben and Scarlet followed.

After running for several minutes through the horribly jumbled contents of the palace (the King had turned it upside-down, after all), Ruben and Scarlet caught up with the King in his main bathroom. He was weeping again, but this time with joy, and clutched in his hands was—his string!

"Rain reminded me that I took a refreshing shower after my breakfast of parched oats!" blubbered the King. "And here it was, hanging to dry, just as I'd left it. I can't thank you enough!"

"Careful!" said Scarlet. "Your string's still a bit wet; look at the beads sliding around on it."

The King sniffed loudly and inspected his string, and the characters on it were, in fact, sliding every which way. The King thought for a moment, then double-knotted each end of the string to keep his characters from sliding off:

```
"Property of His Royal Highness, the King"
```

"Double quotes!" said Scarlet. "Can you use those with Ruby strings?"

"Definitely," said Ruben, "and single- and double-quoted strings work almost exactly the same way." He pried open the King's medicine cabinet to expose a slightly-less-old Computing Contraption, then typed the following:

```
>> double_quotes = "A string's the thing"
=> "A string's the thing"
>> single_quotes = 'for a springly King'
=> "for a springly King"
```

"See?" said Ruben. "Even when we type single quotes, Ruby repeats double quotes back to us. Both work!"

"Though I think I've heard tell," said the King, "that you can put more complicated bits and trinkets in a double-quoted string than a single-quoted one."

"That's true," said Ruben, "but we'll get to that in good time." And he closed the King's medicine cabinet with a gold-plated *click*.

a Smallish PROjEct foR you

Now that you know a bit about strings, numbers, and variables, let's put together a small project: writing a program to reflect and echo the King's string. A *reflection* of something is just that thing backward, so you've probably already guessed that we'll be reverse-ing some strings. On the other hand, an *echo* of something is just that thing repeated a few times, and we'll soon see a way to repeat a string very quickly and easily. You'll weep with joy at how simple and easy it is. You'll tear out the pages of this book and use them to dry your tears.

NOTE *For some of the longer code examples, we'll write Ruby scripts instead of using IRB! Whenever you see a filename in italics above the code, like* kings_string.rb *for the next example, that means you can write the code as a file with the given name and run it using the ruby command. Peek back at Chapter 1 if you don't remember how to do this, or ask the nearest adult to help you. You can download all the scripts that appear in this book at* http://nostarch.com/rubywizardry/. *(But remember, if you're learning to program, try typing things out yourself instead of just reading and running the code!)*

Go ahead and make a new file called ***kings_string.rb***. Then, open your file and type the following. We're going to make a short program that shows off the cool things you can do by assigning variables and how Ruby can play with strings.

kings_string.rb

```
kings_string = "Property of His Royal Highness, the King"
string_reflection = kings_string.reverse
times_to_echo = 3
string_echo = kings_string * times_to_echo
puts kings_string
puts string_reflection
puts string_echo
```

The first four lines are assigning variables. You can tell by the equal sign.

The second line in particular is pretty cool: it defines a variable to hold the `kings_string`, but because the reverse method makes the string backward, `string_reflection` will actually be "gniK eht ,ssenhgiH layoR siH fo ytreporP"!

You might be wondering about the fourth line of code, too:

```
string_echo = kings_string * times_to_echo
```

And you're right to wonder! The * is the Ruby way of saying "multiply by." This means 2 * 2 would equal 4, 13 * 379 would equal 4,927, and so on. *But wait!* you might further wonder, *How can you multiply a string (which is just a bunch of letters) by a number?* The answer is that Ruby is quite the clever robot. When it sees something like this:

```
>> "Hello!" * 3
```

it does this:

```
=> "Hello!Hello!Hello!"
```

So this is how we produce our echo: `kings_string * times_to_echo` will become "Property of His Royal Highness, the King" repeated three times!

`puts` is short for "put string," as in "Put that string on the table where I can see it." As we've seen, it just prints text on the screen. What do you think you'll see when you run your program? Save and close your file, and then run it with `ruby kings_string.rb`. You should see the following output:

```
Property of His Royal Highness, the King
gniK eht ,ssenhgiH layoR siH fo ytreporP
Property of His Royal Highness, the KingProperty of His Royal
Highness, the KingProperty of His Royal Highness, the King
```

Well done!

you know this!

Let's take a minute to review all the stuff you've packed into your brain over the last few pages.

We talked about *strings* and how they're just words or phrases between quotes (single or double quotes are both fine). In fact, since the bits that make up a string don't have to be just letters—they can include punctuation and even numbers, so long as the whole string is between quotes—we say that strings are made up of *characters* rather than letters. You can think of a string as a *literal* string of characters, with each end knotted with either single or double quotes. (You can pick single or double, but the ends have to match: "string' or 'string" won't work!)

You also saw that strings have some handy *methods*, like length and reverse, which are just commands that Ruby knows how to use with strings. You always write the object you want to affect, followed by a dot, followed by the command, like this:

```
"gadzooks".length
```

We talked a bit about *numbers*, which are values in Ruby that work exactly like you think real-life numbers would. Numbers have their very own methods, which include next (for going to the next number) and pred (for going to the previous number):

```
>> 4.next
=> 5
```

Last, we talked about *variables* and how you can use them to give Ruby values special names, like 42 or "chunky bacon". You always write the variable name (which can't contain spaces) on the left, followed by an equal sign, followed by the value:

```
>> bacon_consistency = "chunky"
=> "chunky"
>> number_of_bacon_strips = 3
=> 3
```

And you can get that value back just by typing its name:

```
>> bacon_consistency
=> "chunky"
```

Given what you know, how could you go further with that smallish project we tackled earlier? For instance, what if we changed the number of times_to_echo with next or pred? What would happen if we added a space on the end of the sentence we stored in kings_string? (Hint: It might make our output look nicer. But don't put the space directly on the variable name kings_string—remember, Ruby variable names can't have spaces!) What happens if we try to add a few different strings together with + instead of multiplying them by a number? And what in breakfast's good name is chunky bacon, anyway?

3
Pipe dreams

The Apprentice Plumber's dilemma

The King, Scarlet, and Ruben made their way back from the Royal Bathroom, the King gleefully batting his string about like a big, beardy cat.

"All those waterworks for a string in a shower!" Scarlet said to the King. "I hope you're feeling better now."

"Much," said the King, spinning the beads and trinkets on his string every which way.

"Speaking of waterworks," said Ruben, "do you hear that?" And as they rounded the corner and reentered the King's study, they found themselves ankle-deep in a miniature lake. There was water, water everywhere!

"The Mysterious Pipe!" cried the King. "Look!" And he pointed to the Mysterious Pipe, which was shaking violently and gushing a surprising amount of water from its narrow top.

"Check out the Flowmatic Something-or-Other!" said the King.

"That's not terribly descriptive," Ruben said.

"No, that's what it's called," said the King. "The Flowmatic Something-or-Other™."

"Found it!" said Scarlet, grabbing a square metal box labeled HIS MAJESTY'S FLOWMATIC SOMETHING-OR-OTHER™ on the back of the Pipe. She pried open the cover of the Flowmatic Something-or-Other to find a miniature Computing Contraption with its glowing >> IRB prompt.

"What do I do?" Scarlet asked the King.

"I seem to recall this program uses a `flowmatic_on` variable," the King said. "Try turning it off." He paused a moment. "Hey! I remembered the stuff we learned about variables!"

Scarlet flashed the King a thumbs-up, typed at the prompt, and pressed ENTER:

```
>> flowmatic_on = false
=> false
```

The Mysterious Pipe shuddered once and sputtered, and the water stopped flowing.

"Whew!" said Ruben. "Nice work!" He peered over Scarlet's shoulder at the screen. "How'd you do that? What's `false`? It can't be a string; there are no quotes around it. Is it also a variable?"

"Nope!" said Scarlet. "But it's built into Ruby just like numbers, strings, and variables are. It's called a *Boolean*, and there are actually two of them: `true` and `false`. It looks like the Mysterious Pipe works when `flowmatic_on` is `true` and shuts off when it's `false`."

"Then how was `flowmatic_on` true before?" Ruben asked.

"I don't know!" said Scarlet. "Someone or something must have created that variable."

"Well, it's stopped leaking," said the King, "but it's not really fixed. It should work correctly even when `flowmatic_on` is true! After all, the Flowmatic supplies all the water to the castle; without it, there can be no Royal Baths, Royal Toothbrushings, or Royal Water Balloon Fights! We need the Mysterious Pipe and its Flowmatic to be on without leaking all over the place."

"What about this?" Ruben said, pointing to a line on the Computing Contraption just below the Flowmatic's on/off control:

```
Warning! flow_rate is above 50!
```

"The water must be coming into the Mysterious Pipe too fast," said Scarlet.

"Gadzooks!" said the King. "The flow rate must be above 50!"

"What should we do?" asked Ruben.

The King thought for a minute. "I think it's best that we do what should always be done in these situations," he said. "We should call a professional. In this case, the Royal Plumber!"

Writing and Running Ruby Scripts

While the King calls the Royal Plumber, I'll take a second to explain some more Ruby magic to you. Don't worry, it won't take but a minute.

You see, you don't always have to type commands into IRB one at a time. As mentioned in Chapter 1, you can write a big block of Ruby code and save it as a Ruby *script*. Then, you can run your Ruby script in IRB! (This is a lot like running your code in the terminal with the `ruby` command, as we did in Chapter 1, but IRB will stay open the whole time.) Just start IRB while

you're in the folder that contains your Ruby script, then type `load 'filename.rb'`. That's exactly the same as typing everything in the file into IRB—but this way it's easy to make changes and try again!

Let's try this little guy on for size. Type the following code in your favorite text editor and save it as a file called *flow.rb*. (Look back at Chapter 1 if you need a reminder of how to do this, and don't worry—we'll cover the new #{} syntax in two shakes of a fox's tail.)

flow.rb

```
flow_rate = 100
puts "The flow rate is currently #{flow_rate}."
flow_rate = 100 / 2
puts "Now the flow rate is #{flow_rate}!"
```

If you open IRB, type `load 'flow.rb'`, and press ENTER, you should see:

```
>> load 'flow.rb'
The flow rate is currently 100.
Now the flow rate is 50!
=> true
```

Let's walk through this line by line.

First, `load 'flow.rb'` (it doesn't matter if you use single or double quotes here) tells Ruby to look for a file called *flow.rb* in the current directory (a *directory* is just a fancy name for a folder on your computer). If Ruby finds *flow.rb* and there are no problems with the code in the file, Ruby will run that code just as if you'd typed it bit by bit into IRB. Next, you know what `flow_rate = 100` and `puts` do: the first one sets the `flow_rate` variable to the value 100, and `puts` prints out the string you give it. (You also get a bonus `=> true` from Ruby, which lets you know that loading the file worked.) But you probably want to know: what's this crazy-looking #{flow_rate} business?

Well, strings and variables are different things, but sometimes you might want to combine them—say, to print out a message displaying different values for the flow_rate variable. Rather than making us look up the value of that variable and type it into the string by hand every time we want to use it, Ruby lets us use #{} to say, "Hey! Just insert the value of this variable right into the string." So when you have:

```
flow_rate = 100
puts "The flow rate is currently #{flow_rate}."
```

you get:

```
The flow rate is currently 100.
```

One last thing: remember in Chapter 2 when Ruben said that strings with double quotes (") were very slightly different from strings with single quotes (')? Well, the #{} magic (called *string interpolation* if you want to be super fancy) is possible *only* with double-quoted strings; it can't be done with single-quoted ones. (This is precisely what the King meant in Chapter 2 when he said you could put more complicated bits and trinkets on a double-quoted string than on a single-quoted string.)

That's really all I wanted to show you. And speaking of the King . . .

his majesty's flow control

"Hello?" said the King. (He had been on hold for a while.) "Is this the Royal Plumber?"

"Chuff! Chuff! Chuff!" said the Royal Plumber.

"Oh dear," said the King. "It sounds like the Royal Plumber has come down with a bad case of the Chuffs."

CHUFF! CHUFF! CHUFF!

"Chuffs?" said Scarlet.

"Chuff!" said the Royal Plumber.

"It's a bit like a cold, but coughier and huffier," said the King. "Royal Plumber, could you send down your Apprentice to help us with the Mysterious Pipe? It's been overflowing terribly."

"Chuff!" she said, and hung up.

"I think that was a yes," said the King.

"I think so, too," said Ruben. "It looks like the Apprentice is already here!"

The Apprentice to the Royal Plumber strolled into the King's study carrying a large red toolbox. Ruben and Scarlet found his expression hard to read behind his dark rectangular sunglasses and heavy black beard. The name *Haldo* was stitched in red on the front of his coveralls.

"Haldo!" said the King.

"That's me," said Haldo. "I hear the Mysterious Pipe is on the fritz."

"Definitely," said Scarlet. "Can you help us fix it?"

"I think so," said Haldo, "but I'm just the Apprentice, so it may take me a little while. Let's see what's what." He walked over to the Flowmatic Something-or-Other and looked at the screen for a moment. "I seem to remember there's an *instructions.rb* file in here somewhere." He typed load 'instructions.rb', and this is what came up:

```
 |~~                                                 |~~
 |                                                   |
:$: HIS MAJESTY'S FLOWMATIC SOMETHING-OR-OTHER :$:
 `IIIIIIIIIIIIIIIIIIIIIIIIIIIIIIIIIIIIIIIIIIII`
                ~= Instructions =~

1. Water should flow if flowmatic_on is true and
   water_available is true.
2. If flowmatic_on is false, the message
   "Flowmatic is off!" should appear.
3. If water_available is false, the message
   "No water!" should appear.
4. If the flow_rate is above 50, the warning
   "Warning! flow_rate is above 50!" should
   appear, along with the current flow rate.
5. If the flow_rate is below 50, the warning
   "Warning! flow_rate is below 50!" should
   appear, along with the current flow rate.
=> true
```

"Huh!" said Ruben. "So the problem is that if the flow rate is too high or too low, we only get a message. Ruby doesn't automatically correct the flow rate, so we can end up with a flood."

"We can fix that!" said Scarlet. "We'll write a Ruby program to check the flow rate. If the flow rate is too high, we'll lower it, and if it's too low, we'll increase it!"

Haldo scratched his head. "Well, here's the thing," he said. "I think I know what we need to do, but I haven't learned enough Ruby to enter the right commands. If you kids can give me a hand, though, I think we'll be in business."

"No problem," said Ruben. "Making a Ruby program do different actions based on different conditions is something Scarlet and I know backward and forward."

"It's called *control flow*," said Scarlet, "and it's not hard at all. Take a look!" She opened a new file in her text editor on the Computing Contraption, saved it as *flowmatic_rules.rb*, and typed:

```
flowmatic_on = true
water_available = true
if flowmatic_on && water_available
  flow_rate = 50
end
```

"You've lost me," said the King.

"We'll take it slow," said Scarlet. "First, we assign the variables flowmatic_on and water_available to true. Then, we have the if, which is a *conditional*, on the second line. It means that *if* the code that follows on the same line is true, then everything before end gets run."

"And && is just Ruby's way of saying *and*," said Ruben. "We already know that the fourth line sets the flow rate to 50, so together, the whole thing says, 'If flowmatic_on is true *and* water_available is also true, this program will set the flow_rate variable to 50. end just tells Ruby that if we're not setting the flow rate to 50, we shouldn't do anything—at least, not yet."

"I see," said Haldo. "And that's just the very first of the instructions! Great work. But what happens if the Flowmatic *isn't* on or there *isn't* water available?"

"Well, at the moment, nothing," said Ruben. "But we can fix that." He reached over and added to the *flowmatic_rules.rb* code in his text editor:

```
  flowmatic_on = true
  water_available = true
❶ if flowmatic_on && water_available
    flow_rate = 50
❷ elsif !flowmatic_on
    puts "Flowmatic is off!"
❸ else
    puts "No water!"
  end
```

"I think I'm starting to get this," said the King. "❶ is just what we had before. Then at ❷, we're trying something new: elsif! Does elsif mean 'if the first bit didn't get run, try this next step'?"

"That's exactly it," said Scarlet. "Don't worry about the weird spelling, either! It's just a shorter way of writing 'else, if.' And the ! is just Ruby's way of saying *not*. So if flowmatic_on happens to be false, !flowmatic_on will be true, and vice versa."

"And since there's only one condition left—if the Flowmatic *is* on but there's just no water—the program puts the 'No water!' message at ❸ using an else, which means: 'If none of the other code was run, then run the code that follows,'" Ruben said.

"And all of that's followed by an end, like before," said Scarlet.

"Do you need to add the two spaces before the lines following if, elsif, and else?" asked the King.

"The *indentation*?" said Scarlet. "No, but it sure does look nice."

"That takes care of the first three instructions!" said Haldo. "And I think I'm getting the hang of this. Let's see if I can rewrite the last two instructions in Ruby." He added these lines to his *flowmatic_rules.rb* script:

```ruby
❹ if flow_rate > 50
     puts "Warning! flow_rate is above 50! It's #{flow_rate}."
     flow_rate = 50
     puts "The flow_rate's been reset to #{flow_rate}."
❺ elsif flow_rate < 50
     puts "Warning! flow_rate is below 50! It's #{flow_rate}."
     flow_rate = 50
     puts "The flow_rate's been reset to #{flow_rate}."
❻ else
     puts "The flow_rate is #{flow_rate} (thank goodness)."
   end
```

"Okay, *this* I understand," said the King. "The > means *greater than* and the < means *less than*, so that first bit at ❹ says: if the flow rate is above 50, we show a 'too high' warning and then assign the variable flow_rate to 50. The program then puts a new flow_rate value using string interpolation, like we saw before."

"But at ❺, the program checks if flow_rate is below 50. If it is, we show a 'too low' warning and reset it to 50.

"At ❻, we have the else. If flow_rate isn't greater than 50 or less than 50, that means it's *exactly* 50. So, we just show the flow rate without changing the variable and puts it (thank goodness)." The King smiled, clearly pleased with himself.

"Perfect!" said Ruben. "You can also use <= for *less than or equal to* and >= for *greater than or equal to*, but we don't need those quite yet, I don't think."

Improving flow_rate.rb with Fancier Logical Operators

Ruben studied the screen for a moment. "You know," he said, "I think you could replace the section from ❹ to ❻ with even less code. Check this out!"

```
if flow_rate < 50 || flow_rate > 50
  puts "Warning! flow_rate is not 50! It's #{flow_rate}."
  flow_rate = 50
  puts "The flow_rate's been reset to #{flow_rate}."
else
  puts "The flow_rate is #{flow_rate} (thank goodness)."
end
```

"What do those two vertical lines mean?" asked Haldo. "I haven't seen those before."

"Just like && means *and* and ! means *not*, || means *or*," said Scarlet. "So we're saying, 'If the flow rate is less than 50 *or* it's greater than 50, show a warning and reset it to 50; otherwise, just let us know it's 50 (thank goodness).'

"That works pretty well," she continued, "but we can make it even simpler."

```
if flow_rate != 50
  puts "Warning! flow_rate is not 50! It's #{flow_rate}."
  flow_rate = 50
  puts "The flow_rate's been reset to #{flow_rate}."
else
  puts "The flow_rate is #{flow_rate} (thank goodness)."
end
```

"I know that ! means *not*," said the King, "so is it fair to guess that != means *is not equal to*?"

"It's not only fair, it's right!" said Ruben. "You can use != to mean *is not equal to* and == to mean *is equal to*. But be *really* careful not to mix up = and ==. The first one is used to assign values to variables, and the second is used to check if two things are equal."

"This is amazing," said Haldo. "I think I'm really getting the hang of Ruby control flow. Is there anything else I should know?"

"One more quick thing," Scarlet said. "Because if followed by a negative condition appears all the time in programs, Ruby

came up with another way to write it. Instead of always typing
something like:

```
if flow_rate != 50
  puts "Warning! flow_rate is not 50! It's #{flow_rate}."
end
```

you can instead type unless:

```
unless flow_rate == 50
  puts "Warning! flow_rate is not 50! It's #{flow_rate}."
end
```

"And those two examples are exactly the same," finished
Scarlet. "But if you have elsifs and elses, it's sometimes nicer-
looking to just use ifs."

While Scarlet was talking, Haldo saved their finished
flowmatic_rules.rb file and typed **load 'flowmatic_rules.rb'** at
the IRB prompt. When he pressed ENTER, the Mysterious Pipe
shuddered once, then began to gently vibrate. Ruben and Scarlet
could hear water flowing through the castle walls, and not a
drop was spilled anywhere.

"Huzzah!" said the King. "I can't thank you all enough! But
I do wonder," he continued, "how did the flow rate get set to 100
in the first place?"

"That, I'm not sure about," said Haldo. "There must be
another Ruby program in the castle that has access to the
flow_rate variable and changed it." He rummaged through his
red toolbox and pulled out a flashlight. "I'll look into it right
away," he said.

"Aren't you going to take off your sunglasses?" asked
Scarlet.

"No need," said Haldo, and with that, he opened a small
door on the same side of the room as the Mysterious Pipe
and disappeared into the bowels of the castle, whistling as
he went.

a Biggerish Project for you

You've learned a lot in the last handful of pages, and now it's time to put your newfound knowledge to the test! (Don't worry: I have complete and utter faith in you.) Haldo—now the *Senior Apprentice* to the Royal Plumber, thanks to Ruben and Scarlet—needs your help. While he hasn't tracked down the precise cause of the Mysterious Pipe's overflow, he did briefly find himself in a small but tricky maze. He's asked you to record his adventures in the maze, so let's start by making a new file called *maze.rb*. (Peek back at Chapter 1 if you don't remember how to do this, or ask your local adult for help.) Type the following into your file.

maze.rb

```
puts "Holy giraffes! You fell into a maze!"
print "Where to? (N, E, S, W): "
direction = gets.chomp

puts "#{direction}, you say? A fine choice!"

if direction == "N"
  puts "You are in a maze of twisty little passages, all alike."
elsif direction == "E"
  puts "An elf! And his pet ham!"
elsif direction == "S"
  puts "A minotaur! Wait, no, that's just your reflection."
elsif direction == "W"
  puts "You're here, wherever here is."
else
  puts "Wait, is that even a direction?"
end
```

Run the program by typing `ruby maze.rb` in the terminal and pressing ENTER. You should see something like this (though your output will change depending on which direction you pick):

```
Holy giraffes! You fell into a maze!
Where to? (N, E, S, W): E
E, you say? A fine choice!
An elf! And his pet ham!
```

The print command is new, but never fear: it's almost exactly like puts, except it doesn't add a new blank line after it prints out its text.

This bit is also new:

```
direction = gets.chomp
```

What we're doing here is setting a variable, direction, equal to calling the gets method and then the chomp method right after it. This is a fancy way of saying we're chomping gets. gets is a built-in method (you can think of it as a Ruby command) that *gets* the most recent input the user typed; chomp removes anything extra from the end, like spaces or a blank line. This means that we've now taken whatever the user typed (from gets.chomp) and stored it in our direction variable.

After that, it's all smooth sailing! You've seen string interpolation with #{} already, and everything after that is just checking to see what letter the user entered with == (is equal to) and using if, elsif, and else to control what message the user sees.

You can test out your maze program by typing `ruby maze.rb` from the command line or, after starting up IRB, `load 'maze.rb'`. You can keep rerunning it with different input to see what happens each time!

You can go a bit further, though. (Don't worry, it's seriously a really small maze.) Here are a few ideas:

- How might you add more directions, like NW, SW, NE, SE, up, or down?
- How could you handle accepting lowercase letters for directions?
- A circle has 360 degrees, and turning right is the same as turning 90 degrees. What if you wanted to let your users enter a number so they could turn that many degrees? How could you use <, <=, >, >=, ==, or != to make this work? (This is a bit beyond where we already went, but you can do it! You wouldn't be wandering around in a maze under a castle if you weren't the adventurous type.)

You Know This!

Control flow is tricky stuff, but doing that biggerish project proves you've gotten the hang of it. Let's review some of the things we learned along the way.

We talked about *Booleans*, which can be `true` or `false`. They're part of Ruby just like strings, numbers, and variables are, but they're definitely not strings! Don't put quotes around them, or they won't work right.

We covered *scripts* and how you can run them in IRB using `load 'script_name.rb'`. (You can also run your Ruby programs outside of IRB entirely by typing `ruby script_name.rb` on the command line.) Remember: you need quotes if you're loading a file in IRB, but you don't need quotes if you're typing on the command line! (Computers are very dumb and very picky.)

We explained *string interpolation* using #{} and how you can use it to put the values of variables directly into your strings. This comes in handy a lot, and remember: you can only do string interpolation with double-quoted (") strings. It doesn't work with single quotes (')!

Finally, we learned about control flow using `if`, `elsif`, `else`, and `unless`, and how to combine these with logical operators && (and), ! (not), and || (or), and comparison operators < (less than), > (greater than), <= (less than or equal to), >= (greater than or equal to), == (is equal to), and != (is not equal to). Using all these together, we can see (for example) *if* one thing *and* another thing are true, determine *if* one thing is *less than* another thing, or say we should do something *unless* something *is not equal to* something else. (Whew!)

It's hard to believe, but this is pretty much everything computer programs do: compare values and test to see what is or isn't true. Let's take a minute to kick back, relax, and bask in the glow of all this Ruby know-how. (The next chapter's gonna throw you for a bit of a loop.)

4

Staying

in the

Loop

Ruby on Monorails

"Well," said the King, "all this adventuring's gotten me as hungry as a lumberjack. And I haven't eaten anything since my breakfast of parched oats!"

"It's about lunchtime," said Ruben. "What's there to eat?"

"Nothing here," said the King gloomily. "I'm afraid I pretty much wrecked the Royal Kitchen and Royal Pantry when I turned the palace upside-down looking for my string, and I don't think the cooks have quite gotten everything back in order yet."

"We can go out!" said Scarlet. "I'm sure there are good places to eat in the kingdom outside the palace walls."

The King nodded vigorously. "Of course!" he said. "We'll take the Loop to the Hashery. It's my favorite restaurant!"

"What's the Loop?" asked Scarlet.

"I'm glad you asked," said the King, who was busy pulling on his finest traveling cloak and overbritches. "The Loop is the monorail—a sort of train—that runs throughout the kingdom, taking my subjects anywhere they'd like to go. It's only a few stops to the Hashery from here!"

"Couldn't we take a royal carriage or something?" asked Ruben.

"Where's the fun in that?" replied the King. "Now hurry up—the next Loop train should be arriving outside the palace in just a few minutes."

The King, Scarlet, and Ruben left the King's study and traveled through corridor after corridor of the palace, stepping over and around cooks, maids, butlers, handymen, and a host of other palace employees who were busy righting all the things the King had flipped upside-down in his mad search for his string. Finally, they arrived at the great wooden gate of the palace, and a pair of very strong-looking attendants saluted smartly and pulled the doors open for the trio.

"Where's the Loop stop?" Ruben asked, blinking in the sudden sunshine.

"Just over there," said the King, and pointed to a large metal platform at the top of a small hill near the palace entrance. "See that rail? The Loop train runs on that. It'll come up to the platform in a few minutes, then head out toward the east side of the kingdom."

"It's so high up!" said Scarlet. "Is it safe?"

"Absolutely!" said the King. "You'll see."

After a few minutes of walking, the King, Scarlet, and Ruben arrived at the platform. Just as Ruben was about to ask how long the train would take to get there, a bright red metal train car whizzed up to the platform, and the door opened with a gentle *whoosh*. "Aha! Here we are," said the King. "All aboard!"

The doors closed quickly behind them, and with barely a sound, the Loop train sped away from the palace station. Ruben looked around. "There's no one here!" he said. "A car to ourselves!" He spread out on a plastic bench along one side of the train car.

"No one *at all*," said Scarlet. "Not even a conductor. How's that possible?"

"No need for a conductor!" said the King. "The Loop is fully automatic. It runs entirely on Ruby!"

"Rails running on Ruby?" said Ruben. "Awesome!"

"I'm not so sure," said Scarlet. "We saw how well the Flowmatic Something-or-Other worked without someone keeping an eye on it."

"Oh, I don't think there's anything to worry about," said the King. "The Loop has run for years without any sort of problem."

Ruben pressed his nose to the glass. "We'll be there in no time!" he said. "It looks like the Loop is heading nonstop to the Hashery."

"What do you mean?" said the King.

"We've passed two other platforms without stopping—this is great! Well, maybe not so great for the people on those other platforms, but, you know, more Hashery for us."

The King's eyes went wide. "The Loop should stop at every station if there are people waiting!" he said. "Something must be wrong if we're skipping any."

"Nothing to worry about, huh?" said Scarlet. "We're stuck on an out-of-control train!"

"Awesome!" said Ruben.

"Now, now," said the King. "If this morning's been any indication, I'm sure there's a Computing Contraption around here somewhere that we can pry into to get an idea of what's going on." All three quickly scanned the train, looking for hidden compartments or mysterious devices. It wasn't long before Ruben spotted a square of metallic mesh with a small red button beside it. When he pressed the button, the mesh grid slid up with a slight squeak, revealing the cheerful glow of an IRB >> prompt.

"Found it!" said Ruben, waving Scarlet and the King over.

"Great!" said Scarlet. "Let's see if we can figure out a way to stop this thing."

"Make it quick!" said the King. "We don't want to miss our stop. The Hashery serves breakfast all day, but if you get there late, sometimes they run out of the best dishes. Like hash!"

Scarlet was busy inspecting the Ruby code on the Computing Contraption's screen. "Oh no!" she said. "It looks like we're caught in an *infinite loop*!"

"Sweet breakfast gravy!" cried the King. "What's that?"

while Loops

"An infinite loop is a Ruby instruction that never ends," said Ruben. "In Ruby, a *loop* is a bit of code that runs repeatedly, doing whatever its instructions tell it to until it's supposed to stop. But if you give it a stopping condition that never happens, the code runs forever!"

"Take a look," said Scarlet. "It looks like the code that drives the train will never stop running!" When the King squinted at the screen, this is what he saw.

NOTE   *Just read these next few examples—don't try them out in IRB. These little bits of code (shown in gray) would only work as part of a longer program.*

```
while true
  drive_train_forward
end
```

"I think I've heard of this," said the King. "This loop is a *while loop*, a bit of code that repeats *while* some condition is true. But since this loop starts with `while true`, and true is always true, the loop will call the `drive_train_forward` method forever!"

"Exactly," said Scarlet. "We need a way to tell the loop to stop."

"What about this?" Ruben said, pointing to a yellowed piece of paper tucked next to the Computing Contraption's screen. The King bent forward to read it. "'A Very Brief Guide to the Loop and Its Machinations,'" he quoted. "This looks promising!"

"It says here that there's not only a `drive_train_forward` method but also a `stop_train` method, which should stop the train for us," Ruben said. "Try using that!"

"Sure thing!" said Scarlet. She quickly changed the code in the Computing Contraption to:

```
while true
  stop_train
end
```

As soon as she pressed ENTER, the train made a deep, sad *boooooop* that faded away in just under a second, and as the sound trailed off, the train began to slow. Before they knew it, their train car was standing perfectly still on the monorail track.

"Nice work!" said Ruben.

"Well, you did stop the train," said the King. "But take a look out that window." Ruben and Scarlet ran to where the King pointed and looked out the window at the front of the car. Their hearts sank. "We're stuck between platforms!" said Scarlet. "I can't even see the next one on the track ahead."

"Let's take a look at the Very Brief Guide again," Ruben said. "If whoever designed the Loop program built in a `drive_train_forward` and a `stop_train` method, maybe she also built in a way of figuring out whether the train is at a platform."

Scarlet and Ruben returned to the Computing Contraption and looked over the Very Brief Guide to the Loop and Its Machinations. Meanwhile, the King wondered aloud: "If the loop was an infinite loop, why did the train stop for us at all? Shouldn't it have whizzed by like it did at the other stations?"

"I don't know," said Ruben. "But remember how Haldo said there might have been another program in the kingdom that caused the Mysterious Pipe to overflow? Maybe there was some code running somewhere that told the Loop train to stop for us."

"Maybe," said the King, "but what code, and why? And who wrote it? This is getting stranger and stranger by the minute."

"I think I've found something we can use," said Scarlet. "It says here that the Loop program also has an at_stop? method. If we call that the right way, we should be able to move forward when we're between stops, then stop when we get to a platform!"

"Great!" said Ruben. "And I think I know just how to do it." He stepped up to the Computing Contraption and began to type.

"Don't forget an end for your while loop," Scarlet said. "Just like for if/elsif/else, loops need an end."

"I know, I know," said Ruben. "There, I think this'll do it."

```
while true
  if at_stop?
    stop_train
    break
  else
    drive_train_forward
    break
  end
end
```

"Hold on just a moment," said the King. "What's that break bit do?"

"That tells the while loop to immediately stop," said Ruben. "Otherwise, we'll just stop_train or drive_train_forward forever!"

"It seems we need a way to fix that," grumbled the King.

"I think this new code will do the trick," Ruben said. He pressed ENTER, and the train whirred to life. In less than a minute, the train pulled into the next platform and eased to a halt.

"We did it!" said the King. "And we're at East Bumpspark station! The Hashery is just two more stops from here, at the New Mixico platform."

"Great! We'll be there in no time," said Ruben. But the train just sat there at the East Bumpspark station, doors open, without a soul on the platform. The King, Scarlet, and Ruben stood around awkwardly for a minute or two before the King cleared his throat to break the silence.

"Well," he said. "It looks like we figured out how to stop the train at a platform, but it's not restarting for some reason. Shall we take a second look at the code?"

"Way ahead of you," Scarlet said. "And I think I know what the trouble is—in our while loop, we give the Loop program an instruction to stop if it's at a station and to proceed if it isn't. Well, we're at a station, and the Loop is doing *exactly* what we're telling it to do—it's stopped! We never wrote anything in our loop to tell the train to start again after stopping."

"You're right!" said Ruben. "We need to rewrite the program. Maybe something like this?" And he typed:

```
while !at_stop?
  drive_train_forward
end
```

"That !at_stop? looks a bit ugly to me," Scarlet said. "And Ruby is all about writing beautiful code. Maybe something like this?" She took her turn at the Computing Contraption:

```
until at_stop?
  drive_train_forward
end
```

"Just like if has an unless, while has an until," Scarlet said. "This says that *until* we reach a stop, we should keep driving the train forward."

"That does look much nicer," said the King, "but we still have a problem: we're currently at a stop, so the program won't move us forward! And even if it does, we'll just move forward to the next station and stop, with nothing in the program telling the train to start again."

"You're exactly right," said Scarlet. "We need some way of telling Ruby to move from stop to stop until there are no more stops on the line. Ruben, do you see anything on the list that would tell the train to keep going from one station to the next?"

"Well," said Ruben, "It says here that Ruby's next method can be used in the Loop program to move from one station to another, but I'm not totally sure how we could do that. There's an example in the Very Brief Guide to the Loop and Its Machinations, but it has all these weird-looking square brackets in it. Have you ever seen those before?"

aRRays

While Scarlet explains those funky-looking brackets to Ruben, I'll take a minute to explain them to you. (Scarlet could have explained just as well, but I was getting a little antsy.)

What Ruben's describing looks like this:

```
["East Bumpspark", "Endertromb Avenue", "New Mixico", "Mal Abochny"]
```

A bunch of Ruby objects between square brackets ([]) and separated by commas (,) is called an *array*. Arrays are basically just lists! For example, you could make a Ruby grocery list with an array, like so:

```
grocery_list = ["cheese", "bread", "grapes", "a festive hat for all occasions"]
```

You can put anything in a Ruby array: strings, numbers, Booleans, or even other lists! This is a handy way to set a single variable equal to a whole bunch of values. We'll talk more about arrays in the next chapter, but the important thing to know for now is that arrays can be used with really handy methods (called *iterators*, but don't worry about memorizing that word right away) that let you *iterate through*—that is, go over—each element in the array. Examples are the best way to learn, so try this code in IRB now to see the results:

```
>> grocery_list = ["cheese", "bread", "grapes", "a festive hat for
all occasions"]
>> for item in grocery_list
>>   next if item.length.odd?
>>   puts item
>> end
```

This will print out:

```
cheese
grapes
=> ["cheese", "bread", "grapes", "a festive hat for all occasions"]
```

You see the whole array at the end because even though for will print only what you asked, it gives you back the whole array in case you did something to change it. (We didn't.)

The next method is built into Ruby and does exactly what it sounds like: it moves on to the next item in the array immediately, without calling any other code. In this example, since the string "bread" has a length of 5 and "a festive hat for all occasions" has a length of 31 (both odd numbers), next gets called, and these items in the list don't get printed out (remember, next goes immediately to the next item in the list, skipping any other code before its end). Since "cheese" and "grapes" each have lengths of 6—an even number—and since next is only called if the number of letters is odd, the puts statement gets called, and the item names are printed out.

As for that brand-new for/in bit you just saw, I'll leave it to Scarlet and Ruben to explain that. It sounds like Ruben's got the hang of arrays and iterators, so let's check out the example he's working on in the Loop program.

Putting Arrays and Loops into Action

"I think I understand," Ruben said. "So arrays are just lists of things—strings, numbers, anything we like—and we can set them to a single variable name if we want. Not only that, but we can use loops and iterators to go over the entire array so we can do something for each item, or *element*, in the array if we want."

"Exactly," said Scarlet. "Can I have a look at what you're typing in IRB?" Ruben nodded and turned the Computing Contraption's display toward Scarlet. This is what she saw:

```
stops = ["East Bumpspark", "Endertromb Avenue", "New Mixico", "Mal
Abochny"]
for stop in stops
  next if stop.empty?
end
```

"Good!" said Scarlet. "But what's going on with that for/in part? Is that a kind of loop, like while?"

"Sort of," said Ruben. "Basically it's telling Ruby, 'Hey! *For* each thing *in* this array, carry out the instructions before the end. So, in this case, for each stop in the stops list, go to the next one if the stop has no people waiting there."

"Okay," said Scarlet. "One more question—I saw you define the stops variable and set it to an array, but I didn't see you assign the stop variable anywhere. Why's that?"

"That's just a cool shortcut Ruby lets you take. See, as you go through the array, Ruby moves from each item to the next, and it makes it a lot easier if you can give each item a temporary name while you're working on it. Since this 'temporary' variable only matters inside the for loop, you don't have to declare it— you just say something like for stop in stops, and Ruby knows that stop will take on the value of each item in the stops array in turn. In fact, you can give that variable any name you want, like item or thingy or elf_with_a_pet_ham, but stop makes the most sense, I think."

"I think so, too," said Scarlet. "But something about that for loop looks weird to me. I've read a lot of Ruby code by now, and I don't see many for loops floating around. I do see a lot of these, though!" And she started typing into the Computing Contraption:

```
stops = ["East Bumpspark", "Endertromb Avenue", "New Mixico",
"Mal Abochny"]
stops.each do |stop|
  next if stop.empty?
end
```

"Whoa!" said Ruben. "What's that? Does it do the same thing as my for loop?"

"Yup!" said Scarlet. "And it's only a tiny bit different, but much nicer looking. Instead of the for/in part, we can just call the each method directly on the stops variable. Then we have exactly the same code as before, only it's between do and end instead of for/in and end. The do/end bit actually comes up a lot in Ruby, and it's called a *block*."

"Okay," said Ruben, "that makes sense. But what about the stop between the two vertical lines? Is that like the 'temporary' stop variable from my for loop?"

"Exactly," Scarlet said. "You can think of those vertical lines as being like the sides of a little window that we move along the array: as we put the box over each element in the array, stop is temporarily set to the value of that element."

"In fact," she continued, "You can even write it a bit shorter. Ruby lets you use curly brackets instead of do/end, and since we have only one line of code in our block, it looks even more elegant with the brackets." She typed into IRB:

```
stops = ["East Bumpspark", "Endertromb Avenue", "New Mixico",
"Mal Abochny"]
stops.each { |stop| next if stop.empty? }
```

"This is all very fascinating," said the King, "but will the code *work*? Will we be able to get to New Mixico station before we all starve to death, or—heaven forbid!—the Hashery runs out of hash?"

"I think we're all set!" said Ruben. "And I have a feeling we'll talk a lot more about arrays and blocks after we've had a good meal. Ready, Scarlet?" Scarlet nodded, and on the count of three, they pushed ENTER together. The Loop train car vibrated to life, the doors *whooshed* shut, and the car moved on to the Endertromb Avenue station. The three held their breath as the car doors opened, the car idled . . . and the doors slid shut again! The King began to clap as the car moved on to New Mixico station, and he didn't stop clapping until they left the train, walked down the stairs leading from the platform to the street, and made their way toward the cherry-red doors of the Hashery.

your project, should you choose to accept it

After a careful review of the Loop by the Loop Authority Council for the King, the members of the Council have determined that the Loop *does*, in fact, need a conductor (if only to look after the program and ensure it doesn't end up in any more infinite loops). Surprisingly, no one volunteered for the position, so I went ahead and volunteered you! That's just the sort of guy I am.

Conducting trains is big business, but I think it's safe to start small. We'll just work on a program to report whether the Loop stops at a requested station, and if it does, list all the stops before the requested stop so passengers will know how many stations to expect before theirs. Let's begin by making a new file called *loop_the_loop.rb*. (As always, peek back at Chapter 1 if you don't remember how to do this, or ask your local adult for help.) Then open your file and type the following code.

loop_the_loop.rb

```
❶ we_wanna_ride = true
   stops = ["East Bumpspark", "Endertromb Avenue", "New Mixico",
   "Mal Abochny"]

❷ while we_wanna_ride
     print "Where ya headin', friend?: "
❸    destination = gets.chomp
```

```
❹    if stops.include? destination
      puts "I know how to get to #{destination}! Here's the station list:"
❺      stops.each do |stop|
        puts stop
        break if stop == destination
      end
    else
      puts "Sorry, we don't stop at that station. Maybe another time!"
      we_wanna_ride = false
    end
  end
```

There are a few new bits here, but nothing you can't handle!

First, we set a couple of variables: we_wanna_ride is true, and stops is set to an array of strings ❶. Next, we create a while loop with we_wanna_ride (which starts as true) as the condition ❷. Inside the loop, we use print to print some text on the screen and gets.chomp to get the user's answer ❸.

The include? method ❹ is new! It simply returns true if the array has an element that matches destination and false otherwise. (This is really handy for quickly checking whether an object you want is in a given array.)

The next part at ❺ is a little trickier:

```
stops.each do |stop|
  puts stop
  break if stop == destination
end
```

You've already seen the stops.each do |stop| ... end part, and the break if stop == destination part does exactly what you'd guess: it *breaks* out of the loop as soon as the Loop reaches a stop that equals the destination the passenger wants. It prints out each element before it makes this check, though, so it will always print out at least one stop if that stop is in the array.

You can test out your conductor program by typing ruby loop_the_loop.rb at the command line and pressing ENTER. You should see something like this (of course, you'll probably pick different stops than I did):

```
Where ya headin', friend?: Mal Abochny
I know how to get to Mal Abochny! Here's the station list:
East Bumpspark
Endertromb Avenue
New Mixico
Mal Abochny
Where ya headin', friend?: New Mixico
I know how to get to New Mixico! Here's the station list:
East Bumpspark
Endertromb Avenue
New Mixico
Where ya headin', friend?: Detroit
Sorry, we don't stop at that station. Maybe another time!
```

You can keep rerunning it with different input to see how the output changes each time!

If you want to make your program even more elaborate, here are some other things to think about:

- Right now, the program will keep prompting the user for input as long as the user keeps asking for train stops that are in the stops array. How might you update the program to run only once, even if it recognizes a stop?

- How could you handle accepting lowercase letters for destinations? (Hint: This will be a lot like one of the extra steps you might have taken for your last project.)

- What if a passenger is going the other way on the train (for instance, from Mal Abochny to East Bumpspark)? How could you update your program to work in both directions? Even trickier, what if the train route is a big circle (meaning if a passenger goes from East Bumpspark to Mal Abochny, the next stop after Mal Abochny should be East Bumpspark again)? How could you update your program to print out the right list of train stops if a passenger wants to go all the way around the circle?

You Know This!

I threw a lot at you in this chapter, but if you're conducting trains after reading it, I'm pretty sure you know your stuff. Let's review what we looked at.

We covered *while loops*, which are loops that contain some code between while and end and will continue to run that code as long as the while condition is true. (Beware—if there's no way for the condition to become false, the loop will go on forever and create an *infinite loop!*)

We saw that, just like if has an unless, while has an until. If you can write:

```
while something_is_the_case
  # Do something!
end
```

then you can also write:

```
until !something_is_the_case
  # Do something!
end
```

We also saw that when using a loop or an *iterator* (which is just Ruby code that loops over items in a list), we could call the next method to skip certain elements based on an if/elsif/else or unless statement.

We talked a little bit about arrays, which are basically just Ruby lists, and how we can put anything we want inside them. An array looks like this:

```
my_hobbies = ["Ruby", "eating things", "cat videos"]
```

We learned that we could use a *for loop* or the each method to *iterate*, or go over, an array, and while they work exactly the same, the each method is more common in Ruby.

A for loop looks like this:

```
# Assuming we have an array called todo_list
for task in todo_list
  puts task
end
```

And iterating with each looks like this:

```
# Using do/end
todo_list.each do |task|
  puts task
end

# Or, using curly brackets
todo_list.each { |task| puts task }
```

Finally, we learned a bit about *blocks.* Ruby blocks are just regular Ruby code sandwiched between either do/end or curly brackets ({}). Some methods, like each, take blocks, and we'll learn way more about those after a hearty helping of Ruby know-how at the Hashery.

5
ARRAY of
Sunshine
and
hash on the
RANGE

Big hank's hashery

"Morning, Your Majesty!"
boomed a voice from deep
inside the Hashery.

"Good morning, Big Hank!"
said the King.

"Big Hank?" asked Ruben.
"Who's Big Hank?"

An enormous man with a
bald head and a curly black
mustache emerged from the
back of the restaurant. "I am!"
he said.

The King shook Hank's
hand vigorously. "Great to see

you, Hank! We had a doodle of a time getting here—the Loop was acting up—but I can't wait to sit down to a fine meal of your best hash."

Big Hank frowned, and his mustache drooped noticeably. "The Loop's gone loopy?" he asked. "I wish I could say I were surprised. Things have been going a little haywire here, too."

The King gasped. "You don't mean—"

Big Hank nodded. "Our range is on the fritz," he said. "Until we fix it, I won't be able to cook up anything: no eggs, no breakfast gravy, and certainly none of my famous hash."

The King slumped onto one of the many long oak benches filling the Hashery. "No hash! What could be worse?"

"This hash must be really good," Scarlet said.

"It's the best!" shouted the King, who was on the verge of tears. "But without a working range, there won't be any. And we've come all this way!"

"Now, hang on," said Big Hank. "This isn't the first time Squeaky Jim and I have gotten into a pickle here at the Hashery, and it won't be the last. We'll get this figured out."

"Who's Squeaky Jim?" asked Ruben.

"He's my fry cook," Hank said. "He's not what you'd call a whiz with the kitchen technology—it all runs on Ruby—but he's a heck of a cook. Makes a great omelette, and he's almost mastered my hash recipe."

"Ruby!" Ruben and Scarlet shouted together.

Big Hank raised a heavy black eyebrow. "Do you kids know anything about Ruby?" he asked. "That would be a huge help."

"Absolutely!" said Scarlet. "Show us the kitchen, and we'll take it from here."

"Hooray!" said the King. "These kids are as smart as a whip, Hank," he added. "They'll have your kitchen up and running in no time."

Big Hank nodded. "Sounds good! I've actually got Squeaky Jim using the old griddle in the back, but I think he could use some Ruby help. I'll take another crack at the range, but if you kids and Jim get the orders flowing before I get it fixed, give me a shout and we'll put our heads together."

"Sure thing," Scarlet said. "Lead the way!"

Big Hank motioned for them to follow him and lumbered through row after row of wooden benches toward the back of the Hashery. He stopped at a red metal door with a small window toward the top, tapped on it twice, and shouldered it open. "Jim!" he called. "The King and his friends are here!"

They heard a brief scuffling sound in the corner of the kitchen, followed by the crashing of a dozen or so pots and pans.

"It's okay, it's okay—I've got it!" Squeaky Jim called, his voice cracking twice. He stumbled out from behind a large pile of potato sacks, with a saucepan in each hand and one perched crookedly on his head.

"I know why they call him Squeaky Jim," Ruben whispered to Scarlet.

"Easy, Jim," Big Hank said, taking the pans from Jim. "The King and his friends know a thing or two about Ruby, so I'm asking them to help you out while I tinker with the main range."

Squeaky Jim hastily bowed to the King. "Your Majesty," he said.

"Squeaky Jim," said the King.

Big Hank gestured to the corner of the kitchen Squeaky Jim had just come from. "You'll find the Computing Contraption over there," he said. "I'll be at the range, on the other side of the kitchen." He turned and hefted a sack of potatoes under each arm. "Shout loud if you need me—kitchen's big," he called over his shoulder. And with that, he was gone.

Squeaky Jim cleared his throat. "Big Hank probably told you I'm not a Ruby expert," he squeaked, "but if you can get my griddle working again, I can whip up customer orders like nobody's business." He pulled a stack of orders from his apron pocket. "Most of them are orders for hash and today's special, the Array of Sunshine," he said. "Three sunny-side eggs in row! Best brunch in the kingdom."

"Okay," said Ruben. "We actually just helped the King with the Loop, and we had to use arrays for that. This should be a piece of cake!"

"Eggs," corrected Squeaky Jim.

"Oh, yeah. A piece of . . . eggs," Ruben said.

"Let's get to work," Scarlet said. "I've already got the Computing Contraption open!"

aRRays Within aRRays

"Great!" said Jim. "Since you guys know about arrays, could you create one for me now? The first order is for an Array of Sunshine; that's just three 'sunny_side_up_egg's in a row."

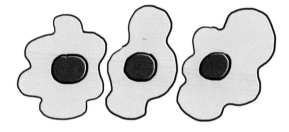

"Sure!" Scarlet said. "It should look something like this." She started typing into the Computing Contraption:

```
>> order_one = ['sunny_side_up_egg', 'sunny_side_up_egg', 'sunny_
side_up_egg']
=> ["sunny_side_up_egg", "sunny_side_up_egg", "sunny_side_up_egg"]
```

When Scarlet pressed ENTER, a small metal track over the griddle began to vibrate. One after another, three eggs rolled down the track, cracked against a small hammer, and dropped sunny-side-up onto the stove.

"That's perfect!" Jim said. "But it looks like a lot of typing, and we're gonna have a lot of orders." His voice cracked again. "Is there any way we could do the same thing with less typing?"

"Yep!" said Scarlet. "You can also create a new array like this:

```
>> order_two = Array.new(3, 'sunny_side_up_egg')
=> ["sunny_side_up_egg", "sunny_side_up_egg", "sunny_side_up_egg"]
```

"Here, we're calling the new method on Array, which creates a list of items. The next part in the parentheses means that the array should have three items," Scarlet explained, "and the last part means that each item should be a 'sunny_side_up_egg'. It's the same as typing all the stuff we did for order_one."

"I remember creating arrays on the Loop with square brackets," Ruben said, "but I've never seen Array.new. What's that do?"

"Remember how Ruby has datatypes like String?" Scarlet asked. Well, Array is another datatype. You can create an array with *array literal* syntax, which is just assigning a variable name to a list in square brackets. You can also create an array by calling the new method on the Array *class*."

"What's a Ruby class?" Squeaky Jim asked.

"We'll get to that in a little bit," Scarlet said. "But the important thing is that classes are like groups of objects in Ruby, and calling the new method on the class name creates a new *instance*, or example, of that class."

"Okay, that makes sense," Ruben said. "And we can put variables in arrays, and we saw earlier that you can put strings in there. What else can go in arrays?"

"Anything!" Scarlet said. "And the items in the array don't even have to be the same thing. Check it out!"

```
>> random_array = [1, 'two', 'sunny_side_up_egg', true]
=> [1, "two", "sunny_side_up_egg", true]
```

"A number, a string, a variable, and a Boolean, all in the same array," Ruben said. "Neat!"

"That's great," Squeaky Jim said, "and the first Array of Sunshine is just about ready. But I have a feeling we're gonna need to cook up a bunch of these—is there any way we can make an array with all of our orders in it? Sort of like a list of lists?"

"Definitely," Ruben said, and Scarlet stepped aside so he could type:

```
>> order_three = ['hash']
=> ["hash"]
>> order_four = ['egg', 'hash']
=> ["egg", "hash"]
>> todays_orders = [order_one, order_two, order_three, order_four]
=> [["sunny_side_up_egg", "sunny_side_up_egg", "sunny_side_up_egg"],
["sunny_side_up_egg", "sunny_side_up_egg", "sunny_side_up_egg"],
["hash"], ["egg", "hash"]]
```

"That's awesome! todays_orders is an array that contains four other arrays: order_one, order_two, order_three, and order_four," Squeaky Jim said. "We'll be done in no time. If we've got our orders packed up in an array, though, how do we get them back out?"

Even More Array Methods!

"There are a few things we can do," Ruben said. "Arrays have lots of cool built-in methods we can use. For example, we can get the first *item* or *element* in an array with the first method, like this:

```
>> todays_orders.first
=> ["sunny_side_up_egg", "sunny_side_up_egg", "sunny_side_up_egg"]
```

"I see," said Scarlet. "The first method gives us the first item in the array! And while we're talking about first, we can get the last element in an array with last!"

```
>> todays_orders.last
=> ['egg', 'hash']
```

"That's order_four," Jim said. "Coming right up!"

"Hang on, though," said Ruben, and he typed quickly into the Computing Contraption:

```
>> todays_orders.empty?
=> false
>> todays_orders.length
=> 4
```

"Whoa, what's that?" Jim asked, pushing his paper fry-cook hat back and scratching his head. "I haven't seen empty? or length before."

"We saw length on strings," Scarlet said. "When we use that method on strings, it tells us how many characters the string contains. For arrays, does it tell us how many items are in the array?"

"Precisely," said Ruben. "And we saw empty? on the Loop train stops, where it just returned a Boolean—true if the stop had no one waiting and false if there was at least one person. This empty? is for arrays, but it works the exact same way."

Then Ruben frowned. "But there are still four orders in the list! We can get some of them with first and last, but how do we get the rest? And how do we remove them from the list as we cook them up?"

Shift! Pop! Insert!

"I think I can help with that," Scarlet said. "We'll need to use a couple of new array methods, though." She reached across Ruben to the Computing Contraption and started typing:

```
>> todays_orders
=> [["sunny_side_up_egg", "sunny_side_up_egg", "sunny_side_up_egg"],
["sunny_side_up_egg", "sunny_side_up_egg", "sunny_side_up_egg"],
["hash"], ["egg", "hash"]]
>> current_order = todays_orders.shift
=> ["sunny_side_up_egg", "sunny_side_up_egg", "sunny_side_up_egg"]
>> todays_orders
=> [["sunny_side_up_egg", "sunny_side_up_egg", "sunny_side_up_egg"],
["hash"], ["egg", "hash"]]
```

"That's perfect!" said Ruben. "How did you pull the very first order out of todays_orders and put it in the current_order variable?"

"With the shift method," Scarlet said. "It does two things at once: it knocks the very first item off the array you call it on, and it *returns*, or spits out, that item!"

"So if you set a new variable equal to calling shift on an array," the King piped up, "you basically move the item from the array to your new variable!"

Ruben and Scarlet turned to the King, who had only just finished studying the many potato sacks littering the kitchen.

"That's . . . actually exactly right," said Scarlet.

"Wonderful!" said the King. "But what if I want to add things onto the front of the array? Or add things onto the back? Or even—dare I say it—take things off the back?"

"Then have we got the methods for you!" Scarlet said. "I don't want to mess up the orders, so I'll show you on my own array called breakfast_items that I'll make up. Take a look!" And she typed the following into the Computing Contraption:

```
>> breakfast_items = ['egg', 'hash', 'gravy', 'biscuit', 'sausage',
'jam']
>> current_food = breakfast_items.shift
=> egg
>> breakfast_items
=> ['hash', 'gravy', 'biscuit', 'sausage', 'jam']
>> current_food = breakfast_items.pop
=> jam
>> breakfast_items
=> ['hash', 'gravy', 'biscuit', 'sausage']
```

"Gadzooks!" said the King. "That's exactly what I wanted—pop removes and returns the last item in the array, and shift does the same thing to the first item!" He watched as Scarlet typed some more.

```
>> breakfast_items.push('egg')
=> ['hash', 'gravy', 'biscuit', 'sausage', 'egg']
>> breakfast_items.unshift('jam')
=> ['jam', 'hash', 'gravy', 'biscuit', 'sausage', 'egg']
```

"Aha! I see: push adds an item to the end of the array, and unshift adds an item to the beginning of the array," the King continued.

"Yup! Just make sure you read the array from left to right," said Scarlet. "The first element is the one all the way on the left, and the last element is the one all the way on the right."

"What if I want to add something to the middle?" asked the King.

Scarlet didn't say anything, but simply typed:

```
>> breakfast_items
=> ['jam', 'hash', 'gravy', 'biscuit', 'sausage', 'egg']
>> breakfast_items.insert(2, 'tea')
=> ['jam', 'hash', 'tea', 'gravy', 'biscuit', 'sausage', 'egg']
```

"Amazing!" said Ruben. "But wait, why is tea the third item in the array?" he asked. "You called the insert method with the number 2, not the number 3!"

"This is one of the weird things about computers," said Scarlet. "They don't start counting at 1, like you or I do. They start at *zero*. If you start counting at 1, tea is in position 3, but if you start at zero, it's one less than that. That's why you have to tell Ruby to insert the tea element at position 2, not position 3, if you want it to be the third item."

"I'm more confused than a bumblebee in a plastic flower factory," the King said gloomily. "And just when I thought I was beginning to understand Ruby."

"Hang on, I think I've got it," said Squeaky Jim, his voice cracking only a little bit. "Is this right?" And he drew a diagram on the back of a hash-stained napkin:

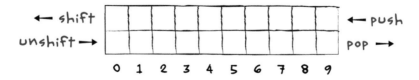

"An array is like a row of boxes," Jim said. "The first one is numbered zero, and the numbers get higher from there. You shift to take something off the front, unshift to add something to the front, push to add something to the back, and pop to take something off the back." He looked uncertainly from Ruben to Scarlet. "Is that right?"

"That's right!" said Ruben and Scarlet together.

"Nice work, my boy!" said the King. "You're picking this up mighty quickly."

"In fact," Scarlet said, "arrays are so much like rows of boxes that you can even get an array element out by asking the array for the element by its box number! See?" She typed into the Computing Contraption:

```
>> breakfast_items
=> ['jam', 'hash', 'tea', 'gravy', 'biscuit', 'sausage', 'egg']
>> breakfast_items[2]
=> "tea"
```

"It's like you're telling the array exactly what box number to grab," Ruben explained. "By saying you want breakfast_items[2], you're telling Ruby you want the array element in slot 2, which is the third element."

Squeaky Jim smiled. "Great!" he said. "But I wonder . . . "

"Wonder what?" asked Ruben.

"Well," said Jim, flipping the last egg and putting it in a paper basket, "it's fine to add and remove things from arrays, and I figure the kitchen's software does that well enough. But what if I wanted to know something about *all* of the orders up front? Is there a way I could go over all of the orders and print them out one by one?"

Iterating with arrays

"Absolutely," said the King. "We saw that on the Loop—what was it called again?"

"*Iterating*," said Ruben. "It works like this!" He reached over to the Computing Contraption and began typing furiously:

```
>> todays_orders.each do |order|
>>    puts "#{order}"
>> end
```

```
["sunny_side_up_egg", "sunny_side_up_egg", "sunny_side_up_egg"]
["hash"]
["egg", "hash"]
```

"Yes, that does look familiar!" said the King. "And that will print out each order in the todays_orders array?"

"You got it," said Scarlet. "But remember, there's a way of writing it with less code than the do/end block." She quickly typed:

```
>> todays_orders.each { |order| puts "#{order}" }
["sunny_side_up_egg", "sunny_side_up_egg", "sunny_side_up_egg"]
["hash"]
["egg", "hash"]
```

"That's right!" said the King. "You can use the curly brackets instead of do/end when there's just one line of code in the block." He scratched his bushy white beard. "Though I'm still a little mystified by these *blocks*."

"We'll talk more about them soon!" said Scarlet. "For now, we should make sure we're all set with arrays and customer orders here in the Hashery."

Squeaky Jim nodded. "I think I get the hang of arrays okay, and we're caught up on orders for the time being," he said, tossing the last order ticket into the trash. "But all this talk about iterating has me wondering if there isn't another problem we can solve."

"What's that?" said Scarlet.

"Well," squeaked Jim, "Big Hank and I have been trying to figure out how best to print out the Hashery menu for our customers. Do you think iterating over an array might be a good way to do it?"

"What's the menu made up of?" asked Ruben.

"In Ruby terms, just strings and numbers," Jim said. "Each string would be an item on the menu, and every item would have a number representing the price. I figure since we can mix strings and numbers in arrays, that might make sense."

"Hmm," said Scarlet. "I don't think so. How would you pair up the menu items and their prices? Even if you just alternated them, you might mess it up with all the pushing, popping, shifting, and unshifting you'd be doing whenever the menu changed."

"You have a point," Jim admitted. "Well, maybe an array of arrays? Each array element could be its own little array, and every little array could just contain a menu item name and its price."

"That's a little better," Ruben said. "At least then your menu names and prices would be together. What do you think, Scarlet?"

Scarlet thought for a moment. "No," she finally said. "I think instead of an array, we want to use a *hash*."

hash in the hashery

I'm sure you're thinking to yourself right now: "Okay, we're in the Hashery. Hash is served. Surely this idea that Ruby has a built-in thing called a *hash* is a big joke, right?"

Well, it's not. It's zero percent joke. Hashes are one of the coolest parts of Ruby, so while Scarlet, the King, Ruben, and Squeaky Jim sort out the differences between breakfast hash and Ruby hashes, I'll take a second to explain them to you.

Arrays are like rows of boxes, right? Each element has its own numbered slot to live in, like items on a grocery list. This is great so long as all the stuff on each line of the list—that is, every element in the array—keeps to itself and does its own thing. But what if you want to show that two elements are somehow related?

Think of a dictionary: in a dictionary, you have a word and its definition. Unlike with a grocery list, you wouldn't say that the words are all on their own lines and the definitions are all on their own lines, since that leaves out the biggest part of the dictionary: the connections between words and their meanings. Squeaky Jim's orders are like a list, and no order really affects any other order, so an array makes sense. But for his menu, where he's got to associate menu items with their prices, he needs something more like a dictionary. And for that, Ruby uses hashes.

Hashes are easier to show than tell (isn't everything?), so check out the following code. It pairs up our heroes (along with Squeaky Jim and Big Hank) with their descriptions. Go ahead and type it into IRB, and notice how we're using curly brackets ({}) instead of square brackets ([]) as we did with arrays:

```
>> our_heroes = {
>>    :the_king => 'the ruler of the kingdom',
>>    :ruben => 'a Ruby wizard in training',
>>    :scarlet => 'a Ruby wizard in training',
>>    :big_hank => 'the owner of the Hashery',
>>    :squeaky_jim => 'a fry cook at the Hashery'
>> }
```

This code takes a variable, our_heroes, and stores a hash in it. Don't be confused by the curly brackets—this isn't a block! Hashes aren't commands; they're just a bunch of what we call *key-value pairs*. A word and its definition are a good example of a key-value pair: the word is the *key*, and the word's definition is the *value*. Just as with a dictionary, you use a hash key to look up a hash value.

Each key-value pair is separated from the next one by a comma, which makes them a bit like arrays. The similarities don't end there! For example, if you had the preceding hash, you could type:

```
>> our_heroes[:the_king]
```

and you'd get:

```
=> "the ruler of the kingdom"
```

This is a lot like looking up array values, only instead of providing the element number inside the square brackets, you write the hash key.

Don't worry that the hash keys look weird right now; those things that look like variables with colons in front of them are called *symbols*, and we'll get to them in the next chapter.

Just as with arrays, you can create a hash with *literal* syntax or with the new method. These two lines of code are "saying" the same thing:

```
>> hashery_menu = {}
=> {}
>> hashery_menu = Hash.new
=> {}
```

Sometimes you'll see an alternate way of writing hashes. Instead of using the little *hash rockets* (=>), some people put the colons after the symbol names, which would make the our_heroes hash look like this:

```
>> our_heroes = {
>>    the_king: 'the ruler of the kingdom',
>>    ruben: 'a Ruby wizard in training',
>>    scarlet: 'a Ruby wizard in training',
>>    big_hank: 'the owner of the Hashery',
>>    squeaky_jim: 'a fry cook at the Hashery'
>> }
=> {:the_king=>"the ruler of the kingdom", :ruben=>"a Ruby wizard in
training", :scarlet=>"a Ruby wizard in training", :big_hank=>"the
owner of the Hashery", :squeaky_jim=>"a fry cook at the Hashery"}
```

Both examples are totally correct Ruby, and you should pick whichever one is easier for you to remember. (I like the colons, since they're faster to type.)

Finally, there are a few neat methods you can call on hashes to get the keys, values, or key-value combinations out of them. For instance, calling the keys method on your hash will give you an array of its keys:

```
>> our_heroes.keys
=> [:the_king, :ruben, :scarlet, :big_hank, :squeaky_jim]
```

You can also call the `values` method on a hash to get an array of its values:

```
>> our_heroes.values
=> ['the ruler of the kingdom', 'a Ruby wizard in training', 'a Ruby
wizard in training', 'the owner of the Hashery', 'a fry cook at the
Hashery']
```

There are a few more hash methods worth knowing about. Just as `empty?` tells you if an array is empty, it also tells you if a hash has no key-value pairs:

```
>> our_heroes.empty?
=> false
>> empty_hash = {}
>> empty_hash.empty?
=> true
```

You can also use `length` to find out how many sets of pairs are in your hash:

```
>> our_heroes.length
=> 5
```

And last but not least, you can use some brand-new hash methods, `has_key?` and `has_value?`, to check whether a hash contains a certain key or value:

```
>> our_heroes.has_key?(:ruben)
=> true
>> our_heroes.has_key?(:trady_blix)
=> false
>> our_heroes.has_value?('a fry cook at the Hashery')
=> true
```

However, you're probably demanding to know: "How can I get all the keys and values of my hash *together*?" Well, the best way to do that is to iterate over the hash. This looks a whole lot like iterating over an array—in fact, there's only one tiny difference!

```
>> our_heroes.each do |hero, role|
>>   puts "#{hero} is #{role}."
>> end
```

Go ahead and try it out. (Make sure you use double quotes
for your puts—remember, you need that if you're going to put
variables in your string.) Did you spot that tiny difference I mentioned? You need both hero *and* role between the pipe characters
(||) in your block. We had just one variable between the pipes for
arrays, but hashes have keys *and* values, so we need to tell the
Ruby block about both. If all goes well, you'll get a list of all of
your intrepid heroes and their stations in life:

```
the_king is the ruler of the kingdom.
ruben is a Ruby wizard in training.
scarlet is a Ruby wizard in training.
big_hank is the owner of the Hashery.
squeaky_jim is a fry cook at the Hashery.
=> {:the_king=>"the ruler of the kingdom", :ruben=>"a Ruby wizard in
training", :scarlet=>"a Ruby wizard in training", :big_hank=>"the
owner of the Hashery", :squeaky_jim=>"a fry cook at the Hashery"}
```

Speaking of our heroes, it sounds like Scarlet and Ruben
have finished explaining hashes to the King and Squeaky Jim.
(I have very acute hearing.) Let's see if they've figured out how
to use hashes to iterate over the Hashery menu.

Rollicking Ranges

"I've got just the idea for iterating over the Hashery menu," said
Squeaky Jim, and this time his voice didn't crack at all. "All we
need to do is—"

At that very moment, Big Hank came lumbering over from
the far side of the kitchen.

"I hate to interrupt," he boomed, "but I'm having a heck of a
time with the range. In fact, there's only one little Ruby detail I
need to get it working, but I'll be a monkey's tax attorney if I can
figure it out. Mind giving me a hand?"

"Sure thing!" said Scarlet. "What's the trouble?"

"Follow me," said Big Hank, and they crossed the enormous kitchen, past counters piled high with eggs, flour, potatoes, and other ingredients, past ovens and spatulas and those little forks with only three prongs, until they reached the gleaming new range on the far side of the kitchen.

"Ain't she a beauty?" Big Hank asked. "Only wish I could figure her out. Here's where I'm stuck." He pointed to the glowing IRB >> prompt on the range's console. It said:

```
>> current_temperature = (300..400)[0]
NoMethodError: undefined method `[]' for 300..400:Range
```

"I overheard what you were saying about arrays," Hank said, "and the instruction manual for the range says it'll go from 300 to 400 degrees. So I figured I could use the square brackets to get the temperature in position zero, which should be 300."

"Oh, I see the problem," said Ruben. "This range doesn't use an array for the temperature! It uses a *range*."

"A range?" Big Hank said.

"That's Ruby's way of giving you a bunch of different values right next to each other," Ruben said. "Ranges don't do all of the things arrays can do, but we can make them into arrays pretty easily. Check it out!" He started typing:

```
>> ('a'..'f').to_a
=> ["a", "b", "c", "d", "e", "f"]
>> ('a'...'f').to_a
=> ["a", "b", "c", "d", "e"]
>> (1..9).to_a
=> [1, 2, 3, 4, 5, 6, 7, 8, 9]
>> (1...9).to_a
=> [1, 2, 3, 4, 5, 6, 7, 8]
>> (1..9).first
=> 1
>> (1..9).last
=> 9
```

"I'll be a Christmas goose!" Hank bellowed. "That's amazing! But I've got a couple of questions. First, what's that to_a bit do?"

"The to_a method turns ranges into arrays," Scarlet said. "Since range values are all right next to each other, Ruby can figure out what the array should look like. See? It works on letters of the alphabet *and* numbers!"

"Not only that," Ruben added, "but once the range is an array, you can iterate over it just like any array."

"I see," Hank said, twirling his mustache. "But answer me this: why d'you get some ranges with two dots and some with three?"

"That's just how you tell Ruby whether or not to include the last thing in the range," Ruben said. "Two dots means 'include the first thing, everything up to the last thing, *and* the last thing between the parentheses in the range,' and three dots means 'include the first thing and everything *up to*, but *not including*, the last thing between the parentheses in the range.'"

"That sounds a bit confusing," Jim squeaked.

"It can be," Scarlet admitted. "That's why I usually stick to the two-dot ranges. It makes more sense to have both numbers in the range."

"Got it," Big Hank said. "Last question. If I want the first thing in the range, I can convert it to an array with to_a and just grab the first element with [0]. But can I also use this first method you just showed me?"

"Of course!" Ruben said, and typed:

```
>> current_temperature = (300..400).first
=> 300
```

With a pleasant *beep*, the range quickly heated up to 300 degrees. The smell of fresh hash began to waft through the air.

"You've done it! I can't thank you kids enough." Big Hank laughed, slinging hash across the range like a gleeful diner cowboy. "I can't help but feel a little silly, though. It was such a small thing!"

"It always feels like that with programming," Scarlet said. "But the more you do it, the more you realize it's *always* some small thing, and you get much better at fixing things quickly."

"Speaking of quick," Big Hank said, "the lunch rush'll be here any minute." He surveyed the kitchen, which was full of ungrated potatoes and unfried eggs. "What do you say—want to grab a quick bite, then maybe give me a hand?" He smiled, and his great black mustache bounced on his face. "Of course, food's on the house. Anything for the King and his friends!"

Ruben and Scarlet looked at each other, then at the King. The King nodded. "We've come all this way," he said. "We might as well stick around a bit longer!"

Order Up!

Now that the Hashery is back at 100 percent, Big Hank and Squeaky Jim (who, now that he's more confident with Ruby, squeaks much less) need your help to get that menu ready for the customers. Jim didn't get a chance to tell us his plan, but I'm pretty sure you've got this one. Easy as pie . . . uh, eggs, right?

Let's begin by making a new file called *hashery_menu.rb*. (Peek back to Chapter 1 if you don't remember how to do this, or ask your local adult for help.) Then open your file and type the following code.

hashery_menu.rb

```
hashery_menu = {
  eggs: 2,
  hash: 3,
  jam: 1,
  sausage: 2,
  biscuit: (1..3)
}

hashery_menu.keys.each do |item|
  puts "Today we're serving: #{item}!"
end

hashery_menu.each do |item, price|
  puts "We've got #{item} for $#{price}. What a deal!"
end
```

```
puts "Here's what a biscuit'll run ya, depending on how much butter
you want:"
hashery_menu[:biscuit].to_a.each do |price|
  puts "$#{price}"
end
```

This is what you and Jim would have put together a little bit ago, so there's nothing new or scary here!

This is the output you'll see when you run the code using the command `ruby hashery_menu.rb`:

```
Today we're serving: eggs!
Today we're serving: hash!
Today we're serving: jam!
Today we're serving: sausage!
Today we're serving: biscuit!
We've got eggs for $2. What a deal!
We've got hash for $3. What a deal!
We've got jam for $1. What a deal!
We've got sausage for $2. What a deal!
We've got biscuit for $1..3. What a deal!
Here's what a biscuit'll run ya, depending on how much butter you
want:
$1
$2
$3
```

There *are* a couple of new combinations of ideas, though, so let's step through them one by one and see how they work. Take a look:

```
hashery_menu = {
  eggs: 2,
  hash: 3,
  jam: 1,
  sausage: 2,
  biscuit: (1..3)
}
```

Here, we're just creating a hash called `hashery_menu`. It's got keys like `:eggs` and `:hash`, and each key is paired with a value, like 2 for `:eggs` and 3 for `:hash`. This is how much we'll charge for the item on our menu.

Next, we have this bit:

```
hashery_menu.keys.each do |item|
  puts "Today we're serving: #{item}!"
end
```

We're using the `keys` method to get a list of all the keys in our hash, then giving that list (or *array*) to the each method. For each key, we're printing out the string: `Today we're serving: #{item}!` So, for example, when we get to the key `:eggs`, we'll print out: `Today we're serving: eggs!` The code loops over each item in our hash and then `puts` each menu item to the screen.

```
hashery_menu.each do |item, price|
  puts "We've got #{item} for $#{price}. What a deal!"
end
```

Things are getting a bit trickier here. When we call the each method on the hash itself, we give the do block both the hash *key* (item) and the *value* of that key (price). For example, when we get to `:eggs` (which is paired with the value 2), we'll print out: `We've got eggs for $2. What a deal!`

```
puts "Here's what a biscuit'll run ya, depending on how much butter
you want:"
hashery_menu[:biscuit].to_a.each do |price|
  puts "$#{price}"
end
```

Finally, we'll work a little Ruby magic with the `:biscuit` in our `hashery_menu`. First, we access its value with `hashery_menu[:biscuit]`. Then, since that value is a range, we can call the `to_a` method on it to make it an array, then use each just as we did before to go through all its items. We'll print out our message saying what a biscuit will cost, and then the do block will print out the possible prices: $1, $2, and $3, each on its own line.

You can test out your entire menu program by entering `ruby hashery_menu.rb` at the command line, and it should look like the output I showed you just a moment ago.

You've got a solid menu going here, but if you want to make Squeaky Jim and Big Hank absolutely weep with joy, try the following ideas on for size.

Your menu has a pretty sweet range in it, and you even convert it to an array! I don't see any regular arrays in your menu, though, and you're *completely* allowed to have arrays as hash values. Why not add a `:random_special` key (for the Special of the Day) with an array of prices as the value? If I told you that you could call the `sample` method on an array to get Ruby to spit out a random element from an array, how might you use it here?

You could get really fancy and `shift`, `unshift`, `push`, or `pop` values onto or off of your `:random_special` array. Looking at the code you've already got, how would you call these methods on the array value of your `:random_special` key?

Speaking of the `push` method, there's a cool shortcut for it in Ruby. It's called the *shovel operator*, and it works like this. The line with the `<<` is exactly the same as `bagel_types.push('cinnamon raisin')`:

```
>> bagel_types = ['plain', 'sesame', 'everything']
=> ["plain", "sesame", "everything"]
>> bagel_types << 'cinnamon raisin'
=> ["plain", "sesame", "everything", "cinnamon raisin"]
```

Try replacing your pushes with `<<`s, and then read more about the shovel operator at *http://www.ruby-doc.org/*. Hint: How could it help you build strings in Ruby?

you know this!

You might feel like your brain is overflowing with all the new array, hash, and range magic we learned, but don't worry—we'll go over everything once more to make sure you've got it all.

Let's start with *arrays*, which are just lists of information. You have two ways of creating arrays. You can use array literal syntax, using square brackets like this:

```
>> breakfast = ['chunky bacon, 'chunky bacon', 'chunky bacon']
=> ["chunky bacon", "chunky bacon", "chunky bacon"]
```

Or you can use `Array.new` to do the same thing:

```
>> breakfast = Array.new(3, 'chunky bacon']
=> ["chunky bacon", "chunky bacon", "chunky bacon"]
```

You found out that arrays can contain anything, including strings, numbers, variables, Booleans, and even other arrays. You learned a whole bunch of *array methods*, including:

- `empty?`, which returns true if an array has no items and `false` if it has at least one item
- `length` or `size`, which do the same thing—return the number of items in an array
- `first`, which returns the first element in an array without removing it
- `last`, which returns the last element in an array without removing it
- `shift`, which returns the first element in an array *and* removes it from the array
- `unshift`, which adds elements to the front of the array
- `push`, which adds elements to the back of the array
- `pop`, which removes and returns the last element of the array
- `insert`, which can add an element anywhere in the array

Whew!

Let's practice a bit in IRB with some more examples to refresh your memory:

```
>> empty_array = []
=> []
>> empty_array.empty?
=> true
```

```
>> not_empty_array = [1, 2, 3, 4, 'I declare a thumb war']
=> [1, 2, 3, 4, "I declare a thumb war"]
>> not_empty_array.empty?
=> false
>> not_empty_array.length
=> 5
>> not_empty_array.first
=> 1
>> not_empty_array.last
=> 'I declare a thumb war'
>> not_empty_array
=> [1, 2, 3, 4, 'I declare a thumb war']
>> first_item = not_empty_array.shift
=> 1
>> not_empty_array
=> [2, 3, 4, 'I declare a thumb war']
>> not_empty_array.unshift(first_item)
=> [1, 2, 3, 4, 'I declare a thumb war']
>> last_item = not_empty_array.pop
=> 'I declare a thumb war'
>> not_empty_array
=> [1, 2, 3, 4]
# We could also do not_empty_array << last_item
>> not_empty_array.push(last_item)
=> [1, 2, 3, 4, 'I declare a thumb war']
# Insert the number 5 at position 4; remember, arrays start counting
at 0!
>> not_empty_array.insert(4, 5)
=> [1, 2, 3, 4, 5, 'I declare a thumb war']
```

We talked about how to access arrays using square brackets:

```
>> junk_drawer = ['lightbulb', 'dead battery', 'some pens', 'old
penny']
=> ["lightbulb", "dead battery", "some pens", "old penny"]
>> junk_drawer[2]
=> "some pens"
```

Finally, we reviewed how to iterate over an array:

```
>> junk_drawer.each do |thing|
>>    puts thing
>> end
lightbulb
dead battery
some pens
old penny
=> ["lightbulb", "dead battery", "some pens", "old penny"]
```

which is exactly the same as:

```
>> junk_drawer.each { |thing| puts thing }
lightbulb
dead battery
some pens
old penny
=> ["lightbulb", "dead battery", "some pens", "old penny"]
```

Next up: *hashes*. Hashes are different from arrays because they aren't just lists. Instead, they associate *keys* with *values* (think: dictionary word with definition). Just like arrays, however, hashes can be created with *literal syntax* or the new method:

```
>> hashery_menu = {}
=> {}
>> hashery_menu = Hash.new
=> {}
```

And, just as with arrays, you can access hash values with square brackets:

```
>> hashery_menu = {
>>    eggs: 2,
>>    hash: 3,
>>    jam: 1,
>>    sausage: 2,
>>    biscuit: (1..3)
>> }
=> {:eggs=>2, :hash=>3, :jam=>1, :sausage=>2, :biscuit=>1..3}
```

```
>> hashery_menu[:jam]
=> 1
```

We saw a few *hash methods*, including empty? (which returns
true if a hash has no key-value pairs and false if it has at least
one pair), length (which returns the number of pairs in a
hash), keys (which returns an array of the keys in the hash),
values (which returns an array of the values in the hash),
has_key? (which returns true if the hash includes a particular
key and false otherwise), and has_value? (which returns true if
the hash includes a particular value and false otherwise).

Here they are again in all their glory:

```
>> hashery_menu.empty?
=> false
>> empty_hash = {}
=> {}
>> empty_hash.empty?
=> true
>> hashery_menu.length
=> 5
>> hashery_menu.keys
=> [:eggs, :hash, :jam, :sausage, :biscuit]
>> hashery_menu.values
=> [2, 3, 1, 2, 1..3]
>> hashery_menu.has_key?(:jam)
=> true
>> hashery_menu.has_key?(:zebra)
=> false
>> hashery_menu.has_value?(3)
=> true
>> hashery_menu.has_value?(42)
=> false
```

We also learned that we could iterate over a hash just like we
can iterate over an array, only we need to put variables for the
key *and* the value between the pipes in our code block:

```
>> hashery_menu.each do |item, price|
>>    puts "#{item} costs #{price}"
>> end
```

```
eggs costs 2
hash costs 3
jam costs 1
sausage costs 2
biscuit costs 1..3
=> {:eggs=>2, :hash=>3, :jam=>1, :sausage=>2, :biscuit=>1..3}
```

Last (but not least), we covered *ranges*. Ranges are just a bunch of Ruby values that happen to be next to each other. We saw that two dots inside the parentheses included both ends of the range, while three dots included the first end but only up to (not including) the second one:

```
>> (1..5).to_a
=> [1, 2, 3, 4, 5]
>> (1...5).to_a
=> [1, 2, 3, 4]
```

We also learned a few *range methods*, including to_a (which turns a range into an array), first (which returns the first item in the range), and last (which returns the last item in the range):

```
>> ('a'..'c').to_a
=> ["a", "b", "c"]
>> ('a'..'c').first
=> "a"
>> ('a'..'c').last
=> "c"
```

All right! We made it. Great work so far—but don't get too cocky. That lunch rush is coming, and the next chapter's gonna get a little crazy.

6

The (Chunky) Bacon to Ruby's hash

Symbols!

"That hash was amazing!" Scarlet said. Ruben nodded vigorously as he shoveled another helping of eggs and hash into his mouth.

"I'm glad you liked it!" said Big Hank. "But that mid-morning rush'll be here any minute, and we need to get cracking if we're going to be ready for it."

Scarlet jumped down from her stool. "We have eggs to fry up, potatoes to grate, sausages to cook, breakfast gravy to make, and biscuits to bake. Anything else?"

Hank twirled his mustache. "I'm not sure," he said. "Let's have a look at that menu you kids and Squeaky Jim cooked up."

"Sure!" Scarlet said, and she called up the Hashery menu on the kitchen's Computing Contraption:

```
>> hashery_menu
=> { :eggs => 2,
     :hash => 3,
     :jam => 1,
     :sausage => 2,
     :biscuit => 1..3 }
```

"This looks good—each order of food is associated with its price in a hash," said Big Hank, "but we should put our breakfast beverages on there, too. Can you add a key with an array as a value to my menu hash?"

"Of course," Scarlet said. "What drinks should we put in it?"

"We've got coffee, orange juice, and tea," said Hank.

"Okay!" Scarlet said. She typed:

```
>> hashery_menu['drinks'] = ['coffee', 'orange juice', 'tea']
=> ["coffee", "orange juice", "tea"]
```

"Aha! So that's how you add a key to a hash," Hank said.

"Yup!" Scarlet replied. "You just type the hash name, then the key name between square brackets—here, we're using 'drinks'—and set the whole thing equal to whatever value you like. See how we updated the hashery_menu?"

```
>> hashery_menu
=> {:eggs=>2, :hash=>3, :jam=>1, :sausage=>2, :biscuit=>1..3,
"drinks"=>["coffee", "orange juice", "tea"]}
```

"Cool!" said Ruben, who had finally finished eating his eggs and hash. "Now we have a list of drinks on the menu." He leaned in close to the glowing screen of the Computing Contraption. "But it looks like the drinks hash key is a string, and the rest are symbols. Does that make a difference?"

"Oh boy, *does* it!" said Squeaky Jim, who had been opening bags of potatoes and cleaning the Hashery's enormous

Grate-O-Matic. He pushed his paper hat farther back on his head and leaned against the machine. "You see—" he began, but as he started to speak, his elbow pushed down the machine's huge switch, turning it on. It roared to life, scaring the sweet peas out of Squeaky Jim and nearly causing him to fall over multiple times as he scrambled to turn it back off.

"You see," Jim squeaked after he finally shut down the Grate-O-Matic, "even though I'm not very good at Ruby, I *have* tried to program the kitchen's Computing Contraption every now and again. One morning, the Hashery was unbelievably busy—one of the biggest mid-morning rushes I'd ever seen!"

"I remember that one," Big Hank said, pulling an armful of sausage links out of a shiny red refrigerator. "Not only did we have a ton of customers, but we were doing a Build Your Own Menu day."

"Build Your Own Menu day?" Ruben asked, scratching his head.

Big Hank nodded and began yanking sausages off the long chain of links and tossing them into an enormous skillet. "Yup. We let customers create their own personal menus, so they could order anything they wanted. We were okay at first—people were building their menus, ordering food, and getting served. But as the morning wore on, the program got slower and slower. By the peak of the rush, we could barely get any orders through! We had to shut down the kitchen's Computing Contraption and do all the orders by hand. It was chaos."

Squeaky Jim nodded. "And I think I know why!"

Hank stopped pulling apart sausage links. "You do?"

"Yup!" Jim said. "I was reading up on Ruby the other day to try to get a bit better at running the kitchen, and I found out that Ruby symbols use up less memory than strings. We were using strings for all the keys in our hashes during Build Your Own Menu day, and as the program went on and on, it used more and more memory until it didn't have enough to do its job."

"Back up a bit," said the King, who was chewing thoughtfully on a raw potato. "What exactly *are* these Ruby symbols? And what do you mean when you say they use less memory than strings?"

The Skinny on Symbols

While Squeaky Jim tries to explain Ruby symbols to the group, I'll give you the rundown. Basically, a Ruby symbol is just a *name*. For instance, if I'm talking about the King and Scarlet is talking about the King, we're both talking about the very same thing— the King! When we talk about symbols (that is, names) in Ruby, we write them with a colon in front, like :the_king. You'll often see the *underscore* (_) in symbol names because, just like variable names, they aren't allowed to have spaces in them.

So how is a symbol different from a string, like 'The_King'? Well, think back to the King's string from Chapter 2. Now imagine that the King has *two* strings with *exactly* the same beads and trinkets on them. While they might have the same *contents*, they aren't the *exact same thing*. But when we both talk about the King, we're not talking about two kings who look exactly like each other: we're talking about *one and the same* king!

If you're still a bit confused, never fear: I've got a couple of code examples that should help clear things right up. Fire up IRB and try this on for size:

```
>> string_one = 'The King'
=> "The King"
>> string_two = 'The King'
=> "The King"
>> string_one.object_id
=> 2184370320
>> string_two.object_id
=> 2184365180
```

Here we're setting two *different* variables to the *same* string value of 'The King'. Then, when you use the object_id method on these two variables, you're asking Ruby to provide the unique number it uses to keep track of every object in a running Ruby program. It's a kind of ID number that Ruby uses to tell objects apart, and no two objects have exactly the same one. On the flip side, if two variables have the same object ID number, they *must* be talking about the very same object.

The object ID numbers you see in IRB won't be *quite* the same as mine, but that's okay! Object IDs get reassigned every time you start a new Ruby program. The important thing is that string_one and string_two, even though they're both equal to 'The King', are *different objects*. Their contents are exactly the same, but just as with our example of the King's string, we're talking about two completely different strings that just happen to have the same thing inside.

Now check *this* out:

```
>> symbol_one = :the_king
=> :the_king
>> symbol_two = :the_king
=> :the_king
>> symbol_one.object_id
=> 466088
>> symbol_two.object_id
=> 466088
```

Here we're setting two different variables, `symbol_one` and `symbol_two`, to the symbol `:the_king`. Again, your object IDs won't be exactly the numbers just shown, but when you compare your object IDs for `symbol_one` and `symbol_two`, you'll see that they're the exact same number! Just like how when we're talking about the King, we're talking about the very same person, both `symbol_one` and `symbol_two` are talking about the exact same object, `:the_king`.

Because symbols are simply names you can toss around, you don't assign values to them. While you can definitely say:

```
>> variable_name = :my_fancy_symbol
=> :my_fancy_symbol
```

you *can't* say:

```
:my_fancy_symbol = some_value
```

If you try this, you'll get a `SyntaxError`. Just as you can't assign a different value to a string or a number by putting it on the left-hand side of the equal sign, you can't assign a different value to a symbol, either.

The only time you'll have symbols on the left-hand side is when you use them in hashes, like this:

```
>> fancy_words = { bloviate: 'To talk at length' }
=> {:bloviate=>"To talk at length"}
```

Remember, we don't need to start our `bloviate` key with a colon if we use the newer hash syntax. If we want to use the older hash rockets (`=>`), we start the symbol with a colon:

```
>> fancy_words = { :bloviate => 'To talk at length' }
=> {:bloviate=>"To talk at length"}
```

But yes! I *do* go on. What you're probably wondering is: what are symbols good for? How is it that they use less memory than strings?

Because a symbol always has only one object ID, it gets created only one time in any given Ruby program. That means you could have a thousand million billion variables that are all set to a certain symbol, and only *one* symbol object gets created. If you were to do that with strings, they'd all have different object IDs, so you'd get *a thousand million billion different strings.* Just like you, Ruby has only a certain amount of memory and can keep track of only so many things at once. If you create a huge number of strings, Ruby will start to run out of memory as it tries to juggle them all, and it will slow way down. Your program might even crash! If you use symbols, Ruby will create fewer objects and use less memory, so programs that use symbols for things like hash keys can run faster than equivalent programs that use strings. This brings us to the thousand-million-billion-dollar question: when should you take advantage of the savings symbols offer?

Basically, any time you need to use a name over and over but don't want to create a brand-new string each time, symbols are the way to go. They're very good for hash keys, and they're also useful for referring to method names. We'll talk about using symbols for method names very soon!

Speaking of soon, I'm pretty sure Squeaky Jim is about to wrap up his explanation of Ruby symbols. Let's see if Ruben, Scarlet, the King, and Big Hank have as good an understanding of them as you do!

Symbols and hashes, together at last

"I think I get it," Ruben said. "Symbols are just names that Ruby uses to refer to one particular object, so if we use symbols as keys in hashes, we're really just referring to the same object over and over."

"That's exactly right!" said Squeaky Jim. "Now you see why we had such a terrible time using strings instead of symbols in our Build Your Own Menu hashes."

"Of course!" Scarlet said. "Each time a customer made a new menu, it made a whole bunch of new strings."

"We had hundreds of customers," Big Hank sighed. "No wonder our Ruby program ran out of memory!"

"Well, I certainly don't want to start adding strings into the menu *now*," Scarlet said. "How can we change the string key to a symbol?" She typed hashery_menu into the Computing Contraption to call up the Hashery menu's contents:

```
>> hashery_menu
=> { :eggs => 2,
     :hash => 3,
     :jam => 1,
     :sausage => 2,
     :biscuit => 1..3,
     "drinks" => ["coffee", "orange juice", "tea"] }
```

"Hmm," said the King. "Can we just change the string key to a symbol key?"

"I don't think so," said Squeaky Jim. "From what I've read, I think the best thing we can do is to delete the string key, then replace it with a symbol key."

"You may be right," Ruben said, "but programming is all about experimenting. I've heard that Ruby has a to_sym method that will turn a string into a symbol. Should we give it a try?"

"Sure thing," Scarlet said, and she typed:

```
>> hashery_menu.keys.last.to_sym
=> :drinks
```

"It looks like it worked!" Ruben said. "Can you bring up the hash again to be sure?"

Scarlet nodded and brought up the Hashery menu again.

```
>> hashery_menu
=> { :eggs => 2,
     :hash => 3,
     :jam => 1,
     :sausage => 2,
     :biscuit => 1..3,
     "drinks" => ["coffee", "orange juice", "tea"] }
```

"Darn!" Ruben said. "Ruby returned a symbolized version of the string `'drinks'`, but it didn't actually change the key in the hash."

"That's probably just as well," said Big Hank. "I've been thinking about our breakfast beverages, and I realized we don't have their prices in the array at all!"

Scarlet slapped her forehead. "That's right!" she said. "We need to have the drinks *and* the prices in there." She thought for a minute. "Wait—if we're associating drinks and their prices, that's just like associating each food item with its price. Can we put a hash inside another hash?"

"Nothing to do but experiment!" said the King. "Why don't you go ahead and delete the "drinks" key like Jim suggested, and then try adding a symbol key with a hash as the value?"

"Okay!" said Scarlet. "Jim, do you know how to delete a key from a hash?"

"I think so," Jim said, and he reached over and began typing into the Computing Contraption:

```
>> hashery_menu.delete('drinks')
=> ["coffee", "orange juice", "tea"]
```

"Whoa, what was that?" said Ruben. "When you deleted the key, it gave you the value back!"

Jim nodded. "That's what the delete method does!" he said. "That way, if we had wanted to use the value of the deleted key for something, we could have saved it into a variable, like this:

```
menu_drinks = hashery_menu.delete('drinks')
```

"But," Jim said, "we *can't* do that now, because the 'drinks' key is gone. See?" He typed again:

```
>> hashery_menu
=> { :eggs => 2,
     :hash => 3,
     :jam => 1,
     :sausage => 2,
     :biscuit => 1..3 }
```

"Nice work!" Scarlet said. "Now all we have to do is test whether we can put a hash inside a hash. Big Hank, what are the prices I should use for the drinks?"

"It's a dollar for coffee, two for orange juice, and one for tea," Hank said. Scarlet typed into the Computing Contraption:

```
>> hashery_menu[:drinks] = { :coffee => 1, :orange_juice => 2,
:tea => 1 }
=> { :coffee => 1, :orange_juice => 2, :tea => 1 }
```

"It worked!" shouted the King. "Great work, everyone!"

"And just in the nick of time!" boomed Big Hank. The group had been so busy crowding around the Computing Contraption and working on getting the Hashery menu just right, they hadn't noticed a steadily growing din. Voices filled the air as customers crowded into the Hashery, and even Big Hank had to shout to be heard above them all: "Spin up the Grate-O-Matic! Attend to the skillets! Bake biscuits like your lives depend on it! The mid-morning rush is upon us, and they're hungry!"

"Aye aye, Hank!" said Squeaky Jim, who not only *didn't* squeak but spun up the Grate-O-Matic and began churning out hash like he'd done it all his life. "Let's get that new menu out to all the customers!"

"The menu! I almost forgot," Hank said. "We do have one more addition to today's specials." And he typed:

```
>> hashery_menu[:chunky_bacon] = 1
=> 1
```

"Chunky bacon?" Scarlet and Ruben asked together.

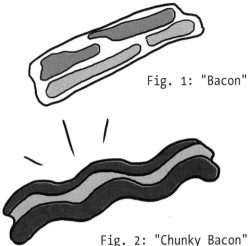

Fig. 1: "Bacon"

Fig. 2: "Chunky Bacon"

Hank smiled and shrugged. "Friend of mine used to come in all the time and order it," he said. "Haven't seen him in a while, so I haven't had it on the menu. But who knows?" He looked out at the growing crowd of hungry Hashery customers. "Maybe today's the day he'll come back."

The Mid-Morning Rush

Now that you know all about symbols, you can handle a mid-morning rush of any size and not worry about slowing down your Ruby program or running low on memory. In fact, you're such a wizard with Ruby symbols that Big Hank and Squeaky Jim have given you a mission that they've so far found impossible: transforming their old Build Your Own Menus so that they use symbols for keys instead of strings!

This may sound like an odd idea at first, but it's just to help make sure you're comfortable using Ruby hashes; you don't have to change all your keys to symbols every time you use them. Hashes are great for storing information like our Hashery menu, and you'll use them time and again whenever you write Ruby—not just for the code in this book.

Earlier, we saw that we couldn't just call to_sym on a hash key and expect it to magically change; instead, we had to delete the key and replace it.

That works okay for a single string key, but Hank and Jim are talking about a thousand million billion strings in hundreds of customer menus—you could never convert them one at a time, even if you wanted to! But what if we could *automatically* run through a hash and do exactly that: grab each string key, delete it, save the key's value, and assign that value to a new symbol key?

Let's make a new file called ***strings_to_symbols.rb***. (As always, peek back at Chapter 1 if you don't remember how to do this, or ask the nearest adult to help you.) Then open your file with your text editor, and type the following:

```
my_own_menu = { 'tater_tots' => 2,
  'fancy_toast' => 3,
  'omelette' => 3,
  'tiny_burger' => 4,
  'chunky_bacon' => 1,
  'root_beer_float' => 2,
  'egg_nog' => 2
}
```

Here, we're creating a brand-new hash called my_own_menu and assigning some values (the prices, which are numbers) to some keys (the menu items, which are strings). Keep on adding to the program; we're not done yet!

```
puts "Object ID before: #{my_own_menu.object_id}"
```

Next, we'll print out the object ID of our menu hash. This is so we can later confirm that although we've made some changes to our hash, it's still the same object; after we make changes to our keys and values, if the ID is the same as it was before, we're talking about the very same hash, just with some different information in it.

Let's keep adding to *strings_to_symbols.rb*. We've got strings for hash keys now, but what we really want are symbols! We'll need to add a bit more code to change our string keys to symbol keys.

```
my_own_menu.keys.each do |key|
  my_own_menu[key.to_sym] = my_own_menu.delete(key)
end

puts "Object ID after: #{my_own_menu.object_id}"

puts my_own_menu
```

Okay, that does it. We call the keys method on the my_own_menu hash to get our keys, then immediately call each on those keys to iterate over them. (Remember that from Chapter 5? Feel free to look back if you need a reminder.)

Here's the really cool part: for each key in the hash, we call delete on the key (which removes it from the hash), but since delete returns the value associated with the key that was deleted, we immediately set this equal to calling to_sym on the key. This is an amazing double whammy: it deletes the original key from the hash while immediately adding the value to a *new* key, and that new key is just the original one turned into a symbol. The result? You change all the keys in your hash from strings to symbols!

We can even prove it's the very same hash, not a copy: we puts the hash's object ID before and after iterating over it, and you'll see in the output that the object ID is the very same both times. That's right—*every* object in Ruby has an object ID, including the hash itself!

Your complete code should look like this:

strings_to_symbols.rb

```
my_own_menu = { 'tater_tots' => 2,
  'fancy_toast' => 3,
  'omelette' => 3,
  'tiny_burger' => 4,
  'chunky_bacon' => 1,
  'root_beer_float' => 2,
  'egg_nog' => 2
}
```

```
puts "Object ID before: #{my_own_menu.object_id}"

my_own_menu.keys.each do |key|
  my_own_menu[key.to_sym] = my_own_menu.delete(key)
end

puts "Object ID after: #{my_own_menu.object_id}"

puts my_own_menu
```

Go ahead and run your code—type `ruby strings_to_symbols.rb` and press ENTER. The output should look like this:

```
Object ID before: 2174149520
Object ID after: 2174149520
{:tater_tots=>2, :fancy_toast=>3, :omelette=>3, :tiny_burger=>4,
:chunky_bacon=>1, :root_beer_float=>2, :egg_nog=>2}
```

You should see the very same object ID printed twice, then a beautiful printout of your hash, complete with symbols for keys instead of strings.

What Else Can You Do with Symbols?

Now that you can solve all of Big Hank and Squeaky Jim's menu woes with ease, you might be wondering what else you can do. As Ruben said, experimenting is a huge part of programming, and there's a lot of experimentation you can do with hashes and symbols. For example, what happens if you call to_sym on a string that contains a space? (You'll still get a symbol, but it will look weird—try it!)

We can also explore hashes within hashes. Remember, we can access a value in a hash like this:

```
>> hash_name[:key]
=> value
```

So how might you go about accessing the value of a hash *inside* a hash? Here's a hint—for our original menu:

```
>> hashery_menu
=> { :eggs => 2,
     :hash => 3,
     :jam => 1,
     :sausage => 2,
     :biscuit => (1..3),
     :drinks => { :coffee => 1, :orange_juice => 2, :tea => 1 } }
```

what do you think `hashery_menu[:drinks][:orange_juice]` will give us back?

Finally, strings have a `to_sym` method that turns them into symbols, but symbols *also* have a `to_s` method (short for "to string") that turns them into strings. How might you update this program to change symbol keys to strings?

you know this!

We only really talked about hashes and symbols in this chapter, but since they're not as easy to understand as numbers or strings (or even arrays), they're worth going over one more time. (Heck, I've been writing Ruby for years, and I *still* think symbols are weird!)

First, we looked at how to add a key and a value to a hash, which is as easy as setting a key in square brackets ([]) equal to a value:

```
my_hash[:key] = value
```

Next, we introduced symbols, which are basically just names; you don't assign values to them, but you can store them in variables if you want to.

For example, this is okay:

```
my_variable = :my_symbol
```

But *this* will cause an error:

```
:my_symbol = some_value
```

The only time symbols can appear on the left-hand side is when we're using them as hash keys, like so:

```
>> my_hash = { ninjas: 'awesome',
>>   wizards: 'pretty rad',
>>   warrior_princesses: 'super tough'
>> }
=> {:ninjas=>"awesome", :wizards=>"pretty rad", :warrior_
princesses=>"super tough"}
```

When you're talking about the King or your teacher or Abraham Lincoln, you're always talking about *exactly* the same person; likewise, symbols always refer to *exactly* the same object. This means they use less memory than strings, because whenever you create a new string—even if it's *all the same* letters as another string—it's a separate object with its own object ID:

```
>> symbol_one = :the_king
=> :the_king
>> symbol_two = :the_king
=> :the_king
>> symbol_one.object_id
=> 466088
>> symbol_two.object_id
=> 466088 # The same!
>> string_one = 'The King'
=> "The King"
>> string_two = 'The King'
=> "The King"
>> string_one.object_id
=> 2184370320
>> string_two.object_id
=> 2184365180 # Different!
```

In general, symbols are good for when you need to use a name over and over, mostly for hash keys and a couple of other neat tricks (which we'll talk more about in later chapters).

When you care about the *content* of something, you want a string; when you care about the *name* of a thing, you want a symbol.

If you're ever unsure whether two objects are the same or different, you can always use the object_id method (which works on any Ruby object) to get an object's ID number. Every object has its very own ID number, which is how Ruby keeps track of which object is which during a program:

```
>> 'The King'.object_id
=> 2187090900
>> { :eggs => 2, :hash => 3 }.object_id
=> 2187097060
>> ['eeny', 'meeny', 'miny', 'moe'].object_id
=> 2187104080
```

Remember, your object IDs won't be exactly the same as the ones shown here, but they should all be different from one another on your computer.

Converting between symbols and strings is a snap! You can use the to_sym method to turn a string into a symbol:

```
>> 'drinks'.to_sym
=> :drinks
```

And you can use the to_s method to turn a symbol into a string:

```
>> :drinks.to_s
=> "drinks"
```

When it comes to deleting keys from hashes, you not only saw that you can do it with the delete method, but you also learned that delete both removes the key-value pair from the hash *and* returns the value, so you can save it in a variable if you want:

```
>> simple_hash = { :one => 1, :two => 2 }
=> { :one => 1, :two => 2 }
>> saved_value_from_hash = simple_hash.delete(:two)
=> 2
```

```
>> simple_hash
=> { :one => 1 }
>> saved_value_from_hash
=> 2
```

Finally, you learned that it's 100 percent allowed to store a hash inside another hash, like so:

```
>> fancy_hash = { :number_key => 42,
>>     :hash_key => { :first_value => 1,
>>        :second_value => 2
>>    }
>> }
=> {:number_key=>42, :hash_key=>{:first_value=>1, :second_value=>2}}
```

You're well into the thick of Ruby now! The good news is that it's pretty much all smooth sailing from here. While there *are* a few tricky concepts ahead, once you've mastered the basic Ruby objects (like numbers, strings, arrays, and hashes), learned how to use a bunch of their methods, and become a whiz at topics like control flow (using if/elsif/else, loops, and iterators), you've covered most of the language. Don't worry if you don't feel perfectly comfortable with Ruby yet; while it doesn't take long to learn the basics, you can take as much time as you want to explore the depths. And that's where we're going next: deeper into the heart of Ruby, where strange-sounding (but powerful!) creatures await.

7
The Magic of
Methods
and
Blocks

A Method to the Madness

"I think that's the last of it!" Squeaky Jim said, sweeping a pile of stray hash into his dustpan. "That was some mid-morning rush!"

"I'll say," said Big Hank. He hefted a huge green compost bag onto his shoulder and grinned at the King, Scarlet, and Ruben. "Thanks for all your help today! We'd have been in a terrible pickle if you all hadn't been here to lend a hand."

"Our pleasure!" said Ruben, who was packing three to-go boxes of hash and eggs. "The food here is terrific!"

"Definitely!" said Scarlet. "Will you be okay for the lunch crowd? We had a lot of fun, and we can help some more if you need it."

Hank laughed as he tossed bag after bag into the kitchen's enormous compost bin. "The Hashery is more of a breakfast and brunch operation," he said. "The lunch crowd is usually pretty thin. I think we'll be okay." He dusted his hands off and looked around. "What are you up to for the rest of the day?"

"Well," the King said, "since we've come down this way, I was thinking we could—"

"Hang on a second. What's this?" Scarlet interrupted, pulling a handful of what had appeared to be stray hash out of Squeaky Jim's dustpan.

Squeaky Jim bent down to look at it. "Mostly mud," he said.

"But what are these little red needles?" she asked. "And this shiny green thing?"

The King pulled a small magnifying glass from his kingly robe and leaned in to get a better look.

"Aha! I've seen those red needles before," said the King. "Those come from the Carmine Pines." He examined the shiny green thing for a minute. "But this," he said, stroking his fluffy white beard, "this is something I've never come across in all my years of kinging about."

"It looks like a scale," Ruben said. "Like from a fish or a lizard!"

"Sweet corn muffins!" said the King. "You're right! But it's too big to be from any normal fish or lizard. Where could it have come from?"

"One thing at a time," Scarlet said. "What are the Carmine Pines?"

"The Carmine Pines are a vast red forest on the eastern edge of the kingdom," the King replied. "Only a few minutes' walk from here, in fact."

Scarlet turned the scale over in her palm. "Have you ever seen anything like this, Hank? Jim?"

"Never," said Jim, and Hank shook his head.

Scarlet thought for a moment. "If this might be a clue to why the Hashery computer malfunctioned, we should investigate," she said. "The sooner, the better!"

The King nodded vigorously. "This way," he said. He turned to Big Hank and Squeaky Jim. "Thanks again for a lovely meal, guys!" he said. "I'll be in again tomorrow!"

"Our pleasure, Your Majesty!" Hank smiled, and he and Squeaky Jim bowed.

Waving goodbye to Hank and Jim, the King, Ruben, and Scarlet stepped out of the Hashery and into the bright, late-mid-morning light.

"Right over there!" said the King, standing on tiptoe and pointing. The red treetops of the Carmine Pines were visible less than a mile away.

"Well, let's get going," Ruben said. "There's still plenty of day left, and it'll only take a few minutes." With that, the three of them set out toward the forest.

"You know," Scarlet said after a while, "I don't think these Ruby malfunctions have been accidents at all."

"Really?" asked the King.

"Think about it!" said Scarlet. "Your string goes missing, the Mysterious Pipe overflows, the Loop goes crazy, and the Hashery's Computing Contraption goes haywire—all in the same day?"

"Well, the string bit might have been my fault," the King said, sheepishly.

"Either way, I think Scarlet's on to something," Ruben said. "I think this is . . . SABOTAGE!"

"Great coats! Sabotage?" said the King. "Who would do such a thing?"

"I don't know," replied Scarlet, "but one way or another, we'll find out!"

After a few more minutes of walking, the trio arrived at the edge of the Carmine Pines. Enormous pine trees towered over them, their red needles glinting in the sun.

Scarlet reached up with one hand and pulled down a handful of needles. She dug through her pocket with her other hand and pulled out the needles she'd found in Jim's dustpan. The King examined both with his magnifying glass for nearly a minute.

"Absolutely the same," he said at last. "These needles are from the Pines, all right!"

"You were right!" said Ruben. "But what do we do now that we're here?"

"I imagine we'll ask for a bit of help from someone who knows the area," the King said.

"How?" asked Scarlet and Ruben together.

"With a Computing Contraption, of course!" said the King.

Scarlet looked around. "But we're in the middle of the forest!" she said. "There are no Computing Contraptions between here and the Hashery."

"Computing Contraptions are everywhere in the kingdom," the King said. "You just have to know where to look." He reached up and pulled on the lowest branch of a nearby tree, and a cleverly hidden Computing Contraption swung out from inside the tree's trunk.

"Wow!" said Ruben. "Now what?"

"Well, I imagine we'll need to use Ruby to figure out who lives here in the Pines," the King said. "Even if we don't find the owner of our shiny green scale, we might at least find someone to help us out."

"Perfect!" said Scarlet. "So there's a directory of people who live in the Kingdom stored in each Computing Contraption?"

"Well, yes," said the King, rubbing his head. "But here's the rub. I don't know much about Ruby, but I *do* recall hearing once that there's actually no built-in method to get a list of all those people."

Ruben sat down on a flat rock. "No method!" he said. "How are we supposed to find someone to help us if Ruby doesn't have a built-in method for it?"

Scarlet thought for a minute. "Well," she said, "I *think* it's possible to write our very own Ruby methods, but I've never actually seen it done before."

"Write our own Ruby methods?" asked the King. "That would be marvelous! Are you sure it's possible?"

"Of course it's possible!" cried a nearby voice. The King and Scarlet both jumped, and Ruben nearly fell off his rock. They all turned in the direction of the voice to see, standing only a few yards away from them . . . a knight, with sword drawn!

"Agh!" Ruben shouted, and tried to hide behind his rock.

"What in the name of midnight snack marzipan is the meaning of this?" demanded the King.

The knight froze, then hastily pushed her visor up on her helmet.

"Your Majesty!" she cried, and bowed deeply. "A bajillion apologies! I didn't recognize you with my visor down." She quickly slid her sword back into its scabbard.

"A lady knight!" said Scarlet.

"No, just a knight," said the King. "After all, if she were a man, you wouldn't say, 'A man knight,' would you?"

"I suppose not," admitted Scarlet.

"Who are you?" Ruben asked.

The knight stood tall and proudly put her hands on her hips. "I'm the Off-White Knight!" she replied.

"Off-white?" asked the King. "Your armor is more of an eggshell color, I think."

"Maybe an ecru," Scarlet said, squinting.

"I think that's a large bird," said the King.

"Enough tomfoolery!" said the knight. "I am the *Off-White* Knight, and now it's time for you to DEFEND yourselves!"

"Agh!" shouted Ruben again, covering his head with his hands.

The knight tried to scratch her head, but ended up scratching the outside of her helmet. "Why are you cowering like that?" she asked.

"Aren't you going to slay us?" Ruben asked.

The Off-White Knight laughed. "Heavens, no!" she said. "In fact, it's my knightly duty to help anyone in the Carmine Pines who needs assistance, so I'll show you how to write your own Ruby methods."

"But it's daytime," said the King.

Ruben and Scarlet gave each other a knowing look.

defining your own methods

The Off-White Knight cleared her throat. "Yes. Well," she said, "what I was trying to say was that you certainly *can* define your own Ruby methods. You simply need to use the special words def and end." She walked up to the cleverly disguised Computing Contraption and began typing.

```
>> def simon_says(phrase)
>>    return phrase
>> end
```

"You start by typing def, which is short for *define*, because you're defining a brand-new method. Next, you type the name of your method, which is simon_says in this case. Then you put the *parameters* next, in between parentheses. For this method, we have just one parameter: phrase."

"The what now?" asked the King, rubbing his head with both hands.

"The parameters," said the Off-White Knight. "They're sort of like placeholders or nicknames for the information you'll give your method when you call it."

"Let me get this straight," said the King. "When you write out what a method does using def and end, that's called *defining* the method."

"That's right," said the knight.

"And when you actually use the method somewhere, that's *calling* the method."

"Indeed!" said the knight. "Sometimes we say *invoke* instead of *call*, but they mean exactly the same thing. You define a method so Ruby knows what it does, and you call the method when you want to use it. Calling a method looks like this," she continued, and typed some more:

```
>> simon_says('Prepare for battle!')
=> "Prepare for battle!"
```

"I'm a bit fuzzy right now," said the King.

"You're a bit fuzzy all the time," said the Off-White Knight, eyeing the King's fluffy beard.

"Yes, yes," said the King, "but I'm also still confused. Could you go over calling the method a bit?"

"Of course!" said the knight. "When we defined the `simon_says` method earlier, we just told Ruby what code to run whenever we use the name `simon_says`. We can then use that code by writing the method name and putting in our own bit of information—the string `'Prepare for battle!'`—where we had the `phrase` parameter before. Like I said, `phrase` is just like a placeholder that sits between the parentheses until we're ready to use the method with `'Prepare for battle!'`.

"What about the parentheses around `'Prepare for battle!'`?" Ruben asked. "I've seen Ruby methods get called without parentheses before."

"You're right!" said the knight. "The parentheses are optional; you usually use them when you define the method, but you can use them or skip them when you call the method. It's all the same to Ruby!"

Return Versus Puts

"All right, I understand defining and calling now," said the King. "But what's this return business, and how is it different from `puts`? Don't they both print things on the screen?"

"Aha!" said the Off-White Knight. "A lot of people find this very confusing, but I think I can show you the difference between return and puts with just a couple of examples."

"Here we define a method called print_sum that prints the sum of two numbers with puts," she said:

```
>> def print_sum(a, b)
>>    puts a + b
>> end
```

"Next, we'll define a second method that *returns* the sum."

```
>> def return_sum(a, b)
>>    return a + b
>> end
```

"Do you see the difference between the print_sum and return_sum methods we defined?" the knight asked. "One puts, the other returns." Scarlet, Ruben, and the King all nodded.

"Perfect!" said the Off-White Knight. "Let's see what that really means for what our Ruby code does. First, we'll call our print_sum method."

```
>> sum = print_sum(2, 3)
5
=> nil
>> sum
=> nil
```

"See that?" said the knight. "puts will print something on the screen for you—in this case, it added 2 and 3 and printed the result 5 to the screen—but it won't *do* anything with the value of 5: it produces nil after doing the printing! When we check out the value of sum, we see that it's nil."

"Now let's call our return_sum method." She typed some more:

```
>> sum = return_sum(2, 3)
=> 5
>> sum
=> 5
```

"*Now* I understand," said the King. "Printing something just makes that value appear on the screen, but *returning* it lets you store that value in a variable, as we did with sum."

"You've got it!" said the knight. "A method is just like a little machine. Things go into it and things come out. The things that go into a method when you call it are its *arguments*, and the thing that comes out is its *return value*.

"If a method doesn't have a specific return value, it returns nil. You know how you always see => nil when you puts or print something? That's because although the puts and print methods write text on the screen, they don't have a return value, so they *return* nil."

"Hang on a moment," said the King. "If a method can automatically return nil when it has no other value to return, why can't we automatically return other values?"

Understanding Method Arguments

"We can!" said the Off-White Knight. "Whenever you're in a method definition, Ruby automatically returns the last bit of Ruby code that gets run. If you want to save some typing, you can leave off the return keyword if the last thing in your method is the return value, and Ruby will automatically return it for you."

"Awesome!" said Ruben "Anything that saves us some typing is good. Now, just to back up a second to the difference between parameters and arguments: parameters are the handy names you put between parentheses in your method *definition* to let your method know what kinds of information it will get, and the arguments are the information you actually give to your method when you *call* it," Ruben said.

"Quite right!" said the Off-White Knight. "Hang on, let me give you another example." She typed furiously into the Computing Contraption, narrating all the while. "Let's define a method called add_things with the parameters thing_one and thing_two and return their sum. That'd look like this:

```
>> def add_things(thing_one, thing_two)
>>    thing_one + thing_two
>> end
```

"Next, we'll *call* the method with the arguments 3 and 7. The return value is 10."

```
>> add_things(3, 7)
=> 10
```

"That's great," said Scarlet, "but what happens if you want to sometimes pass an argument to a method, and sometimes not? If you don't pass the right number of arguments, Ruby throws an error!" She typed into the Computing Contraption:

```
>> def plus_one(number)
>>    number + 1
>> end

>> plus_one 2
=> 3

>> plus_one()
ArgumentError: wrong number of arguments (0 for 1)
```

"Yeah!" said Ruben. "Here, Ruby's saying that it got zero arguments, but it expected one."

"Great point!" said the Off-White Knight. "In that case, you can use *optional* or *default* parameters. Those are special parameters that come with a placeholder value, and if you don't give Ruby arguments for those parameters when you call the method, Ruby inserts the placeholders instead. Let me define a method like that for you," she said, and began typing at the Computing Contraption once more:

```
>> def declare_name(name='The Off-White Knight!')
>>    puts name
>> end
```

"See the equal sign?" she said. "That tells the method to use that string if it's not told otherwise. Now, without any arguments, the method will use the default name," she said. "Let's try calling it!" She typed some more:

```
>> declare_name()
The Off-White Knight!
=> nil
```

"Wow!" said Ruben. "You didn't pass any arguments at all, so the default one was used automatically."

"That's right," said the knight. "And again, because Ruby is super flexible, you don't even need the parentheses to show that you're calling a method!" She typed even more:

```
>> declare_name
The Off-White Knight!
=> nil
```

"That looks a little *too* magical to me," said the King. "If there were lots of code floating around, how would I immediately know the difference between a method with no parentheses and a plain old variable?"

"That's a good point," said the Off-White Knight. She tried to wipe the sweat from her brow, but accidentally knocked her visor down instead. "I often use the parentheses, because they make it clear I'm using a method and not something else, like a variable."

"Now, let's say you *do* want to use your own name," she continued, struggling to push her visor back up. "You just pass it in—with or without parentheses—like this." She typed a few more lines:

```
>> declare_name('Lady Scarlet the Bold!')
Lady Scarlet the Bold!
=> nil

>> declare_name 'Sir Ruben the Fearless!'
Sir Ruben the Fearless!
=> nil
```

"Whew!" said the Off-White Knight. "Let me take a break for just a second. My gauntlets are tired."

what Is nil?

"Of course," said the King. "I'm still a bit hung up on nil, though," he said. "What *is* it?"

"I think I know the answer to that one," Ruben said. "nil is Ruby's way of saying 'nothing at all.' When Ruby wants to express the idea of 'nothing' or 'no value,' it uses nil."

"Is nil true or false?" asked the King.

"Neither!" said Ruben. "It's its very own thing. But it *is* one of two *falsey* values in Ruby—the other is false."

"What do you mean by 'falsey'?" asked the King.

"I mean that if you use nil in an if statement, it will be the opposite of true," Ruben said. "This should look familiar." He typed into the Computing Contraption:

```
>> if nil
>>   puts "This text won't be printed!"
>> end
```

"Your code didn't print anything on the screen!" said the King.

Ruben nodded. "That's because Ruby will never treat if nil as a true condition. To Ruby, saying 'if nothing' and 'if false' are the same, so it will never run the code between if nil and end." He thought for a moment. "Remember the if statement?" he asked.

The King nodded vigorously. "As if it were only yesterday!" he said.

"It was today," said Ruben.

"Tomato, tomato," said the King, pronouncing the word the same way both times. Ruben and Scarlet looked at each other and shrugged.

"Anyway," said Ruben, "The if statement takes a bit of Ruby code and does one thing if that code is true and something else if it's false. nil is always treated like false in if statements, so to make something happen if a value is nil, you might think you have to do this:

```
>> if !nil
>>   puts "But I will get printed!"
>> end

But I will get printed!
=> nil
```

"But there's a piece of built-in Ruby code we've already seen that means the same thing as 'if not': unless!" Ruben typed some more:

```
>> unless nil
>>   puts "But I will get printed!"
>> end

But I will get printed!
=> nil
```

"unless has the exact same meaning as 'if not.' When we say 'Stay up late *if* you're *not* sleepy,' that means the same thing as 'Stay up late *unless* you're sleepy,'" Ruben explained.

"I've seen this before!" said the King. "We use unless in Ruby anytime we'd otherwise use if and !."

"Right!" said Ruben. "Both false and nil will behave the same way when used in an if or unless statement, but it's important to remember that nil's not the exact same thing as false." He continued typing:

```
>> nil == false
=> false
```

"Did you see that => nil at the end of the unless example?" the Off-White Knight asked. "That's what I was talking about. nil is the return value of puts. Check it out!" She reached over Ruben's head and typed some more:

```
>> puts 'Prepare for nil!'
Prepare for nil!
=> nil
```

"One last thing about nil," said the knight. "Not only is it *not* the same thing as false, it's *not* the same thing as zero! Zero is a number; nil is simply nothing at all."

"I think I've got it now," said the King.

Splat Parameters

"Right," said the knight. "Then we're on to more method magic! I showed you how to make a method take an optional argument, but Ruby also lets you tell a method to take *any number* of arguments. *Splat parameters* are the way to tell a Ruby method, 'Hey, I'm going to pass you a whole list of things to use. I don't know how many, so just deal with whatever number I send!'" The knight flexed her fingers a few times. "They work like this," she said, and began typing:

```
>> def declare_knights(*knights)
>>    puts knights
>> end
```

```
>> declare_knights('Lady Scarlet', 'Sir Ruben', 'The Off-White
Knight')
Lady Scarlet
Sir Ruben
The Off-White Knight
=> nil
```

"You can think of the asterisk (*) in our first line as a little splat mark that tells the method to take the whole messy bucket of arguments, no matter how many, and do something with them," the Off-White Knight said.

"I see the little splat next to the parameter name," said the King, "but not in the method body and not when you call the method. Is the * only used when you define the method and only between the parentheses?"

"Exactly," said the knight. "Ruby is very smart—you only have to tell it something once! As I mentioned," the Off-White Knight continued, "Ruby realizes that the last thing that appears in your method body is probably the thing you want to return. So, as I mentioned earlier, if you want to save some typing, you can leave off the return keyword if the last thing in your method is the return value. Ruby does it automatically! That means that this:

```
>> def add(a, b)
>>    return a + b
>> end

>> add(1, 3)
=> 4
```

is exactly the same as this!

```
>> def add(a, b)
>>    a + b
>> end

>> add(1, 3)
=> 4
```

"Wonderful!" said Scarlet. "I'll definitely remember that trick when writing my own methods."

"And now," said the Off-White Knight, pulling her sword out of its scabbard, "it's time for you to YIELD!"

"Agh!" shouted Ruben, covering his head with his hands again.

Block Methods

The Off-White Knight struggled to get her sword back into its scabbard. "You really should do something about that cowering habit," she said. "What I was saying is, you need to use the yield keyword when you write your own Ruby methods that take blocks."

"Oh," Ruben said, slowly putting his hands down again.

"Wait, you can write your own Ruby methods that take blocks?" Scarlet asked.

"Of course!" said the knight. "You'd write it like so," she said, and typed in the Computing Contraption:

```
>> def my_block_method
>>    yield
>> end
=> nil
```

"First," said the knight, "we define a method, my_block_method, using def. Next, we use the yield keyword to tell the method to let the code inside the block run; when you call the method with a block, whatever happens in the block is what the method does! Let's look at some examples."

```
>> my_block_method { 1 + 1 }
=> 2
```

"Here, we're calling my_block_method and passing in a block that just adds 1 + 1, so my_block_method returns 2. We can also do other things, like print text:

```
>> my_block_method { puts 'Hello from the block!' }
Hello from the block!
=> nil
```

"my_block_method lets the code in the block run, so it prints out Hello from the block! We see the nil because puts prints out text on the screen, but the value it returns is nil," the knight explained.

"What's a block, again?" the King asked.

"A block is just a bit of Ruby code between curly brackets or between do and end," said the knight. "You've probably seen built-in methods like each that use blocks, but now you can create your own methods that use blocks!"

"That's amazing!" said Scarlet. "But can you use splat parameters and blocks together?"

"You can!" said the knight. "You can pass regular, default, *and* splat arguments to any method you write, and they can be in any order."

The knight cracked her knuckles and typed into the Computing Contraption, explaining as she went along. "Let's build a little something we can use to quickly and easily introduce ourselves," she said. "After all, we knights are always having to go around introducing ourselves as we sally forth into a new town."

```
>> def all_about_me(name, age=100, *pets)
>>   puts "My name is #{name}"
>>   puts "I'm #{age} years old"
>>   if block_given?
>>     yield pets
>>   else
>>     puts pets
>>   end
>> end
=> nil
```

"We're not done yet," said the knight, "but let's go over this. First, I defined the all_about_me method to take three parameters. We see a regular old name parameter and an age parameter, which defaults to 100 if no age is passed in when the method is called."

"But you could have written the age parameter with its default first, then the name one," Ruben said.

"You got it," said the knight. "Finally, the *pets splat parameter! That can come in any order with respect to the regular or default parameters, but we happened to put it at the end."

"I get that part," said the King, "but what's this block_given? business?"

"That's a built-in Ruby method," said the knight. "It returns true if the method was passed a block as an argument and false otherwise. I wrote the all_about_me method so it yields to the block if there is one, sending the list of pets to the block; otherwise, it just uses puts to print out the pets. Don't worry if block_given? doesn't make perfect sense now—we'll be seeing more of it later on."

"Why is it yield pets and not just yield?" Scarlet asked.

"An excellent question," said the knight. "Earlier, we just wanted to let the block handle everything that was passed to our method, so we simply typed yield. Now, though, we want our block to care only about pets, so we specifically give only our list of pets to the block."

The knight's fingers moved again across the Computing Contraption, giving their newly defined method a try.

```
>> all_about_me('Ruben', 12, 'Smalls', 'Chucky Jim')
My name is Ruben.
I'm 12 years old.
Smalls
Chucky Jim
=> nil
```

"That's me!" said Ruben. "That's amazing. What else can we do?"

"Well," said the Off-White Knight, "We can use that block I mentioned earlier! Look what happens if we pass a block to our method, then refer to the pets we pass in with pets:

```
>> all_about_me('Ruben', 12, 'Smalls', 'Chucky Jim') { |pets| puts
pets.join(' and ') }
My name is Ruben.
I'm 12 years old.
Smalls and Chucky Jim
=> nil
```

"This looks a lot like the last example," said Scarlet. "But the block is pretty tricky. What's it doing?"

"I'll walk you through it! First, `{ |pets| puts pets}` would simply tell Ruby: 'Hey, block! I'm going to pass you a variable, pets, and you should print it out.'"

"But then `all_about_me` would just print out the array elements, and it wouldn't look very nice," Scarlet said.

"Exactly!" said the knight. "So I'm also using a built-in Ruby method, `join`. Ruby array elements can be joined to make strings, so I'm using `join` to turn the array of pets into a string with ' and ' in the middle."

"Could you show us another example?" Ruben asked.

"Sure," said the knight. "Here's one where we can use `join` to turn an array of numbers into a string with `'plus'` between each number:

```
>> [1, 2, 3].join(' plus ')
=> "1 plus 2 plus 3"
```

"There's always something new to discover in Ruby," marveled the King.

Into the Dagron's Lair

"Speaking of discoveries," said Scarlet, "that reminds me!" She rummaged around in her pockets. "Have you ever seen anything like this before?" She held out the glittering green scale for the Off-White Knight to examine.

"Great googly moogly!" said the Off-White Knight. "That scale looks like it belongs to the Dagron!"

"You mean the *dragon*," Ruben offered.

"No, the Dagron," said the Off-White Knight. "That's her name. Though she *is* a dragon."

"A lady dragon!" said Ruben.

"No, just a dragon," said the Off-White Knight. "If she were a man, would you call her a man dragon?"

"I guess not," admitted Ruben. He looked around nervously. "But there's really a dragon in the Carmine Pines?"

"Not to worry," said the knight. "The Dagron is a very power-ful dragon, but she's also wise and well mannered. In fact, I'm surprised you found one of her scales anywhere trouble's been brewing. That doesn't sound like the Dagron I know."

"Well, it *sounds* like we'd best find her and ask what's going on," said the King. "Lead the way, madam knight!"

"To the Dagron!" said the Off-White Knight, flipping her visor down over her eyes. "This way!" The knight set off deeper into the forest, and the King, Scarlet, and Ruben followed.

After walking for a few minutes, they began to hear a low, rhythmic *whooshing* sound, like someone squeezing bellows on a fire.

"What's that?" Ruben whispered.

"The Dagron!" whispered the knight. "Here she is!" And before they knew it, they found themselves in front of an enor-mous dragon curled up in a shining green circle, asleep.

"Dagron!" the knight called, pushing her visor up on her helmet.

The Dagron didn't open her eyes. "Yes?" she boomed, a thin plume of smoke rising from her right nostril.

"I've brought some guests to see you, including the King!"

The Dagron's eyes flashed open, focusing immediately on the four of them. The Dagron unfurled herself and reared up to her full height; her head nearly reached the tops of the pines around her.

"Your Majesty!" said the Dagron, and she bowed so low that her head nearly brushed the earth.

"Madame Dagron," said the King. "We've come with a somewhat . . . unusual question." The King nodded toward Scarlet. "Does this belong to you?"

Scarlet pulled the scale from her pocket and held it out to the Dagron. The Dagron stared at it for a few seconds, then shook her head slowly.

"I don't think that's one of mine," said the Dagron, "but I *do* have a great many scales. If you'd like, you can check to see if I'm missing one."

The group spent almost an hour examining the Dagron, looking for a loose or missing scale. Scarlet and Ruben searched high and low. The Off-White Knight quested mightily. The King took a short nap beneath a tall red pine.

"Well, there's no doubt about it," Scarlet finally said, holding the mystery scale near the tip of the Dagron's tail. "This is definitely *not* one of the Dagron's." She put the scale in her pocket and sat glumly next to Ruben on a rock.

"Though I'm pleased not to be a suspect in these strange goings-on," said the Dagron, "I *am* sorry to disappoint you." She thought for a moment. "While I'm not certain I can help, I may know someone who can."

Scarlet perked up. "Who?" she asked.

"Wherefore the Wand'ring Minstrel," said the Dagron. "He frolics and sings all throughout the Carmine Pines and has been almost everywhere in the kingdom. If anything strange is going on, I'm sure he'd know about it."

Ruben jumped off his rock. "Can you take us to him?" he asked.

"Certainly," said the Dagron. "It may take us a while to find him, though."

Scarlet stood and dusted herself off. "Actually, I'll bet we can find him pretty quickly," she said. "Now that we know how to define our own Ruby methods, I might know *just* the thing!"

You Know This!

Between defining your own methods, creating your own methods that use blocks, and learning about things like splat and default arguments, your head's probably feeling pretty full! Let's take some time to review what we talked about in this chapter.

First, you learned how to write your own methods. We start our method definition with def, followed by the name of the method and then a list of parameters between parentheses. Finally, we type whatever code we want our method to perform and then finish it all up with end, like so:

```
>> def multiply_by_three(number)
>>    number * 3
>> end

>> multiply_by_three(2)
=> 6
```

You also learned that methods can have *default* or *optional* parameters. If we provide an argument to a method that takes an optional parameter, the method will use that argument; otherwise, it'll use whatever its default is:

```
>> def multiply_by_three(number=2)
>>    number * 3
>> end

>> multiply_by_three
=> 6

>> multiply_by_three 3
=> 9
```

If we want a method that takes any number of arguments, we can use *splat parameters* by putting an asterisk (*) before our parameter name:

```
>> def print_all_the_names(*names)
>>    puts names
>> end

>> print_all_the_names('Larry', 'Curly', 'Moe')
Larry
Curly
Moe
=> nil
```

Speaking of nil, you learned that methods that don't have an explicit *return value* will return nil, which is Ruby's way of saying "nothing at all." Remember, returning a value is different from just printing it on the screen!

```
>> puts 'Beware the Dagron!'
Beware the Dagron!
=> nil
```

In fact, when it comes to return values, it's more common to leave off the return and let Ruby automatically return the result of the last bit of code it runs. So while you *can* write this:

```
>> def just_return_two
>>    return 2
>> end

>> just_return_two
=> 2
```

It's much better Ruby style to write this:

```
>> def also_returns_two
>>    2
>> end
```

```
>> also_returns_two
=> 2
```

Finally, we saw that if we want to define a method that takes a block, we just need to use the handy yield keyword. We can yield without parameters to give control over to the block, or we can pass parameters in order to give the block arguments to work with.

```
>> def block_party
>>    yield
>> end

>> block_party { puts 'Hello from the block!' }
Hello from the block!
=> nil

>> def block_party_part_two(name)
>>    yield name
>> end

>> block_party_part_two('Haldo') { |name| puts "This is #{name}'s
party!" }
This is Haldo's party!
=> nil
```

You learned a lot in this chapter, but keep in mind: if you're ever curious about what a method does or what arguments it expects, you can always look up the Ruby documentation at *http://ruby-doc.org/*. Just make sure to ask your local adult before going online!

Speaking of looking up new things, we'll be covering a bit of new Ruby code in the next chapter—specifically, how to organize, create, and control our very own Ruby objects.

8

EVERYTHING
Is an
OBJECT
(almost)

THE SUBJECT OF OUR STORY
Is an OBJECT

Scarlet ran to the Computing Contraption. "Do you know the name of that directory of everyone in the kingdom?" she called to the King. "It's a hash that associates everyone's name with his or her address."

"Let's see," said the King. "Ah, yes! I'm pretty sure it's called citizens."

Scarlet nodded and began typing into IRB. When she pressed ENTER, this is what she saw:

```
>> citizens
=> {
  :aaron_a_aardvark => 'A van down by the river',
  :alice_b_abracadabra => 'The green house with two chimneys',
```

```
:trady_blix => 'Mal Abochny',
# ...and so on and so forth
```

The King peered over her shoulder. "That's it!" he said. "But whoa! There must be a bajillion people in the kingdom! How will we find Wherefore?"

Scarlet typed some more:

```
>> citizens.size
=> 24042
```

"Yeah, the hash is definitely too big to go through by hand," Scarlet said, "but I bet we can write our own method to find him!"

Ruben studied the citizens hash for a minute. "Remember how we could get the value of a hash key by typing the hash name, then the key in square brackets?" he asked.

"Yep," Scarlet said.

"Well," Ruben said, "what if we just write a method that takes a person's name and the citizens hash, then tries to find that name in the hash?"

"Ruben, you're a genius!" Scarlet said. She quickly typed:

```
>> def find_person(name, people)
>>   if people[name]
>>     puts people[name]
>>   else
>>     puts 'Not found!'
>>   end
>> end
```

"Hang on, hang on. What's all this?" the King asked.

"Just a quick method I whipped up," Scarlet said. "See? It's called find_person, and it takes a person's name as a symbol and a hash of people as parameters. If it finds the name in the hash, it prints it out; otherwise, it says the name's not found!" She typed:

```
>> find_person(:wherefore, citizens)
=> One half mile due east!
```

"There it is!" Scarlet said. "It found the `:wherefore` key in the `citizens` hash."

"One half mile due east!" said the Off-White Knight. "That should only take a few minutes, and east is that way. Let's go!"

The Dagron rose to her full height, blotting out the sun for an instant. "I'll come as well," she said. "Wherefore and I are old friends, and we haven't spoken in some time. It will be good to see him again."

"Well, then," said the King, "lead the way!"

The Off-White Knight and the Dagron turned and headed toward the late morning sun, and the King, Scarlet, and Ruben followed. The trees became taller and closer together as they walked, and after a few minutes, the sun could only be seen as a warm red light through the tops of the Carmine Pines.

"Hold on a second," Ruben said, stopping and turning his head to one side. "Do you hear that?"

They all paused. The King cupped his hand to his ear, shook his head, wiggled his little finger around in his ear, then cupped his hand to it again. "I don't hear anything," he said.

"I think I hear it too," said the Dagron. "It's—"

"Music!" cried Ruben. "It's coming from over there!" He pointed a little to the right of where they'd been headed.

"Let's go!" said Scarlet, and the group pressed on into the Pines.

The music grew louder, and after walking through a particularly dense thicket of trees, the group found themselves on the edge of a small meadow. In the very center, perched on a wide tree stump, was a man in a scarlet tunic and archer's cap with a long white feather in it. He was playing a pink mandolin and occasionally stopping to furiously scribble on a long roll of parchment with a quill pen, which sported the same type of long white feather as his cap.

"Wherefore!" boomed the Dagron.

The man on the stump stopped scribbling and looked up. A wide grin broke out across his face. "The Dagron!" he called. "Wonderful to see you! Come in, come in, come in."

Led by the Dagron, the group crossed the meadow and circled around Wherefore. Wherefore leapt nimbly from his stump, removed his cap, and bowed deeply.

"Friends," he said, "welcome to my forest stronghold!" He gestured to the stump. "It's not much to look at now, but I've always had a weak spot for a fixer-upper. And I," he said, "am your humble host, Wherefore the Wand'ring Minstrel." Wherefore replaced his cap on his head. "I know, of course, the Dagron, and I've met the Off-White Knight before." He looked at the King and pressed his palms together. "Your Majesty," he said. "I've not had the pleasure of meeting you before, but it *is* a pleasure."

"Likewise," said the King. "We've heard much about you!"

Wherefore turned to Ruben and Scarlet. "Which leaves you fine rapscallions. What do you call yourselves?"

"I'm Scarlet," said Scarlet, "and this is Ruben."

"Hi!" said Ruben.

"Hello and hello!" said Wherefore. "Wonderful to meet you. I'm afraid you've caught me at a bit of a bad time, though." He sighed. "I've spent all morning writing a ballad, and it's hardly half done. I've got to get back to it immediately if I'm going to finish it before nightfall."

"A ballad?" said Scarlet.

"Oh, yes," Wherefore said, "you see, I'm something of a businessman. I operate a small-time ballad delivery service with dozens of customers. The only catch is," he said, "that this means I do in fact have *dozens* of customers, and each ballad takes me hours to write. I can hardly keep up!" He pulled a handkerchief from his tunic pocket and mopped his brow.

The Dagron hummed thoughtfully, exhaling little puffs of smoke. "You know," she said, "I think I can be of service." She looked around the nearly empty meadow. "But I'll need a little Ruby magic. Do you happen to have a Computing Contraption nearby?"

Wherefore laughed. "*Do* I have a Computing Contraption!" he said, and he stepped on the largest root of the tree stump. The stump shuddered, then rose a few feet out of the ground. It rotated slowly as it emerged, revealing the familiar glow of a Computing Contraption screen!

Classes and Objects

"Wonderful," said the Dagron, coiling herself around the stump and leaning in close to the screen. "Now then! Every object in your Ruby program has a unique ID number," she said. "You'll find that objects you create usually have much higher numbers than objects Ruby creates. See?" She touched the screen of the Computing Contraption with her claw and said, "Ruby has a few objects that are very familiar, like 0 or true. Each object in Ruby has its very own ID number, and that's how Ruby keeps track of them all. Have a look!"

```
>> 0.object_id
=> 1
>> true.object_id
=> 20
```

"Built-in Ruby objects like these get ID numbers from Ruby automatically when IRB starts or the script loads," the Dagron continued. "Ruby also gives IDs to Ruby objects we create in our programs, but they're very high numbers. This is because Ruby comes with so many built-in objects for us!" She touched the Computing Contraption again, and more text appeared:

```
>> :baloney.object_id
=> 1238088
>> "The Ballad of Wherefore the Wand'ring Minstrel".object_id
=> 2174481360
```

"How did she do that?" Ruben whispered to the Off-White Knight. "She didn't even type anything!"

"She doesn't need to," the knight whispered back. "Dragons are magical creatures, and the Dagron is one of the most magical of all."

"But where do all these objects come from?" the Dagron asked. Wherefore sat cross-legged on the ground and looked up expectantly at her.

"From *classes*," the Dagron said, answering her own question. "You can think of Ruby classes as little machines that make objects of a certain type, and each object in Ruby knows what class it belongs to. We can use the class method to ask objects what their classes are. To start, Ruby numbers are from the Fixnum class. Behold!" she said, and more code appeared on the screen:

```
>> 7.class
=> Fixnum
```

"A string's class is naturally . . . String!" she continued:

```
>> 'Odelay!'.class
=> String
```

"That's nice to know," interrupted the King, "but what *good* does it do us?"

"I was just getting to that," said the Dagron. "When you know what class a Ruby object is, you can use the new method to make a new object of that class. You've seen this before, yes?" She gestured at new code on the screen:

```
>> greeting = 'Hello!'
```

"Yup!" said Ruben.

"Well, now you can do *this*!" said the Dagron, touching the Computing Contraption once more.

```
>> greeting = String.new('Hello!')
=> "Hello!"

>> greeting
=> "Hello!"

>> greeting.class
=> String
```

"You see?" said the Dagron, folding her claws. "Every object in Ruby has a class, which we can find with the class method. Not only that, but every object is created by a class with the new method, and it's the class's job to produce objects of a particular type!"

"So the class is like a cookie cutter, stamping out particular kinds of cookies," said Wherefore, hitting his palm with his closed fist in a stamping motion. "Gingerbread men, chocolate chip cookies, sugar cookies shaped like snowflakes. And the objects are the cookies!"

"That's a very good way of thinking about it," said the Dagron.

"When's lunch?" asked Wherefore.

"I'm afraid I still don't quite understand," the King interrupted. "And I'm still a bit mystified as to what makes classes so important."

"I think I can help with that one," said Scarlet. "When we're dealing with numbers or strings, the helpful things classes do might not be obvious. But if we're creating our *own* objects with their *own* new classes, classes become a way of creating a bunch of objects from a template. For example, if we have a `Minstrel` class, we can make a bunch of minstrels!"

"How?" asked the King.

Creating Our First Class, Minstrel

"I'm glad you asked! Let's give it a try," said the Dagron. She touched the Computing Contraption, and more code filled the screen.

NOTE   *For some of these longer code examples, we'll write Ruby scripts! Whenever you see a filename in italics above the code, like* minstrel.rb *for the next example, that means you can type the code into your text editor and save it as a file with the given name.*

minstrel.rb

```ruby
class Minstrel
  def initialize(name)
    @name = name
  end

  def introduce
    puts "My name is #{@name}!"
  end

  def sing
    puts 'Tralala!'
  end
end
```

"Now then," the Dagron said, clearing her throat, "let's have a look. The `class` keyword tells Ruby you'd like to make a new class," she said. "Just like you use `def` and `end` to tell Ruby you're defining a new method, you use `class` and `end` to tell Ruby you'd like to create a new class.

"After `class`, you type the name of the class, which can be whatever you like," the Dagron explained. "Class names, however, *always* begin with a capital letter, like `Minstrel`." Wherefore had turned his parchment over and was taking notes as quickly as he could on the back of his ballad. "We're creating the `Minstrel` class, so we can make lots of new minstrels."

"Between `class` and that final `end`, you can add any methods you wish, just as you would define them outside a class," the Dagron continued. "In the `Minstrel` class, I defined three: `initialize`, `introduce`, and `sing`."

Ruben leaned in close to the Computing Contraption's screen. "Why does that `@name` variable have an `@` in front of it?" he asked.

"All in good time," said the Dagron.

NOTE *To follow along with the Dagron, we'll need to load her script into IRB. When we want to use code in IRB from a file we've written, we just start IRB while we're in the folder that contains our Ruby script, then use the `load` command to load the file. Load* minstrel.rb *like this:*

```
>> load 'minstrel.rb'
=> true
```

Now let's give the Dagron's code a try!

"First, let's look at the `Minstrel` class's `initialize` method. This gets called whenever we make a new instance of the class with the `new` method. Have a look!" The Dagron added more code to the screen.

```
>> wherefore = Minstrel.new('Wherefore')
=> #<Minstrel:0x000001052c77b0 @name="Wherefore">
```

"When we call `Minstrel.new`, we make a new minstrel. Because `initialize` takes a single parameter, `name`, we pass in a name when we call the `new` method. See the `@name="Wherefore"` bit there? It means `wherefore`'s name is `'Wherefore'`!" The Dagron puffed thoughtfully for a second. "So if there's any code you want to run as soon as a new instance of your class is created, you put it in the definition of your class's `initialize` method."

"Got it," said the King.

"Now all that `Proc.new` stuff makes way more sense!" said Ruben. "We were just making new procs whenever we called `new`!"

"That's right!" said the Off-White Knight. "`Proc` is a built-in Ruby class, and whenever we call `new`, we create a new one. We basically have a little factory that generates new procs whenever we want. And that's all classes are: little factories that make objects!"

"Precisely," puffed the Dagron, and she almost seemed to smile.

"What about the other two methods you added?" Scarlet asked.

"Ah, yes," said the Dagron. "Our `wherefore` is a `Minstrel`, so he has access to those methods automatically."

```
>> wherefore.introduce
My name is Wherefore!
=> nil
```

"You see?" she said. "The `introduce` method prints a string with the minstrel's name in it, which in this case is Wherefore. And not only can he introduce himself, he can also sing!"

```
>> wherefore.sing
Tralala!
=> nil
```

"We've talked about how classes make objects of a certain type," said the Dagron, "but we haven't really mentioned what an object *is*. It's quite simple: objects are just little collections of values! You can think of them as buckets of information—a thing that might have a name, or a size, or a color. Each object gets methods from its class that let us talk about its name or size or color, and that's what makes up our Ruby code."

"All right," said the King, "I think I understand why classes are so important now: they let you reuse your code for many objects without having to rewrite all the information and methods each time, and Ruby code is made up of objects. But let's go back to Ruben's question—what was that kooky spiral we saw on wherefore's @name?"

"The at sign (@) just shows Ruby that it's a special kind of variable—the kind that talks about an object's value, like its name or size or color! I'll explain that a little more. Let's try out an example using weezards," said Wherefore.

"You mean wizards," said Scarlet.

"No, weezards," said Wherefore. "Short wizards. Wee things. Weezards."

"Very well," said the Dagron. "But to get there, I'll need to explain the four different kinds of Ruby variables."

"Four kinds!" exclaimed the King. "I thought there was only one!"

"The variables you're used to seeing are called *local variables*," said the Dagron. "They're very good for creating a variable that you're going to use quickly. But once we start writing our own methods and classes, we'll need to create variables that can be defined inside those method and class definitions but are used much later—for example, when we finally call a method or create an instance of a class."

"The other three kinds of variables," the Dagron continued, "are *global variables*, *class variables*, and *instance variables*. It may seem confusing that we use different kinds of variables in different places, but once you get the hang of it, it's very easy."

"What do you mean by different places?" Scarlet asked.

"*Scopes*," said the Dagron.

Variable Scope

Oh man, this is getting good. We're getting into the real meat of the language! *Scope* is a very important idea in Ruby, and I got so excited, well, I just couldn't contain myself. I hope it's okay if I take a second to explain scope to you while the Dagron explains it to our intrepid heroes. It'll take but a minute.

This might come as a surprise to you, but not all variables are available for you to use willy-nilly at any point in a Ruby program. There are times in your program where even though you've defined a variable, if you try to use it, Ruby will complain and say it doesn't exist! What could this mean?

What it means is this: at any given point in your program, only *some* of the variables and methods you've defined can be seen. The collection of variables and methods that can be seen at any given time in your program defines the current scope; you can use anything that's in scope, and you can't use anything that's out of scope.

What determines your variable's scope in Ruby? For now, here's a good rule of thumb: new scopes are created inside a method definition, inside a class definition, and inside a block. So if you're using the run-of-the-mill local variables we've been using, this will work perfectly:

```
>> regular_old_variable = 'Hello!'
=> "Hello!"
```

We're just setting a regular_old_variable to the string 'Hello!'. Pretty standard stuff.

Next, we'll define a variable within a method:

```
>> def fancy_greeting
>>   greeting = 'Salutations!'
>> end
=> nil
```

Here, we're defining the variable named greeting inside a method named fancy_greeting. You've seen method definitions before, so there's nothing new here, either!

Next, we'll revisit blocks:

```
>> 3.times { |number| puts number }
0
1
2
=> 3
```

You're a block expert by this point, so you've got this too: we're calling the times method on the number 3 and passing it a block. Inside the block, we use the variable number to keep track of which number we're on, and we print out each number from 0 to 2 in turn. (Don't forget that computers start counting things at 0, not 1.)

These Variable Errors Will Shock and Surprise You!

What might surprise you, though, is that some of this stuff will cause Ruby to throw an error! Let's look at these one by one. In the following code, we start by defining a variable. But that regular_old_variable exists outside the class definition of FancyThings (in the outer *scope*), so it *doesn't* exist inside the class definition!

```
>> regular_old_variable = 'Hello!'
=> "Hello!"

>> class FancyThings
>>   puts regular_old_variable
>> end
NameError: undefined local variable or method `regular_old_variable'
for FancyThings:Class
```

Inside class definitions, you get a brand-new set of local variables (the kinds of variables you've seen all along so far), so Ruby rightfully tells you that inside the class, you don't have anything called regular_old_variable yet.

The same goes for method definitions: they get their own sets of local variables, too, so when you define regular_old_variable within a method, it doesn't exist outside the method definition:

```
>> def fancy_greeting
>>   puts regular_old_variable
>> end

>> fancy_greeting
NameError: undefined local variable or method `regular_old_variable'
for main:Object
```

Another error!

And, as you might have already guessed, the number variable in our block example is *local* to the block. It stops existing as soon as the block is over, so if we try to use it again after the block is finished, we get an error!

```
>> 3.times { |number| puts number }
0
1
2
=> 3

>> puts number
NameError: undefined local variable or method `number' for
main:Object
```

Here, for each number from 0 to 3, Ruby puts the number passed into the block. Now, here's where blocks get interesting: just as with methods or classes, a variable defined in a block stops existing when the block is finished. *Unlike* methods and classes, though, blocks can access variables and information that are outside them! In this case, our block knows about the number 3 and so knows that the variable number should take on each number between 0 and 3. Once the block is finished, though, Ruby no longer cares about number, so it causes an error if we try to use it again.

When I first learned that Ruby could see variables in some parts of a program and not others, I scratched my head for a good while, and I'm sure you're asking yourself the exact same thing I asked myself then: "If that's true, how on Earth can I use variables that I make inside classes or methods elsewhere in my program?" Well, as luck would have it, the Dagron's about to tell us!

Global Variables

"Let's start with *global variables*, which can be seen from anywhere in the program. An example might help," said the Dagron, and she touched the Computing Contraption's screen with her claw:

```
>> $location = 'The Carmine Pines!'

>> def where_are_we?
>>   puts $location
>> end

>> where_are_we?
The Carmine Pines!
=> nil
```

"Here," said the Dagron, "we create a variable called $location that's equal to the string 'The Carmine Pines!'. Then we create a method, where_are_we?, that tries to access $location. Normally, this wouldn't work, but because $location is a global variable, we get 'The Carmine Pines!' when we call the where_are_we? method!"

"Aha! I've seen this kind of variable before," said the Off-White Knight. "I recognize it by the dollar sign it starts with! Global variables can be useful, since they can be seen anywhere in a Ruby program. You can define a global variable outside a method, inside a method, in a class, anywhere you want, and if you try to use it anywhere else in your program, it will just work. But," she said, holding up one finger, "if the variable can be seen anywhere in the program, it can also be *changed* anywhere in the program, and it's not always clear when or how that change happened."

Scarlet nodded. "That's right!" she said. "Remember when we found out that something was altering the variables in the Flowmatic Something-or-Other? Imagine how bad it would be if all our variables could be changed anywhere in our programs at any time!"

"Perish the thought!" said the King, shuddering. "We certainly don't want *that*. All right, so we won't use global variables if we can help it! What are the other sorts of variables we can use?"

Class Variables

"A wise choice, Your Majesty," said the Dagron. "Another type of variable we can use is a *class variable*, which is useful if we want a class to save some information about itself. Just as all global variables start with $, all class variables start with @@, and a class can have as many class variables as it wants. A class variable can be seen from inside the class and by any instances of the class; all instances share the same class variable. Now, Wherefore, we'll use your weezard example." She blew a smoke ring at the Computing Contraption, and this code filled the screen:

weezard.rb

```
class Weezard
  @@spells = 5

  def initialize(name, power='Flight')
    @name = name
    @power = power
  end

  def cast_spell(name)
    if @@spells > 0
      @@spells -= 1
      puts "Cast #{name}! Spells left: #{@@spells}."
    else
      puts 'No more spells!'
    end
  end
end
```

"We've defined a Weezard class with a class variable called @@spells," said the Dagron, "as well as two methods: initialize, which sets up the name and power for a particular weezard, and cast_spell, which any weezard can use. Let's go ahead and use new to create two new weezards with some special powers. Don't forget to load the code you just wrote first!"

```
>> load 'weezard.rb'
=> true
>> merlin = Weezard.new('Merlin', 'Sees the future')
=> #<Weezard:0x00000104949260 @name="Merlin", @power="Sees the
future">
>> fumblesnore = Weezard.new('Fumblesnore', 'Naps')
=> #<Weezard:0x0000010494c500 @name="Fumblesnore", @power="Naps">
```

"Here's the interesting thing about our weezards," the Dagron continued. "Even though Merlin and Fumblesnore have different powers, they're interacting with the same variable, @@spells! Each time they use cast_spell, the spell variable decreases by one. Take a look."

```
>> merlin.cast_spell('Prophecy')
Cast Prophecy! Spells left: 4.
=> nil

>> fumblesnore.cast_spell('Nap')
Cast Nap! Spells left: 3.
=> nil
```

"So when you create a class variable, there's just one copy for the whole class, and any instances you create all share that one class variable?" Ruben asked.

"That's right," said the Dagron.

"It's kind of weird that all weezards share a fixed group of spells, isn't it?" asked Wherefore. "Wouldn't it make sense for each weezard to have his own set of spells?"

Instance Variables

The Dagron nodded. "Sometimes it makes sense for the class that creates objects to keep track of certain information, but not all that often," she said. "For that reason, we don't end up using a lot of class variables in Ruby; it's mostly *instance* and *local* variables. In fact, with instance variables, we can give each weezard her own set of spells," the Dagron continued, and more code appeared on the screen. "An instance variable can be seen from inside the class and by any instance of the class, just like class variables. The big difference is that each instance gets its very own copy of the variable!"

weezard_2.rb

```
class Weezard
  def initialize(name, power='Flight')
    @name = name
    @power = power
    @spells = 5
  end

  def cast_spell(name)
    if @spells > 0
      @spells -= 1
      puts "Cast #{name}! Spells left: #{@spells}."
    else
      puts 'No more spells!'
    end
  end
end
```

"See how we've moved the @@spells variable from a variable that belongs to the class to a @spells instance variable inside the initialize method?" asked the Dagron. "Variables that start with @ are *instance variables*. They're called instance variables because each *instance*, which is what Ruby calls an object created by a class, has its own copy."

"So when we create instances of the Weezard class with the new method, each instance will get assigned its own @spells variable?" Scarlet asked.

"Precisely," said the Dagron. "In fact, let's do that now. We'll create our weezards, just as we did before."

```
>> load 'weezard_2.rb'
=> true
>> merlin = Weezard.new('Merlin', 'Sees the future')
=> #<Weezard:0x0000010459e160 @name="Merlin", @power="Sees the
future", @spells=5>
>> fumblesnore = Weezard.new('Fumblesnore', 'Naps')
=> #<Weezard:0x000001045a13d8 @name="Fumblesnore", @power="Naps",
@spells=5>
```

"This looks just like it did the last time we created weezards!" grumped the King.

"It's very similar," admitted the Dagron, "but there *is* one important difference. Look what happens when each weezard casts a spell!"

```
>> merlin.cast_spell('Prophecy')
Cast Prophecy! Spells left: 4.
=> nil

>> fumblesnore.cast_spell('Nap')
Cast Nap! Spells left: 4.
=> nil
```

"They each have their own @spells variable!" said Scarlet. "That's why fumblesnore's spell count wasn't affected when merlin cast a spell."

"Exactly right," said the Dagron. "Even though their @spells variables have the same names, each instance gets its own copy, so they don't conflict with each other. Not only that, but because instances of classes can always access their instance variables, any instance variables we define in our classes' initialize method can be used by the newly created objects."

"That's why we do things like @name = name in our initialize method definitions," said the Off-White Knight. "It makes sure that when we pass in the name argument, each instance saves a copy in @name."

Local Variables

"Speaking of local variables," said the Dagron, "let's have a look at those, shall we? They should be quite familiar, but they're worth a second look. A *local variable* can be seen only in its current scope, which means it can be seen only in the method or class where it's defined."

New code appeared on the Computing Contraption's screen:

```
>> class YeOldeClass
>>   local_variable = 'I only exist inside the class!'
>> end

>> puts local_variable
NameError: undefined local variable or method `local_variable' for
main:Object

>> def yet_another_method
>>   another_local = 'I only exist inside this method!'
>> end

>> puts another_local
NameError: undefined local variable or method `another_local' for
main:Object
```

"So really, local variables can be seen only inside the methods or classes where they're defined, or we can use them outside *all* class and method definitions," Scarlet said.

"That's right," said the Dagron. "There is a special scope in Ruby called the *top-level scope*, so if you define local variables outside *any* method or class definition, Ruby can see them. Have a look!"

```
>> local_variable = "I'm the top-level local variable!"

>> def local_in_method
>>   local_variable = "I'm the local variable in the method!"
>>   puts local_variable
>> end

>> puts local_variable
I'm the top-level local variable!
=> nil

>> local_in_method
I'm the local variable in the method!
=> nil
```

"You see?" said the Dagron. "Local variables can even have the exact same variable names, as long as they're in different scopes! Ruby knows that the method definition gets its own set of local variables, so it doesn't complain that there are two with the same name."

"So local variables can be seen only in the classes or methods where we define them, or in this special top-level scope that's outside any class or method," said the King. "But global variables can be seen anywhere, and if we create an instance of a class, the instance can see any instance variables we created when we defined the class."

"Precisely," said the Dagron.

"And the class can see its own class variables," the King continued.

"Correct!" said the Dagron. "In fact, it's not just instances that can have methods like initialize, introduce, and sing; even *classes* can have their own methods!"

"Just when I was starting to get this!" moaned the King. "How is that possible?"

"Because," replied the Dagron, "Ruby classes *are also objects*!"

"I need to sit down," said the King.

"You *are* sitting down," said Wherefore.

"So I am," said the King, who was sitting cross-legged between the Off-White Knight and the Wand'ring Minstrel. "Go on, Madame Dagron," he said. "How can we add a method directly to a class itself, and not just an instance of a class?"

Objects and self

"Well," said the Dagron, "Ruby keeps a special built-in variable named self around at all times, and self refers to whatever Ruby object we're currently talking about." She was talking quickly now, and small sparks leapt from her mouth as she continued. "So all we need to do is use self to define a method inside our class, and instead of adding that method to the instance, we add it to the class itself."

"Perhaps an example would make things clearer," said the Off-White Knight. She reached over and typed into the Computing Contraption:

monkey.rb

```ruby
class Monkey
  @@number_of_monkeys = 0

  def initialize
    @@number_of_monkeys += 1
  end

  def self.number_of_monkeys
    @@number_of_monkeys
  end
end
```

"Here I've created a Monkey class," said the knight. "It has a @@number_of_monkeys class variable that will keep track of how many monkey instances we create, as well as the initialize method we've seen in classes before. When we call new on Monkey to create a new monkey, it will add 1 to the @@number_of_monkeys."

"What about that `self.number_of_monkeys` method?" asked Ruben.

"That's a class method!" said the knight. "It's a method of the `Monkey` class itself, and when we call it, it will return the `@@number_of_monkeys`. Let's have a look! First, we'll load that script, and then we'll create a few monkeys."

```
>> load 'monkey.rb'
=> true
>> monkey_1 = Monkey.new
=> #<Monkey:0x000001048fccf8>
>> monkey_2 = Monkey.new
=> #<Monkey:0x00000104902310>
>> monkey_3 = Monkey.new
=> #<Monkey:0x00000104907900>
```

"Good!" said the Off-White Knight. "Now that we have some monkeys, let's ask the `Monkey` class how many monkeys there are." She typed into the Computing Contraption:

```
>> Monkey.number_of_monkeys
=> 3
```

"Amazing!" said Wherefore. "But why not ask an individual monkey how many monkeys there are?"

"Well," said the knight, "first, it doesn't quite make sense to ask a monkey instance how many other instances there are—that's the class's business, not the instance's! But more importantly, because we used `self` when we defined the `number_of_monkeys` method, it's only a method of the class, not its instances! See?" She typed some more:

```
>> monkey_1.number_of_monkeys
NoMethodError: undefined method `number_of_monkeys' for
#<Monkey:0x000001048fccf8>
```

"There we are," said the Dagron. "The `Monkey` class has its very own `number_of_monkeys` method now, but it's only on the class itself; the monkey instances themselves don't have that method."

"In fact," said the knight, "adding methods onto classes is common enough that Ruby has its own shorter syntax for it. It looks like this!" And she typed some more:

monkey_2.rb

```
class Monkey
  @@number_of_monkeys = 0

  def initialize
    @@number_of_monkeys += 1
  end

  class << self
    def number_of_monkeys
      @@number_of_monkeys
    end
  end
end
```

"See that?" she asked. "Instead of defining the number_of_monkeys method on the class with self.number_of_monkeys, I used class << self to tell Ruby: 'Hey! Every method I define until I say end is a method for the class, not its instances.' Look what happens when I call the method on Monkey without creating any instances."

```
>> load 'monkey_2.rb'
=> true
>> Monkey.number_of_monkeys
=> 0
```

"Now look what happens if I create an instance and call the method again," said the knight.

```
>> monkey = Monkey.new
=> #<Monkey:0x0000010490af60>
>> Monkey.number_of_monkeys
=> 1
```

"See? It's just like using `self.number_of_monkeys`," the Off-White Knight said, beaming.

"Very interesting," said the Dagron. "I'd never seen `class <<` `self` before."

"Really?" asked Wherefore.

"No one knows everything," said the Dagron. "Not even me!"

"Many people find the `def self.method_name` syntax easier to understand," said the knight, "so it's perfectly fine to use that whenever you need to add a method to a class."

"Of course," said Scarlet, "and now `self` makes so much more sense to me! It just refers to whatever the Ruby program is 'talking about.' And in this case, `self` is the class we're inside!"

Methods and Instance Variables

"Precisely," said the Dagron. "And with that, I have but one more trick to show you. You see, while it's very easy to create instance variables for our instances, it's not always so easy to get at them. See what I mean?" she said, and as she spoke, new code began to fill the screen:

```
>> class Minstrel
>>   def initialize(name)
>>     @name = name
>>   end
>> end
```

"I've re-created our `Minstrel` class from before, but with only an initialize method," said the Dagron. "No introduce or sing methods! Let's create an instance, like we did earlier."

```
>> wherefore = Minstrel.new('Wherefore')
=> #<Minstrel:0x000001049637c8 @name="Wherefore">
```

"Now," said the Dagron, "see how our minstrel instance has the name 'Wherefore'? (You can tell by the `@name="Wherefore"` bit.) Let's try to get to it."

```
>> wherefore.name
NoMethodError: undefined method `name' for
#<Minstrel:0x000001049637c8 @name="Wherefore">
```

"You see," said the Dagron, "while `wherefore` has a `@name` instance variable, it doesn't have a name *method*. And when it comes to Ruby, all that matters are methods. In order to make `wherefore.name` actually work, we need to write a method to reach the `@name` instance variable."

"Does that mean we'll need to define a method in the `Minstrel` class called `name`?" Scarlet asked.

"That's exactly right," said the Dagron, and the code on the screen changed under her claw:

another_minstrel.rb

```
class Minstrel
  def initialize(name)
    @name = name
  end

  def name
    @name
  end
end
```

"Now we have a `name` method that returns the `@name` instance variable," said the Dagron. "Let's see what happens when we create a new minstrel with this `name` method and try to use it!"

```
>> load 'another_minstrel.rb'
=> true
>> wherefore = Minstrel.new('Wherefore')
=> #<Minstrel:0x000001049637c8 @name="Wherefore">
>> wherefore.name
=> "Wherefore"
```

"Huzzah!" cried the King. "We've done it! We've changed the minstrel's name with the name method."

"Truly wonderful," said Wherefore, "but what if we want to change the minstrel's name to something else?"

"Well," said the Dagron, "let's see if we can do that with the code we have now." She added more code to the Computing Contraption's glowing screen:

```
>> wherefore.name = 'Stinky Pete'
NoMethodError: undefined method `name=' for
#<Minstrel:0x000001049637c8 @name="Wherefore">
```

"We can *get* the name," said the Dagron, "but we can't *change* it; Ruby's complaining that our instance has no method that changes names. It's looking for a method we haven't written yet!"

Ruben studied the screen. "It's that NoMethodError again," he said. "It looks like Ruby wants the Minstrel class to have a method called name=!"

The Dagron nodded. "If we want to *change* the @name, we have to write a special method called name= to do it," she said. "If you write the name of a method with an equal sign at the end, Ruby understands it to mean: 'I want this method to change the value of something.' So to change the @name," she finished, "we'd add a bit more code."

She added the name= method to the rest of the code for all of them to see:

another_minstrel_2.rb

```
class Minstrel
  def initialize(name)
    @name = name
  end
```

```
def name
  @name
end

def name=(new_name)
  @name = new_name
end
end
```

"Now we have a new method, name=, that takes a single parameter, the new_name," said the Dagron. "This should tell Ruby to let
us change the name simply by calling wherefore.name = 'some new
name'! Let's give it a try. First, we'll create a new minstrel."

```
>> load 'another_minstrel_2.rb'
=> true
>> wherefore = Minstrel.new('Wherefore')
=> #<Minstrel:0x000001049637c8 @name="Wherefore">
>> wherefore.name
=> "Wherefore"
```

"Next, we'll try to change its name."

```
>> wherefore.name = 'Stinky Pete'
=> "Stinky Pete"

>> wherefore.name
=> "Stinky Pete"
```

"That's amazing!" said Ruben. "But writing all these methods
to get and set instance variables sure is hard work. Is there any
faster way to do it?"

The Dagron nodded. "As it turns out, there is," she said.
"There are three built-in shortcut methods for reading and writing instance variables: attr_reader, attr_writer, and attr_accessor.
Here's how they work." She touched the Computing Contraption
with her claw, and these words appeared:

```ruby
class Minstrel
  attr_accessor :name
  attr_reader :ballad

  def initialize(name)
    @name = name
    @ballad = 'The Ballad of Chucky Jim'
  end
end
```

"For example, if you pass the symbol :name to attr_reader, it will automatically create a method called name that will read the instance variable @name. attr_writer will automatically create a method called name= that will change the value of @name, and attr_accessor will create both the name and name= methods." The Dagron clicked her claws. "In this case, I've called attr_accessor with :name and attr_reader with :ballad, which should mean I can both get and change the minstrel's name, but can only read his ballad without changing it. Let's create a new minstrel to test out."

```
>> load 'another_minstrel_3.rb'
=> true
>> wherefore = Minstrel.new('Wherefore')
=> #<Minstrel:0x0000010413c0e0 @name="Wherefore", @ballad="The
Ballad of Chucky Jim">
```

"Perfect," said the Dagron. "Let's see if attr_accessor lets us get and change the minstrel's name, like we could before."

```
>> wherefore.name
=> "Wherefore"

>> wherefore.name = 'Wherefive'
=> "Wherefive"

>> wherefore
=> #<Minstrel:0x0000010413c0e0 @name="Wherefive", @ballad="The
Ballad of Chucky Jim">
```

"Now let's see if we can read the minstrel's ballad, but not change it; that's what attr_reader is supposed to do," said the Dagron. She filled in more code on the Computing Contraption:

```
>> wherefore.ballad
=> "The Ballad of Chucky Jim"

>> wherefore.ballad = 'A Song of Mice and Friars'
NoMethodError: undefined method `ballad=' for
#<Minstrel:0x0000010413c0e0>
```

Wherefore shook his head in amazement. "Extraordinary!" he said. "With these Ruby tools, I'll be able to write ballads in no time at all."

"This is one of the most amazing parts of Ruby," said the Off-White Knight. "When we design programs around objects, we're doing something called *object-oriented programming*, and it lets us write programs that describe real-life things like minstrels and ballads. Everything becomes a thousand times easier!"

"This is marvelous, truly marvelous," said Wherefore. "I can't thank you enough. How can I possibly repay you?"

"Well," Scarlet said, "actually, we were looking for you to ask whether you'd seen anything unusual happening in the kingdom. Ruby systems all over the kingdom have been breaking all day, and we're starting to think none of the problems is an accident."

"Show him the scale!" Ruben said.

"Oh, yeah!" Scarlet said, and she pulled the glittering green scale from her pocket. "Have you ever seen anything like this? We thought at first it might have belonged to the Dagron, but we checked and she isn't missing a one."

"Hmm," said Wherefore. "Quite the quandary. No, I don't think I've seen any creature with scales like this, but I *did* see something strange out here in the Pines not an hour ago."

The King, Ruben, and Scarlet exchanged startled looks.

"What was it?" Scarlet asked.

"Well," said Wherefore, "I only caught a snippet of conversation, but it was a few voices, talking in low tones behind that thicket yonder. I went to see what was going on, but they ran when I got near—three, maybe four of them," he said.

"Who were they?" asked the King.

"I didn't see," said Wherefore, "but the part I overheard was dastardly indeed. They said something about not having made a big enough impact, and how they were going to see the Queen about whatever it is they were doing. I'll bet my hat that when they fled, they were heading straight for the castle!"

"The castle! The Queen!" cried the King. "Oh my biscuits, oh my gravy! If these are our saboteurs, the Queen could be in terrible danger!"

"We've got to get back there, and fast!" said Scarlet. "Off-White Knight, Dagron, can you help us?"

The knight frowned thoughtfully. "I'm honor bound to stay in the Pines and to help anyone who wanders through," she said. "But my duties are also to the King and Queen. I can spread the word as quickly as possible that trouble's afoot and send as many friends to the castle as I can!"

"Please do!" said Scarlet. "What about you, Dagron?"

The Dagron shook her head. "Magic and wisdom come at a price," she said. "I'm not able to leave the Carmine Pines. However, there *is* a shortcut back to the castle."

"Where?" asked Ruben.

"The underground passage!" said Wherefore. "Yes, I know it. Follow me, I'll take you there!"

The King, Scarlet, and Ruben thanked the Off-White Knight and the Dagron and, waving goodbye, hurried to catch up with Wherefore, who was already halfway across the meadow. They all plunged headlong along a twisty path of roots and knotted tree trunks, and after a few minutes of breathless running, they arrived at an enormous red pine tree, bigger than all the ones around it as far as they could see.

"Going down!" cried Wherefore, and knocked on the trunk three times. With a pleasant *ding*, a door slid open in the side of the trunk, revealing a cramped elevator car.

"Take the elevator to the sub-sub-basement," he said, stuffing the three of them inside. "You'll find a long, narrow passage that heads off to the west. Take that as far as you can, then look for a large black pipe. There'll be words written on it that say—"

"—*the Mysterious Pipe!*" cried Ruben and Scarlet together. "We saw Haldo disappear down into the lower levels of the castle earlier today; this passage must connect to the same place!"

"Then you know your way!" said Wherefore. "Goodbye and good luck—in the meantime, I'll help the Off-White Knight and the Dagron send help your way." And with that, the elevator doors slid shut, and the King, Scarlet, and Ruben began to descend deep into the earth.

Dial-a-Ballad, or the Minstrel's Delivery Service

Now that we've taught Wherefore the Wand'ring Minstrel all about Ruby objects and classes, it's time to help him create his very own Ballad! Otherwise, he won't be much of a minstrel. Don't worry, though—now that you know all about classes and how they work, creating a simple class to help Wherefore write faster, better ballads will be a breeze.

Let's begin by making a new file called *ballad.rb* and typing the following code.

ballad.rb

```
class Ballad
❶   attr_accessor :title
    attr_accessor :lyrics

❷   @@number_of_ballads = 0

❸   def initialize(title, lyrics='Tralala!')
      @title = title
      @lyrics = lyrics
      @@number_of_ballads += 1
    end

❹   def self.number_of_ballads
      @@number_of_ballads
    end
  end

❺ ballad = Ballad.new('The Ballad of Chucky Jim')

❻ puts "Number of ballads: #{Ballad.number_of_ballads}"
  puts "Ballad object ID: #{ballad.object_id}"
  puts "Ballad title: #{ballad.title}"
  puts "Ballad object ID again!: #{ballad.object_id}"
  puts "Ballad lyrics: #{ballad.lyrics}"
```

It's hard to believe, but you now know so much Ruby that there's actually nothing new here! You've seen all this stuff before: creating classes and instances of classes, using attr_accessor, using class and instance variables, adding methods to classes and instances, the whole shebang. Let's step through it line by line and have a look at the output.

First, we create a Ballad class at ❶ with a title and lyrics we can both read and change (thanks to attr_accessor).

Next, at ❷, we set up a class variable, @@number_of_ballads, to track the number of ballads our class creates, and our initialize method at ❸ both sets the name and lyrics of the ballad and adds 1 to the @@number_of_ballads.

For the last part of our class definition, we add a number_of_ballads method at ❹ on the Ballad class itself; that will let us get the @@number_of_ballads later.

Finally, we create a new ballad with Ballad.new at ❺, then print out some interesting facts about our ballad at ❻.

You can run the code in your file by using the terminal to go to the folder where you saved *ballad.rb*, then typing **ruby ballad.rb** on the command line.

Your object IDs will be slightly different from mine, but you should see something like this:

```
Number of ballads: 1
Ballad object ID: #<Ballad:0x0000010413e0e0>
Ballad title: The Ballad of Chucky Jim
Ballad object ID again!: #<Ballad:0x0000010413e0e0>
Ballad lyrics: Tralala!
=> nil
```

We've just proved that our self.number_of_ballads method works, that our object ID doesn't change once we create an object, and that we can get to all of the information we've stored in our ballad with the magic of attr_accessor.

All that's well and good, but the *really* interesting part is how you take it further! For example, you can start small by writing code to change the title of a ballad you create or to update its lyrics after it's created. (Do you think this will change the object ID?)

You could also add more attr_readers, attr_writers, or attr_accessors. You could add more methods (what about a playing_time method to return how many minutes long the ballad is?). You could add class methods or create additional ballads.

You could even take on the greatest challenge of all: actually writing the lyrics to "The Ballad of Chucky Jim"! The world is your oyster. (If you don't like oysters, then the world is your cupcake.)

You Know This!

You learned a fair amount in this chapter, but nowhere near as much as you crammed into your noggin with methods! Learning about objects and classes was practically a vacation! Even so, let's take the time to go over it all one more time, just to make sure you've got it all.

Objects and Classes

You already knew that just about everything in Ruby is an object, but in this chapter, you learned more about objects and took a closer look at object IDs. An object's ID number is like a fingerprint: every object has its very own, and no two objects have exactly the same one. As a general rule, objects created by Ruby have lower object ID numbers than objects you create:

```
>> 0.object_id
=> 1
>> :minstrel.object_id
=> 465608
```

We also saw that *classes* are how we can create a whole bunch of objects with similar characteristics. We create classes with the class keyword, like so:

```
>> class Monkey
>>    # Class magicks go here!
>> end
```

Creating classes is all well and good, but classes don't really do much for us until we *instantiate* (create) an object from that class. You can think of classes as cookie cutters and the objects they create as cookies: the cookie cutter (class) makes a bunch of things that are all very similar, but the thing we're most interested in is the cookie itself (the object).

For instance, we can define a `Monkey` class with our class keyword, and we instantiate it—that is, we make a *particular* monkey from our `Monkey` class cookie cutter—by calling `Monkey.new`:

monkey_review.rb

```ruby
class Monkey
  @@bananas = 5

  def initialize(name)
    @name = name
  end

  def eat_banana
    @@bananas -= 1
    puts "Ate a banana! #{@@bananas} left."
  end
end
```

Great! So far we've got a `Monkey` class with two methods and a class variable. The class variable `@@bananas` keeps track of how many bananas there are for *all* monkey instances, the `initialize` method sets the monkey's name when `Monkey.new` is called, and eat_banana decreases `@@bananas` by 1.

Next, let's create a couple of monkeys:

```
>> load 'monkey_review.rb'
=> true

>> socks = Monkey.new('Socks')
=> #<Monkey:0x000001052c77b0 @name="Socks">

>> stevie = Monkey.new('Stevie')
=> #<Monkey:0x00000104ca38e8 @name="Stevie">
```

Now we can have each monkey eat a banana and see what happens:

```
>> socks.eat_banana
Ate a banana! 4 left.
=> nil
```

```
>> stevie.eat_banana
Ate a banana! 3 left.
=> nil
```

Did you notice how our `Monkey` class's `@@bananas` class variable was reduced every time *any* monkey instance ate a banana? Remember, that's because class variables are shared by all instances of that class.

We can assign any combination of local, instance, class, and global variables in combination with our classes, as shown here:

monkey_review_2.rb

```
class Monkey
  $home = 'the jungle'
  @@number_of_monkeys = 0

  def initialize(type)
    @type = type
    @@number_of_monkeys += 1
    puts "Made a new monkey! Now there's #{@@number_of_monkeys}."
  end
end
```

Here, we've changed our `Monkey` class to have a global `$home` variable (`'the jungle'`), a `@@number_of_monkeys` class variable that keeps track of how many instances the `Monkey` class has created, and a `@type` instance variable that lets each individual monkey be of a different type.

```
>> load 'monkey_review_2.rb'
=> true

>> blue = Monkey.new('blue monkey')
Made a new monkey! Now there's 1.
=> #<Monkey:0x00000104aafb40 @type="blue monkey">

>> silver = Monkey.new('silver monkey')
Made a new monkey! Now there's 2.
=> #<Monkey:0x00000104ab3b28 @type="silver monkey">
```

```
>> gold = Monkey.new('golden monkey')
Made a new monkey! Now there's 3.
=> #<Monkey:0x00000104ab7c00 @type="golden monkey">
```

See how each @type is unique to each monkey, but they all change the same @@number_of_monkeys variable?

Finally, every part of the program also has access to the $home variable, since it's global:

```
>> puts "Our monkeys live in #{$home}."
Our monkeys live in the jungle.
=> nil
```

Variables and Scope

This can all be a bit tricky to keep straight, so I've created the following handy-dandy table to help you remember the differences between local, global, instance, and class variables.

Variable type	Looks like	Where can it be seen?
Local	odelay	Inside the top-level scope, method, or class where it's defined.
Global	$odelay	Anywhere!
Instance	@odelay	Inside the class where it's defined or in any instance of the class. Each instance gets its own copy.
Class	@@odelay	Inside the class where it's defined or in any instance of the class. Each instance shares the same class variable with all other instances.

Remember, it's usually not a good idea to use global variables, because not only are they visible everywhere in our program but they can also be *changed* from anywhere in our program. When things can be changed from a bunch of places, it can be hard to figure out what part of our program made the change if something unexpected happens. I'm showing you global variables so you know what they are and how they work, but in almost every situation, they're much more trouble than they're worth.

As you saw in the last example, we could reach the $home variable from outside the class definition because it was defined as global (global variables start with a $). We can only ever get at a variable if it's in the proper scope. Let's review some examples from earlier in the chapter:

```
>> local_variable = 'Local here!'
=> "Local here!"
```

Our local_variable exists in this outer scope, but it doesn't exist inside the class definition:

```
>> class OutOfTowner
>>    puts local_variable
>> end
NameError: undefined local variable or method `local_variable' for
OutOfTowner:Class
```

The local_variable doesn't exist inside the method definition, either!

```
>> def tourist
>>    puts "Can you take our picture, #{local_variable}?"
>> end

>> tourist
NameError: undefined local variable or method `local_variable' for
main:Object
```

Our variable number exists inside the block, but it's gone as soon as the block's code is finished:

```
>> 3.times { |number| puts number }
0
1
2
=> 3
>> puts number
NameError: undefined local variable or method `number' for
main:Object
```

We discovered that Ruby has a built-in variable, self, that refers to whatever object the method will be called on, and we can use self to add methods directly to classes (instead of just the objects they create), as shown here:

monkey_review_3.rb

```
class Monkey
  @@number_of_monkeys = 0

  def initialize
    @@number_of_monkeys += 1
  end

  def self.number_of_monkeys
    @@number_of_monkeys
  end
end
```

You've seen this before! It's our Monkey class with a @@number_of_monkeys class variable, an initialize method that increases that variable every time we make a new monkey, and a self.number_of_monkeys method that means that we can call Monkey.number_of_monkeys to find out how many we've created so far:

```
>> load 'monkey_review_3.rb'
=> true
>> Monkey.number_of_monkeys
=> 0
```

It's 0 right now, but if we create a monkey, we'll see that number go up!

```
>> monkey = Monkey.new
=> #<Monkey:0x0000010490af60>
>> Monkey.number_of_monkeys
=> 1
```

If you're ever unsure of the value of self in a particular part of your program, you can always puts self to see what it is.

We also learned that if an object has an instance variable that we want to see or change, we have to write methods to do it. We *can* write these methods ourselves as follows:

minstrel_review.rb

```ruby
class Minstrel
  def initialize(name)
    @name = name
  end

  def name
    @name
  end

  def name=(new_name)
    @name = new_name
  end
end
```

Here, we've set a `@name` in our `initialize` method, which means that any time we call `Minstrel.new`, we pass in a name for that minstrel. The `name` method gets that `@name` variable for us, and the `name=` method allows us to assign a `new_name` to the minstrel . . .

. . . but we can also use the shortcuts `attr_reader` (to read an instance variable), `attr_writer` (to change an instance variable), and `attr_accessor` (to do both). All we do is pass the instance variable name as a symbol, like so:

minstrel_review_2.rb

```ruby
class Minstrel
  attr_accessor :name
  attr_reader :ballad

  def initialize(name)
    @name = name
    @ballad = 'The Ballad of Chucky Jim'
  end
end
```

Here, we've used attr_accessor and passed it a :name symbol to have it automatically create name and name= methods for us; we called attr_reader with :ballad, so we only get a ballad method to read the @ballad instance variable. Check out what happens if we try to change our ballad!

```
>> load 'minstrel_review_2.rb'
=> true

>> wherefore = Minstrel.new('Wherefore')
=> #<Minstrel:0x0000010413c0e0 @name="Wherefore", @ballad="The
Ballad of Chucky Jim">

>> wherefore.ballad
=> "The Ballad of Chucky Jim"

>> wherefore.name
=> "Wherefore"

>> wherefore.name = 'Wherefive'
=> "Wherefive"

>> wherefore.ballad = 'A Song of Mice and Friars'
NoMethodError: undefined method `ballad=' for
#<Minstrel:0x0000010413c0e0>
```

Object-Oriented Programming

Finally, we learned that writing programs that revolve around classes and objects is called *object-oriented programming* (*OOP*). Our minstrel is a good example of an object: a piece of code that acts just like something in the real world! It has attributes (facts about itself) as well as behavior, which is just a way of talking about the methods the object knows how to use. We can define the behavior of any minstrel with a Minstrel class, as follows.

```ruby
class Minstrel
  attr_reader :name

  @@number_of_minstrels = 0

  def initialize(name)
    @name = name
    @@number_of_minstrels += 1
  end

  def sing(song_name)
    puts "Time to sing a song called: #{song_name}!"
    puts 'Tralala!'
  end

  def self.number_of_minstrels
    @@number_of_minstrels
  end
end
```

Our class has an attr_reader for :name (meaning we can read the name, but not change it), as well as a @@number_of_minstrels class variable that keeps track of how many instances we've created and an initialize method that gives our minstrel a name and increases the @@number_of_minstrels.

It also has two methods: one, sing, is a method of minstrel instances and sings a little song, and the other, self.number_of_minstrels, is a method of the Minstrel class and tells us how many minstrels we've created so far.

Let's see them in action!

```
>> load 'minstrel_review_3.rb'
=> true

>> wherefore = Minstrel.new('Wherefore')
=> #<Minstrel:0x000001031eac68 @name="Wherefore">
```

```
>> Minstrel.number_of_minstrels
=> 1

wherefore.sing('A Tail of Two Foxes')
Time to sing a song called: A Tail of Two Foxes!
Tralala!
=> nil
```

Voilà! We can create a new minstrel, call `Minstrel.number_of_minstrels` to see that we've created one, and then call our minstrel instance (`wherefore`)'s sing method to hear his ballad "A Tail of Two Foxes."

Things are starting to get a bit suspenseful around here, so I'm gonna go grab a bag of popcorn—be right with you. In the meantime, go on ahead to see what the King, Scarlet, and Ruben find when they get back to the castle, and get ready for even more object-oriented Ruby magic!

9
Inheriting
the
Magic
of
Ruby

her majesty's menagerie

The King, Ruben, and Scarlet raced westward along the underground passage toward the castle.

"How much farther?" panted Ruben.

"I'm not sure," said the King, "but Wherefore told us to go as far as we could, and then we'd be at the Mysterious Pipe." He thought for a moment. "It can't be too far, though," he said at last. "These are the Ambrose Caverns, and while they stretch beneath the entire kingdom, I know Haldo has managed to get between the castle and places farther than the Pines in a matter of minutes."

"That's right! Haldo knows these tunnels," said Scarlet. She ran in silence for a minute or two. "What if . . ." she began.

"What if what?" asked Ruben.

"Well, what if whoever's causing all this trouble is someone Haldo let in? Or what if Haldo's *one of them?*"

"Bite your tongue!" said the King. "Haldo's been in my service since he was a boy. He'd never do anything to hurt us or this kingdom!"

"We should consider every possibility," Scarlet said.

"Even so," said the King, "all suspects are innocent until we prove them guilty. If we're lucky, we'll catch these scoundrels red-handed when we arrive at the castle!"

"Which will be any minute," Ruben said. "Look!"

Up ahead, the narrow tunnel opened up into a wide cavern. The King, Scarlet, and Ruben jogged into the open space, then stood for a moment, catching their breath.

"This is it," said the King, "the basement *below* the basement below the castle! Now we just need to find the Mysterious Pipe and climb back up into my Royal Study."

"And there it is!" said Scarlet. In the darkness, they could just make out the outline of the Mysterious Pipe in the far corner.

The trio walked up to the base of the pipe, which was gurgling softly.

"Now what?" asked Ruben. "The Mysterious Pipe is full of water! How are we supposed to climb up it?"

"Well, we turned the Flowmatic Something-or-Other on before," Scarlet said. "We can turn it back off!" She felt around the bottom of the pipe until she found the familiar boxy shape of a Computing Contraption, then flipped open its lid. The glow of the IRB prompt illuminated their faces.

"Right!" said the King. "What variable did we change before?"

"flowmatic_on!" replied Ruben.

Scarlet quickly typed into the Computing Contraption:

```
>> flowmatic_on = false
=> false
```

With a slow *booooop* and a *glug-glug* sound, the Mysterious Pipe shut down and emptied.

"Well done, Scarlet!" said the King as he walked to the far side of the Pipe. He grabbed a large metal wheel jutting out of the side and gave it a spin. The wheel turned several times, and with a hollow *clank*, the door to which it was attached eased open.

"Into the Mysterious Pipe!" cried the King, and the three climbed inside.

Ruben looked straight up and squinted. "I can't even see the light at the top!" he said. "This Pipe is huge! Hellooo!" he called, and the Mysterious Pipe echoed: *Hello! Ello! Lo!*

"It'll take forever to climb, if we can even do it at all!" said Scarlet. She thought for a moment. "I might have an idea." She turned to Ruben and the King. "Do you trust me?" she asked.

"With my life!" said the King.

"To the end!" said Ruben.

"All right, then," said Scarlet. "Hold your breath!" She reached around to the Computing Contraption on the side of the Mysterious Pipe and typed:

```
>> flowmatic_on = true
```

She slammed the metal door shut, and in an instant, the pipe filled with water.

For a moment, the three floated at the bottom of the Mysterious Pipe, holding their breath. Then the entire pipe began to tremble slightly, and with a deep *whoosh*, the force of the water propelled the King, Scarlet, and Ruben straight up!

In just a few seconds, the three of them began to slow down, and they found themselves floating just inches from the narrow top of the Mysterious Pipe. The King reached down and pushed on the latch of the pipe's door, and in a flood of water, the trio tumbled out onto the floor of the King's Royal Study.

"Genius! Absolutely genius!" the King sputtered.

"Thank you," said Scarlet, taking a small bow. "But we've got to get to the Queen! Do you know where she is?"

"She should be back from Her Royal Majesty's Hacktastic Ruby Conference," said the King, "so I imagine she's up in her Royal Office. Let's go!" And with that, he dashed out of the room.

Ruby and Scarlet followed. "The Queen was at a Ruby conference?" Scarlet asked as they raced up the stairs.

"Indeed!" said the King. "It might surprise you to learn that although I'm rather new to all of this Ruby business, my wife is quite the hacker."

"That's amazing!" said Ruben. "Maybe she'll be able to help us fix all these Ruby malfunctions and catch the bad guys causing them."

"I hope so. Ah! Here we are," said the King, and he skidded to a halt in front of an enormous wooden door with golden handles.

He pulled down on both handles at once, swung the doors open, and rushed inside.

The Queen was seated at her desk in a high-backed chair, furiously typing at a Computing Contraption.

"They tried to break into my Computing Contraption!" she said. "The very idea!"

"They who?" asked Scarlet and Ruben together as they followed the King into the Queen's Royal Office.

"I don't know!" said the Queen, still typing. "There were four of them, and I caught them at my Computing Contraption, trying to figure out my password. Luckily, I'm a stickler for security."

"That she is," said the King, wringing out his fluffy white beard. "She won't even let me buy gummy bears on the Internet!"

"For good reason," said the Queen, and she stopped typing. "The last time I let you do that, you sent a small fortune to someone claiming to be the Gummy Bear King!" She paused, looking at Scarlet and Ruben. "I don't believe we've met," she said. "Who might you be?" She looked the three of them up and down. "And why are you all so wet?"

"I'm Ruben," said Ruben, "and this is Scarlet. We're helping the King find whoever's responsible for all the Ruby malfunctions going on, and we ran all the way from the Carmine Pines and swam up through the Mysterious Pipe to do it!"

"Well, you've come to the right place!" said the Queen. "I'm going to track down those ne'er-do-wells if it's the last thing I do." She began typing again.

"Did you get a good look at any of them?" asked Scarlet. "Were there any clues? Did you see or hear anything that might help us catch them?"

"I didn't see their faces," the Queen said, "but I overheard them trying to figure out my Computing Contraption's password. There were four of them—it sounded like two boys and two girls. I got home early from the Hacktastic Ruby Conference and thought I'd

try out some of the Ruby tricks I learned, and when I came up to my office, I caught them in the act! They ran when I shouted at them to surrender, and I sent the palace guards after them. In the meantime, I've been working to increase the security on my Computing Contraption to ensure it's completely immune to attack."

"Did they get anything from your Computing Contraption?" Scarlet asked.

"Thank heavens, no," said the Queen. "They didn't get my password, but we'd be in terrible trouble if they had. With that, they could access any system in the kingdom with no restrictions!"

"These villains are escalating!" said the King, pacing around the Queen's office. "We've got to catch them as quickly as possible, before they strike again. We might not be so lucky next time."

The Queen nodded. "I've instructed the guards to bring any suspects they catch directly to us for questioning," she said. "In the meantime, I've upgraded all the security on my Computing Contraption. The only thing left to do is update some of my Ruby programs to make them more secure, too!"

"Ruby!" said Ruben. "That happens to be our specialty. Can we help?" he asked.

The Queen smiled. "That would be lovely," she said. "While I'm something of an expert in more than a few programming languages, I'm pretty new to Ruby." She slid over in her chair, and Ruben and Scarlet clambered up beside her.

"First things first," said the Queen. "Do you know how to create a Ruby class?"

a Brush-Up on Classes

"I think so," said Ruben. "May I create any class I want?" The Queen nodded, and Ruben typed into her Computing Contraption:

```
>> class Animal
>>   attr_accessor :name
>>
>>   def initialize(name, legs=4)
>>     @name = name
>>     @legs = legs
>>   end
>> end
=> nil
```

"I see!" said the Queen. "You've defined an Animal class. You're using attr_accessor to automatically make a method to access the names of your animals, and the initialize method sets the animal's @name and number of @legs whenever a new animal is created."

"Yup!" said Ruben. "And if we create an animal with Animal.new but don't give it a number of legs, it'll be 4 by default."

The Queen nodded. "That makes sense to me. Why don't you go ahead and create a couple of animals?"

Ruben typed some more:

❶ ```
>> monkey = Animal.new('George', 2)
=> #<Animal:0x00000104953940 @name="George", @legs=2>
```
```

```
❷ >> monkey.name = 'Kong'
   => "Kong"

❸ >> dog = Animal.new('Bigelow')
   => #<Animal:0x00000104950178 @name="Bigelow", ❹@legs=4>
```

"Wonderful! At ❶, we've created monkey, an instance of the Animal class, and created it with the name 'George' and 2 legs. Next, at ❷, we've changed our monkey's name to 'Kong' to show that our attr_accessor lets us both read *and* change the name.

"Finally, at ❸, we've created a second instance of the Animal class, dog, with the name 'Bigelow'. Since we didn't create our dog with a number of legs, it gets four by default, as you can see by the return value at ❹."

a Couple of Classes

The Queen thought for a moment. "Yes, this will do nicely. Now then," she continued, "imagine if instead of just having monkey and dog as instances of Animal, we decided we wanted to have Monkey and Dog as separate classes instead. How could we do it?"

"Well, we could do something like this," Ruben said, and he typed:

```
>> class Monkey
>>     attr_accessor :name
>>
>>     def initialize(name)
>>       @name = name
>>       @legs = 2
>>     end
>> end
=> nil
```

"Precisely," said the Queen. "That defines a Monkey class, and the monkeys it creates will have @names and two @legs. The attr_accessor also automatically creates a name method for each monkey so we can get its name. To create a new monkey from the class, we use `Monkey.new` and pass its name as a string value. Like this!" She typed into the Computing Contraption:

```
>> monkey = Monkey.new('George')
=> #<Monkey:0x00000104bdf3a8 @name="George", @legs=2>

>> monkey.name
=> "George"
```

"We can do the same thing for our `Dog` class," Ruben continued. "We know that pretty much every dog has four legs, so it'll look just like the `Monkey` class, only the class name will be different and the number of `@legs` will be 4." He typed into the Computing Contraption:

```
>> class Dog
>>   attr_accessor :name
>>
>>   def initialize(name)
>>     @name = name
>>     @legs = 4
>>   end
>> end
=> nil
```

"Just like we can create new monkeys with `Monkey.new` and pass in a string for the monkey's name, we can create new dogs with `Dog.new` and pass in a string for the dog's name!" Ruben said.

```
>> dog = Dog.new('Bigelow')
=> #<Dog:0x00000104be3d18 @name="Bigelow", @legs=4>

>> dog.name
=> "Bigelow"
```

"That's certainly one way to create a couple of classes," said the Queen, "but it looks like you had to write a lot of the same code for both your `Monkey` and your `Dog` class."

"That's true," said Ruben. "Is that okay?"

Inheritance and DRY Code

"Well," said the Queen, "any time you find yourself writing something more than once, you should ask yourself whether you *have* to. Good code—unlike my husband here," she said, stifling a laugh as the King poured water out of the sleeves of his kingly robe, "—should be *DRY*."

"I know that one!" said the King, shaking drops of water off his string and replacing it in his pocket. "It stands for *Don't Repeat Yourself.*"

"He knows that one because he repeats himself all the time," the Queen whispered to Scarlet and Ruben. "But yes," she said, "if you avoid repeating yourself in your code, you save lots of time! Also, if you ever have to change something, you only need to change it *one* place, not several."

"I like the sound of that!" said Ruben, "but how can we make our class code more DRY?"

"With *inheritance*," said the Queen.

"Inheritance!" said Scarlet. "I think I've heard it mentioned before, but I'm not sure what it is."

"I'll show you," said the Queen, explaining as she typed into the Computing Contraption. "We've already created a class called `Animal`. What if we could use that class as a way to create both our `Monkey` *and* `Dog` classes?"

```
>> class Dog < Animal
>>   def bark
>>     puts 'Arf!'
>>   end
>> end
=> nil
```

"The `class Dog < Animal` part means that the `Dog` class *inherits from* the `Animal` class. It says to Ruby: 'Make a new class called `Dog` that knows how to do everything `Animal` does,'" the Queen said. "Then we just add a method, like we'd normally do. Here, I'm adding a bark method for `Dogs`, since dogs know how to bark." She rolled up her sleeves.

"Here's the amazing part: because `Dog` inherits from `Animal`, new dogs can do anything animals can do *and* anything dogs can do. They'll have a `name` method and a default of four legs, and know how to bark!"

```
>> dog = Dog.new('Bigelow')
=> #<Dog:0x00000104c89218 @name="Bigelow", @legs=4>

>> dog.name
=> "Bigelow"

>> dog.bark
Arf!
=> nil
```

"Astounding!" said the King.

"Isn't it?" said the Queen. "It also means that instead of typing all that class definition business again for our `Monkey` class, we can just inherit from `Animal` again. Because we inherit from `Animal`, we get our `name` method and a default `@legs` value of 4, *plus* we'll get this neat new `make_sounds` method I added just for monkeys."

```
>> class Monkey < Animal
>>   def make_sounds
>>     puts 'Eeh ooh ooh!'
>>   end
>> end
=> nil
```

"Now we can create a new monkey with a name and two legs. Not only can we change its name with the `name=` method we inherited from `Animal`, but we can also `make_sounds`!"

"We can get the name and change it?" Ruben asked.

The Queen nodded. "Remember, we inherited from `Animal`, and `Animal` has `attr_accessor :name`. That automatically creates a `name` method for getting the name and a `name=` method for setting the name. See?"

```
>> monkey = Monkey.new('George', 2)
=> #<Monkey:0x00000102deaed8 @name="George", @legs=2>

>> monkey.name = 'Oxnard'
=> "Oxnard"

>> monkey.make_sounds
Eeh ooh ooh!
=> nil
```

"Wow!" said Scarlet, "That's amazing—the monkey and the dog have their own methods, but they also can do anything an Animal can do!"

"That's what makes inheritance so wonderful!" said the Queen. "Given our Animal class from before, which had an attr_accessor for :name and an initialize method that set the @name and @legs instance variables, we can make two new classes that inherit that information and add some new things—like a bark method for Dog instances and a make_sounds method for Monkey instances.

"Inheritance in Ruby works exactly as it does in real life," the Queen continued. "Just like you might have inherited your father's eye color or your mother's math smarts, objects in Ruby can inherit information and methods from other objects."

"Oh!" said Ruben. "So not only can we use classes to create lots of similar objects and avoid writing extra code, but we can even write classes that borrow code from other classes?"

"On the nose," said the Queen. "We might want to use inheritance in our code if two classes have what I like to call an 'is-a' relationship, as in 'a monkey *is a* kind of animal' or 'a dog *is a* kind of animal.'"

"But a Dog would never inherit from a Monkey," said Scarlet, "because a dog *isn't* a kind of monkey."

"Exactly," said the Queen.

"Could you show us the syntax again?" said Scarlet. "This is a good trick and I want to remember it."

Subclass and Superclass

"Of course," said the Queen. "When you have one class that inherits from another, you use the class keyword, just like always. Then you write the name of the class that will inherit, which we call the *subclass* or the *child class*, and then a <. You can think of that little < as the tip of an arrow that says, 'Put all the powers and abilities of the class on the right into the class on the left!' To finish up, you then write the name of the class you're inheriting from to the right of the <, which we call the *superclass* or *parent class*. Finally, you just define any new methods as you normally would. It looks like this," she said, and typed:

super_and_subclass.rb

```
❶ class MySuperclass
    def say_hello
      puts 'Hello!'
    end
  end


❷ class MySubclass < MySuperclass
    def say_goodbye
      puts 'Goodbye!'
    end
  end
```

"Here we have two classes, MySuperclass and MySubclass," the Queen explained. "MySubclass inherits from MySuperclass on line ❷, so instances of MySubclass not only have the say_goodbye method defined in the MySubclass class, but they can also use the say_hello method they inherit from MySuperclass! Let's see what happens when we create a new instance of MySubclass."

```
>> load 'super_and_subclass.rb'
=> true

>> subby = MySubclass.new
=> #<MySubclass:0x00000104a4c478>

>> subby.say_hello
Hello!
=> nil

>> subby.say_goodbye
Goodbye!
=> nil
```

"I created an instance of MySubclass called subby using MySubclass.new," said the Queen. "Just like I promised, subby can use both the say_goodbye method defined in MySubclass as well as the say_hello method defined in MySuperclass, because MySubclass inherits from MySuperclass and can therefore do anything MySuperclass knows how to do."

"Thanks!" said Scarlet, "I think I've got it now." She studied the screen for a few seconds. "Is it possible for a class to inherit from more than one other class?" she asked.

"Alas, no," said the Queen. "You can have only one class name on the left side of the < and one class name on the right side. However!" she continued, "there *is* a Ruby trick that lets you mix the behavior of several classes into one, which we'll get to in a little while."

"Okay," said Ruben, "but what if you want your subclass to have a different version of a method than the superclass has?"

Overriding Methods: Pirates are People, Too

"Now *that*, we can do," said the Queen. "Any subclass can override a method it inherits from its superclass at any time. Let's have a look. We'll create a superclass called `Person` and subclass called `Pirate`, with a `speak` method for both. Of course, pirates and regular people speak pretty differently, don't they?" Scarlet and Ruben nodded. "So," the Queen continued, "the two `speak` methods will be different." She typed into the Computing Contraption:

pirates_and_people.rb

```
❶ class Person
     attr_reader :name

     def initialize(name)
       @name = name
     end

     def speak
       puts 'Hello!'
     end
   end

❷ class Pirate < Person
     def speak
       puts 'Arr!'
     end
   end
```

"Starting at ❶, I've defined the `Person` class with an `attr_reader` `:name`, so we'll be able to get and change the name of any `Person` instances," the Queen said. "The `initialize` method sets the `name` to the string we'll pass in when we call `Person.new`, and the `speak` method just prints out `'Hello!'`"

"With you so far!" said the King.

"Next, at ❷, I've defined the `Pirate` class to inherit from `Person`, so `Pirate` instances will be able to do anything a `Person` instance can do," said the Queen. "But! I've given `Pirate` its very own `speak` method that prints 'Arr!'. We'll see how that works in a moment. First, let's go ahead and create an instance of each class to make sure we can create it and get its name without any trouble."

```
>> load 'pirates_and_people.rb'
=> true

>> esmeralda = Person.new('Esmeralda')
=> #<Person:0x00000104bfaa90 @name="Esmeralda">

>> rubybeard = Pirate.new('RubyBeard')
=> #<Pirate:0x00000104bfedc0 @name="RubyBeard">

>> esmeralda.name
=> "Esmeralda"

>> rubybeard.name
=> "RubyBeard"
```

"Now, let's test our speak method," the Queen said. "Because Pirate created its own speak method, instances of Pirate will use that one instead of the one inherited from Person," she explained. "But since we didn't change the name and name= methods given to Pirate by attr_reader :name, which it inherited, we can get and change names the same way for both people and pirates!"

```
>> esmeralda.speak
Hello!
=> nil

>> rubybeard.speak
Arr!
=> nil
```

"That's really cool," Ruben said, "but when would we decide to override a method?"

"Any time one class inherits from another and you want *most* of the same behavior, but not all," said the Queen. "In this case, we want a Pirate to be a Person and to be created like one, but we want to make sure our Pirates sound like pirates. So we simply override the methods we want to be different between regular old people and pirates!"

"That makes sense," said Scarlet, "but what if we want a little of both? That is, what if we want to *modify* a method we inherit, but not completely *replace* it?"

Using super

"I'm so glad you asked," said the Queen. "That's absolutely something Ruby lets us do—all we need is the super keyword. Using the Animal class we created earlier, we'll create a new version of a method that already exists, just like we did with the speak method, and add our new code. Then, we'll use super to tell Ruby: 'Okay, I'm done adding new things to this method! Now have it do all the things the superclass's version of the method does.' It works like this," she said, and typed:

super_dog.rb

```
class Dog < Animal
  def initialize(name)
    puts 'Just made a new dog!'
    super
  end
end
```

"Now we can create a Dog class that inherits from Animal, just like before," said the Queen.

```
>> load 'super_dog.rb'
=> true

>> dog = Dog.new('Bigelow')
Just made a new dog!
=> #<Dog:0x00000104c6f020 @name="Bigelow", @legs=4>
```

"Here, though, we've given Dog its own initialize method, which Dog instances will use instead of the one inherited from Animal," the Queen continued.

"Just like pirates used their own speak method instead of the one from Person," Ruben said.

"Exactly!" said the Queen. "We added our own puts statement to the Dog initialize method to print out a message, but then we used super to tell Ruby: 'Okay! Now, use Animal's initialize method.' All super does is call the version of the method from the superclass! Since Animal's initialize method sets the @name and the @legs instance variables for us, you see not only @name="Bigelow" but @legs=4!"

"Gracious me, that's astounding," said the King, who had finally dried himself off. "Is there anything Ruby *can't* do?"

"That's nothing," said the Queen. "Now the real fun begins. We'll use inheritance, method overriding, and super to create some trusty friends to defend us against the intruders in our kingdom!"

Protecting the Kingdom with GuardDogs and FlyingMonkeys

"But before we do that," said the Queen, "let's get back to our Dogs and Monkeys. First, I'll redefine a Dog class, since it's been a bit since we looked at it." She typed into her Computing Contraption:

guard_dog.rb

```
class Dog < Animal
  attr_accessor :name

  def initialize(name)
    @name = name
  end

  def bark
    puts 'Arf!'
  end
end
```

"Our Dog class inherits from Animal and will be initialized with a name, and it will have a bark method to let it bark whenever it likes," said the Queen. "Next, I'll create a brand-new class that inherits from Dog. Let's keep adding to *guard_dog.rb*!" She typed into the Computing Contraption:

guard_dog.rb

```
class GuardDog < Dog

❶   attr_accessor :strength

❷   def initialize(name, strength)
      @strength = strength
      super(name)
    end

❸   def bark
      puts 'Stop, in the name of the law!'
    end

❹   def attack
      puts "Did #{rand(strength)} damage!"
    end
  end
```

"Here, I've created a GuardDog class that inherits from Dog. At ❶, we have an attr_accessor for :strength, so we'll be able to set and get the strength of our new guard dog. Next, I added an initialize method at ❷ that partly overrides the one from Dog: it sets the GuardDog's @strength, then calls super with just the name to use Dog's initialize method, which sets the @name. At ❸, I completely overrode the bark method from Dog and gave GuardDog its own phrase to say.

Finally at ❹, I added a brand-new attack method that prints out a string saying how much damage the dog did. That method uses Ruby's built-in rand method to choose a random number between zero and whatever the GuardDog's strength is."

"Wow!" said Ruben. "That's amazing! And I didn't know you could call super with arguments."

"Oh, yes," said the Queen. "If you call super by itself, it calls the superclass's initialize method with all of the arguments the subclass's initialize method got. GuardDog takes one more argument than Dog—it takes strength as well as name—and that would cause an error if we tried to give both of those to Dog, which is created only with a name. So we call super with just name to make sure that Dog's initialize method gets the number of arguments it expects."

Every GuardDog has his day

"Now then," the Queen continued, "let's create a new GuardDog and test it out!"

```
>> load('guard_dog.rb')
=> true
>> rex = GuardDog.new('Rex', 7)
=> #<GuardDog:0x0000010334e168 @strength=7, @name="Rex">
>> rex.strength
=> 7
>> rex.bark
Stop, in the name of the law!
=> nil
>> rex.attack
Did 1 damage!
=> nil
>> rex.attack
Did 4 damage!
=> nil
```

"Now we've got a special kind of dog—a GuardDog—with its own set of methods!" The Queen said. "We partly overrode its initialize method because we wanted it to have strength, but then we used super to finish creating it like a regular dog. We overrode bark because we wanted our GuardDog to have the bark method, then finished up by adding a completely new attack method that GuardDogs have but Dogs don't."

"I'm starting to get it now," said Ruben. "We use inheritance to minimize the amount of code we have to retype, and we override methods when we want to make exceptions and give our sub-classes special behavior!" The Queen nodded.

"Don't forget super," Scarlet said. "We use that when we want to partly change the behavior of a method in a subclass, but not completely replace it."

The King furrowed his brow. "This makes sense, but could we see a bit more?" he asked. "It's an awful lot to keep in my head all at once."

Once More, with Feeling!

Ruben nodded. "Could we have one more example, just to be sure we understand?" he asked.

"Of course," said the Queen. "Here's another example of inheritance, method overriding, and super, this time using our trusty Monkey class. Let's make Monkey look like this," she said, and typed:

flying_monkey.rb

```
class Monkey < Animal
  attr_reader :name, :arms

  def initialize(name, arms = 2)
    @name = name
    @arms = arms
  end

  def make_sounds
    puts 'Eeh ooh ooh!'
  end
end
```

"Here, we have a Monkey class. Using attr_reader, we can get (but not change) our monkey's name and number of arms, which defaults to 2. We also have a make_sounds method that prints out a string."

"Looks pretty standard," said the King.

"Next," the Queen continued, "we'll create a `FlyingMonkey` class that inherits from `Monkey`. We'll keep adding to *flying_monkey.rb!*" She typed into her Computing Contraption:

flying_monkey.rb

```
❶ class FlyingMonkey < Monkey
❷   attr_reader :wings

❸   def initialize(name, wings, arms = 2)
      @wings = wings
      super(name, arms)
    end

❹   def throw_coconuts
      coconuts = rand(arms)
      damage = coconuts * wings
      puts "Threw #{coconuts} coconuts! It did #{damage} damage."
    end
  end
```

"For our `FlyingMonkey` class," said the Queen, "we first inherit from `Monkey` ❶. Next, we add an attr_reader for :wings so we know how many wings our `FlyingMonkey` has ❷. We initialize the flying monkey with a certain number of @wings, but then call super to have the `Monkey` class take care of setting the @name and number of @arms ❸. We then define a brand-new throw_coconuts method ❹ that uses Ruby's built-in rand method to calculate how much damage the flying monkey can do by throwing coconuts. The number of coconuts is a random number between zero and the flying monkey's number of arms, and the damage is that number multiplied by the number of wings the monkey has, because monkeys with more wings can fly higher."

"Okay!" said the Queen. "Let's create a flying monkey and test out his methods."

```
>> load 'flying_monkey.rb'
=> true

>> oswald = FlyingMonkey.new('Oswald', 6, 4)
=> #<FlyingMonkey:0x000001013d1718 @wings=6, @name="Oswald", @arms=4>
```

```
>> oswald.make_sounds
Eeh ooh ooh!
=> nil

>> oswald.throw_coconuts
Threw 3 coconuts! It did 18 damage.
=> nil
```

"Amazing!" said Scarlet. "We create the FlyingMonkey by using its own initialize method for wings, then letting Monkey finish up by setting the name and number of arms. And because FlyingMonkey inherits from Monkey, a flying monkey can not only throw_coconuts but can also use Monkey's make_sounds method!"

"Huzzah!" said the King. "I'll bet that monkey is excellent at throwing coconuts, too. Which I suppose is only natural for a flying monkey."

"And I'll bet he makes very good monkey sounds," added Ruben.

"I guess that makes sense," said Scarlet, "but something's been bothering me: why does our GuardDog know how to *talk*?"

"He's a very smart dog," said the Queen.

"Very," said the King.

"Speaking of," said the Queen, "I think it's high time we put our guard dogs and flying monkeys to work!" She pressed a button on the arm of her chair, and her Computing Contraption began to hum. In a matter of seconds, doors slid open on all sides of her office, and dozens of guard dogs and flying monkeys emerged!

"Taco Tuesdays!" said the King. "And I thought all these gadgets and hacking conferences were a waste of time and money."

"On the contrary," said the Queen. "I think they just might save the kingdom!"

The King opened his mouth to speak, but at that very moment, a bright red telephone began ringing madly on the Queen's desk. She picked it up. "Hello?" she said. She waited a moment, and then her eyes went wide. "Stay right where you are! We're on our way!" She hung up and jumped from her chair. "The guards have news!" she said. "They're down in the Royal Stables. Quickly now, let's go!"

And with that, the four of them dashed from the Queen's office and headed for the stables out back, the guard dogs charging ahead and the flying monkeys following close behind.

Che Queen's Machine

This is getting exciting! While the King, the Queen, Ruben, and Scarlet go catch the bad guys, let's jump in and help the Queen create a Ruby class to help keep all her royal business secret; after all, there's only so much GuardDogs and FlyingMonkeys can do! I'm thinking some kind of login account for her Computing Contraption that's a bit more secure than what she's been using so far might be just what we need; we don't want anyone breaking in again anytime soon. So, we'll set up an Account class with a password for the Queen to use to log in to her computer.

Let's begin by making a new file called *secrecy.rb* and typing the following code.

```
❶ class Account
     attr_accessor :username, :password
❷   def initialize(username, password)
       @username = username
       @password = password
     end
   end

❸ class SuperSecretAccount < Account
❹   def initialize(username, password)
       @reset_attempts = 0
       super(username, password)
     end

❺   def password=(new_password)
       while @reset_attempts < 3
         print 'Current password?: '
         current_password = gets.chomp
         if @password == current_password
           @password = new_password
           puts "Password changed to: #{new_password}"
           break
         else
           @reset_attempts += 1
           puts "That's not the right password."
           puts "Attempt #{@reset_attempts} of 3 used up!"
         end
       end
     end

❻   def password
       'The password is secret!'
     end
   end

❼ regular = Account.new('Your name', 'your password')
   super_safe = SuperSecretAccount.new('Your name', 'your password')

❽ regular = Account.new('Your name', 'your password')
   super_safe = SuperSecretAccount.new('Your name', 'your password')
```

```
puts "Your regular account password is: #{regular.password}"
regular.password = 'Something else!'
puts "Your regular account password is now: #{regular.password}"

puts "If we try to see the secret account password, we get: #{super_
safe.password}"

changed_password = 'Something else!'

puts "Trying to change your secret account password to: #{changed_
password}..."
super_safe.password = changed_password
```

This is a long one, so let's go through it step-by-step.

First, we create a basic Account class at ❶ that sets up some instance variables (check them out in the initialize method at ❷). Instances of the Account class can have their @username and @password read and changed by any Ruby code that happens to want to, thanks to the attr_accessor for both :username and :password.

We're off to a pretty good start! This code lets us create an account for someone and lets that person set her password, just as you might do for a website or your email. The problem, though, is that this code lets *any* Ruby code change the user's password, which we definitely don't want.

To fix that, we create our SuperSecretAccount class at ❸ that inherits from Account, and here's where things get interesting. First, SuperSecretAccount's initialize method also takes a username and password, and it passes these to super to let Account take care of setting those instance variables ❹. The SuperSecretAccount also creates a new instance variable, @reset_attempts, to keep track of how many times a user tries to log in.

Next, the SuperSecretAccount class overrides the password= method ❺ (one of the two created by Account's attr_accessor :password), so it requires a user to enter her old password in order to change it. If she enters the correct password, the program updates the password and immediately breaks out of the while loop; if she tries unsuccessfully three times, the program exits without changing the password.

After that, the SuperSecretAccount class overrides the password method at ❻ (the other one created by Account's attr_accessor :password) and makes it print the string The password is secret! instead of giving up the password as it normally would. Finally, we create a couple of accounts ❼ and try getting and setting the passwords ❽.

You can run the code in your file by typing **ruby secrecy.rb** from the command line. Make sure you're in the same folder as your *secrecy.rb* file and type:

```
$ ruby secrecy.rb
```

Here's the output I get (yours might be a little different, depending on what you enter when you run the script):

```
❶ Your regular account password is: your password
  Your regular account password is now: Something else!
❷ If we try to see the secret account password, we get: The password
  is secret!
❸ Trying to change your secret account password to Something else!...
  Current password?: lasers
  That's not the right password.
  Attempt 1 of 3 used up!
  Current password?: ninjas
  That's not the right password.
  Attempt 2 of 3 used up!
  Current password?: your password
  Password changed to: Something else!
```

First, we see our program print out our regular account's password, followed by the new password after we change it ❶. That was too easy!

Next, at ❷, we see that our secret account correctly hides the password from prying eyes, printing out only The password is secret! if we try to look at it.

Finally, we try to change our secret account password at ❸. We put in two wrong passwords (lasers and ninja) before finally entering the correct password, your password, and our Ruby program prints out that we successfully updated our password to Something else!.

Feel free to play around with the code. What happens when you try to get and set the password on the regular account in *secrecy.rb*? What about when you try to change the super_safe one?

What happens if we try to set the password on our super_safe account and pass in the correct current password? The wrong one? Try passing in the wrong password a bunch of times. What happens?

Once you're done exploring the code, you can try thinking about all the cool stuff we could do to make it even better. For example, what methods could we add to the Account or SuperSecretAccount to make them even more useful? (Maybe a reset_password method, in case you've completely forgotten your password?) What methods might SuperSecretAccount override from Account? Are there any that might use some of the functionality of Account but not all of it? How could we go about doing that? (Hint: super would be involved.)

Lastly, Ruby does have some built-in methods that can help make your code more secure (or at least control which methods can be called). If you like, you can read all about it in the Ruby docs: *http://ruby-doc.org/core-2.0.0/Module.html#method-i-private*.

you Know this!

You learned some tricky stuff in this chapter, but I'm confident you've got a good handle on it. Just to be sure, let's go through it all once more.

First, we reviewed how to create a Ruby class using the class keyword.

```ruby
class Greeting
  def say_hello
    puts 'Hello!'
  end
end
```

Next, you found out that Ruby classes can share information and methods with each other through *inheritance*: just as a person can inherit traits from her parents, one Ruby class can inherit information and behavior from another. The class that does the inheriting is called a *subclass* or *child class*, and the class it inherits from is called the *superclass* or *parent class*.

Inheritance syntax looks like this:

```
class Dog < Animal
  def bark
    puts 'Arf!'
  end
end
```

In this example, because `Dog` inherits from `Animal`, instances of the `Dog` class (made with `Dog.new`) can use any of the methods defined in the `Animal` class.

We also learned about *method overriding* and the super keyword. Method overriding is just writing a method in a subclass that has the same name as a method in the superclass; when we create an instance of the subclass, it will use the subclass's version of the method instead of the superclass's. You'd want to override the superclass's method any time you want different or more specific behavior in the subclass. For example, say you're writing a game where your wizard is a hero (class `Wizard < Hero`), and wizards use magic in their attack method instead of the game's default `sword`.

You can override a method like so:

```
class Hero
  def initialize(name)
    @name = name
  end

  def attack
    puts "Swung sword for #{rand(5)} damage!"
  end
end

class Wizard < Hero
  def attack
    puts "Cast spell for #{rand(20)} damage!"
  end
end
```

We can see this in the following example: the hero's pretty good with a sword, but the wizard knows how to cast spells!

```
>> aragorn = Hero.new('Aragorn')
=> #<Hero:0x0000010334e398 @name="Aragorn">

>> aragorn.attack
Swung sword for 4 damage!
=> nil

>> gandalf = Wizard.new('Gandalf')
=> #<Wizard:0x000001033627f8 @name="Gandalf">

>> gandalf.attack
Cast spell for 17 damage!
=> nil
```

If we want to change only *part* of a method, we use super; we add whatever extra functionality we want, then call super to call the superclass's version of the method, like so:

```
class Wizard < Hero
  def attack
    super # This calls Hero's attack method
    puts 'But I also know magic! You shall not pass!'
  end
end
```

The attack method is doing two things. First, it calls the superclass's version of attack using super (that is, the attack defined in Hero that just prints the Swung sword message). Then it prints an additional message (But I also know magic! You shall not pass!). You'd do this when you want to modify the behavior of the superclass's method, but not replace it completely.

```
>> gandalf = Wizard.new('Gandalf')
=> #<Wizard:0x000001032d4278 @name="Gandalf">

>> gandalf.attack
Swung sword for 2 damage!
But I also know magic! You shall not pass!
=> nil
```

Last but not least, you saw that you can call super with arguments in order to send the right arguments to the superclass's method:

```ruby
class Dog
  attr_accessor :name

  def initialize(name)
    @name = name
  end
end

  class GuardDog < Dog
  attr_reader :strength

  def initialize(name, strength)
    @strength = strength
    super(name)
  end
end
```

Now when we create a GuardDog, it adds its own @strength and lets Dog take care of adding the @name:

```ruby
>> mook = GuardDog.new('Mook', 2)
=> #<GuardDog:0x00000102fcfca8 @strength=2, @name="Mook">
>> mook.name
=> "Mook"
>> mook.strength
=> 2
```

All right! At this point, you're a class master. Well, *almost*—just as there are ways to update and change your methods, there are ways to update and change your classes; you can even mix behaviors from a bunch of different classes into the Ruby classes you create! The last piece of the Ruby class puzzle is *modules*, and if we hurry, we can get down to the Royal Stables just in time to learn all about them.

10 a horse of a different color

Utter panda-monium

The King, the Queen, Ruben, and Scarlet spiraled down staircase after staircase toward the Royal Stables. Just when Ruben and Scarlet thought there would be no end to the twisty maze of stairs, the Queen reached a huge set of heavy oak doors and threw them open. They all ran blinking into the sudden light of the fields behind the palace, and only a stone's throw away stood the entrance to the Royal Stables.

"Over here!" said the Queen. "Quickly now!"

They ran to the front gate of the stables, where two of the Queen's guards were waiting. Each held a very familiar-looking Senior Apprentice to the Royal Plumber by the arm.

"Haldo!" gasped Ruben.

"Now, now," said the King. "I'm sure there's a reasonable explanation for all this." Despite his words, the King looked worried. He turned to Haldo. "Haldo, what in the name of the Hashery's glorious breakfast hash is the explanation for all this?"

Before Haldo could respond, the Queen approached the guards. "Haldo isn't who I saw in my Royal Office," she said. "There were four of them, and they were much shorter. Please release him."

The guards nodded and dropped Haldo's arms.

"Thank you, Your Highness," Haldo said, brushing himself off.

"Why are you down here at the stables?" asked the King.

"That's what we were just asking him," said the guard with the crooked nose.

"I was trying to explain," said Haldo. "You see, after searching through the Ambrose Caverns and finding nothing, I returned to my work as the Senior Apprentice to the Royal Plumber. I'd learned so much from Scarlet and Ruben about Ruby, though, that I could do a day's work in just a few hours. I had a bit of spare time on my hands, so I took on the job of Part-Time Apprentice to the Royal Stableman as well."

"Marvelous," said the King, visibly relieved that Haldo was not the villain they'd been chasing. "A veritable jack-of-all-trades!"

"I'm not sure I'd go that far," Haldo said, blushing slightly.

"Your Majesties," said the guard without the crooked nose, "we chased a group of hooded figures from the Queen's office, but lost track of them once they got out here to the stables. When we saw what had happened, Haldo was the only one around. We thought he might be involved, so we called the Queen." He shrugged. "Turns out Haldo had come out to see what the trouble was and try to help."

"One moment," said the Queen. "When you saw *what* had happened in the stables?"

The guards exchanged an uneasy look. "You'd better come see," said the guard with the crooked nose.

The group hurried into the stables. The two guards pointed to the first stall, and the King, the Queen, Ruben, and Scarlet peered inside.

"Strangest horse I've ever seen," said the King.

"That . . . is a panda," said Ruben.

"And it's red!" moaned the Queen. "Good heavens, what's happened here?"

"It's not supposed to be red?" Scarlet asked.

"Not at all!" said the Queen. "All royal pandas are supposed to be purple!" She ran to the next stall, then the next, then the next. "This one's blue!" she cried. "And this one's yellow! Not a single panda is purple!" She threw up her hands. "Whoever heard of a Purple Panda-monium Parade with pandas of every color *except* purple?"

"Wait, the pandas were purple, but now they're not?" said Ruben. "Aren't they *born* purple?"

"And what, exactly, is the Purple Panda-monium Parade?" Scarlet asked.

"One at a time," said the Queen. She turned to Ruben "No, the pandas aren't born purple. They're born white, but we feed them special extra-nutritious food that turns them purple. As for the parade," she said to Scarlet, "We hold it once a month to celebrate the peace and prosperity of the kingdom. We figure if there's going to be a little craziness in our lives, we should at least be in control of it." She sighed. "Of course, given all the chaos today, we won't be able to hold the parade."

"Not so fast," said Scarlet. "I'll bet we can fix this! It sounds like someone must have tampered with the pandas' food. Where is it?"

"Over here," said Haldo. "The food is prepared by the Panda Provisionator 3000."

They all walked past the rows of stalls to the far side of the stable, where a huge round machine covered in dials and switches hummed away. A familiar-looking screen glowed in its center.

"A Computing Contraption!" said Ruben. "Does the Panda Provisionator 3000 run on Ruby?"

"Absolutely," said Haldo. "Ever since you kids helped me fix the Mysterious Pipe, I've been learning as much Ruby as I can. I daresay I've gotten pretty good," he said, hooking his thumbs behind the straps of his overalls. "I've even gotten the hang of the Panda Provisionator here."

"Could you tell us if someone's messed with the pandas' food?" Ruben asked.

"And can you fix it?" asked the Queen, looking anxious.

CReatiNG moDules

"I think so," said Haldo. "Let's have a look." He opened a file called *colorize.rb* on the Computing Contraption, and this is what the group saw:

```ruby
module Colorize
  def color
    [:red, :blue, :green, :yellow].sample
  end
end
```

"Aha!" said Haldo. "I see the trouble here. Someone's changed the color method to return a random color as a symbol—either red, blue, green, or yellow. That's what the sample method does," he explained. "It picks a random item from an array."

"That's why the pandas are all different colors *except* purple!" Ruben said. "But wait a minute—there's nothing about panda food in this file. And what does the first line mean?"

"That? That means this code is a *module*," said Haldo, scratching his heavy black beard. "You can think of a Ruby module as a bucket of handy information and methods that we can use whenever we need it."

"It looks kind of like a class," said Scarlet.

"It's very much like a class!" said Haldo. "Like classes, modules have their own methods. In fact, that's all modules really are: just collections of methods!"

"Then what's the difference between classes and modules?" Ruben asked.

"Modules are actually *exactly* like classes, only we can't make new modules with the new method," Haldo explained. "First, let's do a lightning-quick review of classes." He started up IRB and typed:

```
>> class FancyClass; end
=> nil
```

"That just creates a new, empty class called FancyClass," Haldo explained.

"What's that semicolon for?" Scarlet asked.

"It's just a way of telling Ruby you're done with a line of code," Haldo said. "Normally in IRB you do that by pressing RETURN or ENTER and starting a new line, but since our class and module definitions are empty, we can just use the semicolon to tell Ruby we're done with one line and we're starting a new one." He shrugged. "Some people don't like to use semicolons. To each her own! Now, let's create an instance of our FancyClass."

```
>> FancyClass.new
=> #<FancyClass:0x000001044d80c8>
```

"You've created instances of classes before, right?" Haldo asked. Scarlet and Ruben nodded. "Good!" he said. "Now, let's create a module and try to create an instance of it."

```
>> module ImportantThings; end
=> nil

>> ImportantThings.new
NoMethodError: undefined method `new' for ImportantThings:Module
```

"Trying to create an instance of a module causes an error because modules don't have the new method that classes do," Haldo said.

"So if you can't create instances of a module," Ruben said, "what *can* you do with it?"

"I'll show you!" said Haldo. "Let's create a module of our own." He typed:

```
>> module Bucket
>>   MAX_BITS_AND_TRINKETS = 100

>>   def announcing_bits_and_trinkets
>>     puts 'Step right up! Bits and trinkets available now!'
>>   end
>> end
=> nil
```

"What's MAX_BITS_AND_TRINKETS," Scarlet asked, "and why is it in all caps?"

Constants

"That's a *constant*," said Haldo. "Constants are like variables, only their values don't change once you set them. They start with a capital letter—for example, class and module names are constants—and while you *technically* can reassign them during your Ruby program, Ruby will warn you if you do. See?" He typed:

```
>> RUBY = 'Wonderful!'
=> "Wonderful!"

>> RUBY = 'Stupendous!'
(irb):2: warning: already initialized constant RUBY
=> "Stupendous!"
```

"When you create your own constant that isn't a class or module—that is, just a name for a value that won't change—you usually write it in ALL CAPS," Haldo said.

"Can you use constants only inside modules?" Ruben asked.

"Nope!" Haldo said. "You can use them anywhere in your Ruby program. I just bring them up now because class names and module names are technically constants, since they start with a capital letter."

"That's pretty cool," said Scarlet, "but how do we get to our ALL CAPS constants and methods if they're stuck inside a module?"

"I'm glad you asked," Haldo said, smiling. "Let's have a look!" He typed some more:

```
>> class Announcer
>>   include Bucket
>> end
=> Announcer
```

"Here, I've made an Announcer class that *includes* the Bucket module. Our Bucket module contains a constant, MAX_BITS_AND_TRINKETS, which is set to 100, and a method, announcing_bits_and_trinkets, that prints some text on the screen.

When we include a module in a class, the constants and methods in that module can be used by any instance of the class. Because we've included Bucket in Announcer, an Announcer can now use any of the constants and methods defined in Bucket! Let's create an instance of Announcer and see what happens when we use a method we defined in Bucket."

```
>> loud_lucy = Announcer.new
=> #<Announcer:0x00000103f0c5b8>

>> loud_lucy.announcing_bits_and_trinkets
Step right up! Bits and trinkets available now!
=> nil
```

"Wow!" said Ruben. "loud_lucy knows how to use the announcing_bits_and_trinkets method, even though it's defined in the Bucket module!"

Extending your Knowledge

"Exactly!" said Haldo. "But include isn't the only way to get constants and methods defined in modules into other classes. Have a look at this." He typed some more:

```
>> class Announcer
>>    extend Bucket
>> end
=> Announcer

>> Announcer.announcing_bits_and_trinkets
Step right up! Bits and trinkets available now!
=> nil
```

"If we extend the module Bucket into the class, then those constants and methods can be used by the class itself," Haldo explained. "In this case, the class Announcer—instead of its instance, loud_lucy— can use the method. You usually end up wanting your instances to have the method rather than your classes, so in my experience, you tend to include more often than you extend."

"Remember when I said there was a Ruby trick that lets you mix the behavior of several classes into one?" asked the Queen. "This is how you do it!"

Mixins and Inheritance

"Wait," said Ruben. "So you can have a class that inherits from another class *and* includes modules to add extra methods?"

"See for yourself!" replied Haldo, and he typed:

```
>> module Enchanted
>>    def speak
>>      puts 'Hello there!'
>>    end
>> end
=> nil
```

"First, I've just created an Enchanted module with a single speak method."

```
>> class Animal
>>    def initialize(name)
>>      @name = name
>>    end
>> end
=> nil
```

"Next, I've created an Animal class that takes care of setting the names of the Animal instances we create."

```
>> class Dog < Animal
>>    include Enchanted

>>    def bark
>>      puts 'Arf!'
>>    end
>> end
=> nil
```

"In the next step, I've created a Dog class that inherits from Animal and includes Enchanted. If we've done everything right, our

Dog instances should be able to use the Dog bark method *and* the Enchanted speak method. Let's try it now!"

```
>> bigelow = Dog.new('Bigelow')
=> #<Dog:0x000001049df148 @name="Bigelow">

>> bigelow.bark
Arf!
=> nil

>> bigelow.speak
Hello there!
=> nil
```

"When we use a module this way, we call it a *mixin*," Haldo said, "because you're mixing new constants and methods into an existing class. Basically, Dog now gets the powers of Animal and Enchanted, even though it only directly inherits from Animal. We can include as many classes as we like! Assuming we defined all these modules somewhere, we could use them all in a row:

```
class Dog
  include Enchanted
  include Magical
  include AnythingWeLike
  # ...and so on and so forth
end
```

"So if you had a Dog class and the modules Enchanted, Magical, and AnythingWeLike," said the King, "if you were to make a dog with the Dog class, that dog could use any of the methods defined in Enchanted, Magical, or AnythingWeLike."

"Exactly," Haldo said. "We could also extend our class with as many modules as we wanted." He continued typing:

```
class Dog
  extend Enchanted
  extend Magical
  extend AnythingWeLike
  # ...and so on and so forth
end
```

"That's amazing!" said Scarlet.

"But hang on just a second," Ruben said. "That means that somewhere on the Computing Contraption, there's a file for the panda food that includes the Colorize module?"

Requiring another File

"Absolutely correct," said Haldo. "It happens to be called *panda_food.rb*. Take a look!" And he opened the file for them all to see. "This is the code that controls the pandas' food."

NOTE   *The next few examples are just for you to follow along and read for now—running this code as is will cause an error! We'll run this example ourselves later in the chapter.*

```ruby
require './colorize'

class PandaFood < Food
  include Colorize

  attr_reader :calories

  CALORIES_PER_SERVING = 1000

  def initialize
    @calories = CALORIES_PER_SERVING
  end
end
```

"Here's how it works," Haldo said. "Let's pick one of the pandas—Hogarth's my favorite—and see if we can figure out what's going on with his food." He opened up IRB and typed:

```
>> hogarths_food = PandaFood.new
=> #<PandaFood:0x00000104480850 @calories=1000>

>> hogarths_food.calories
=> 1000
```

"attr_accessor gives us access to the @calories instance variable, which is 1000," Haldo explained. "Now let's take a look at the color!"

```
>> hogarths_food.color
=> :yellow
```

"Hmm," said Haldo. "Can that be right? Let's try it again."

```
>> hogarths_food.color
=> :blue
```

"There you have it!" Haldo said. "You see? That's our trouble. Other Ruby programs running in the Panda Provisionator 3000 check the color of the panda food when they give instructions to the machine to make it, and they're getting colors like yellow and blue, but not purple!"

"Then the pandas ate the food and changed color!" said Ruben. "Wow, that must happen pretty quickly."

Haldo nodded. "The pandas were just fed. It actually takes a while for them to change from white to any other color, but once they've taken on a color, eating different-colored food will make their color change instantly."

"So switching them back should be a piece of cake!" said Scarlet. "We just need to change the color back to purple." She studied the screen for a minute. "Hey Haldo," she said, "what's this require bit do?"

"I'm glad you caught that," said Haldo. "The require method pulls in Ruby code from a file *outside* the file you're currently working in! So you don't need it for IRB when you're just messing around, but if you've written out a Ruby file, you can use require to pull in code from a separate file. You don't even need to type the *.rb* file extension; you just type require, then the name of your file as a string, and you can use that code immediately."

He created a file called *test_colors.rb* and began typing:

```
❶ require './colorize'
❷ class TestColors
❸   include Colorize
  end

  test = TestColors.new
❹ puts test.color
```

Haldo closed the file. When he ran it with ruby test_colors.rb, this is what they saw:

```
$ ruby test_color.rb
blue
$ ruby test_color.rb
yellow
```

"See?" Haldo said. "We can create our own file called *test_colors.rb*, then require the *colorize.rb* file inside it ❶. Once we do that, we can create our own TestColors class ❷, include the Colorize module from the *colorize.rb* file we saw earlier ❸, and then use the color method ❹!"

"Nice!" said Ruben. "But why do we need the ./ in front of colorize?"

"That's a little complicated," said Haldo, "but the short answer is that when you want to require a Ruby file, you need to tell Ruby where to look for it. ./ says, 'Look in this folder right here!' If we needed to require something from a folder *outside* the one we're in, we'd use *two* dots to tell Ruby to go up one folder. This can be confusing," Haldo finished, "so I drew a couple of pictures to help myself remember. I think I still have them!" He rummaged around in his pocket for a moment, then pulled out a piece of paper, unfolded it, and showed it to the King, the Queen, Scarlet, and Ruben.

Haldo's Fancy Diagram

requires
1.rb 2.rb

require
'./2.rb'

require
'../2.rb'

fancy/ 1.rb
2.rb

require
'fancy/
2.rb'

1.rb fancy/

by: haldo

"I get it!" said Scarlet. "One dot and a slash means 'look in the current folder,' two dots and a slash means 'go up one folder and look there,' and anytime we need to go into folders within folders, we just use folder names separated by slashes."

"Exactly right," said Haldo.

"But is there ever a time when you *don't* need to use dots or slashes?" she asked.

"That's also a bit complicated," said Haldo, "but the short answer is yes. I can show you sometime, but there's a way to use the Internet to download collections of Ruby files other people have written, called *gems*, to use in your own code!"

"That sounds amazing!" said Scarlet.

"It is!" said Haldo. "When we get to the bottom of this mystery, I'll be glad to show you."

"I think I've got a handle on all this," interrupted the King, "but I've been wondering about constants since you brought them up. Is including a module in a class the only way to get to its constants?"

Looking Up Constants

"Not at all!" said Haldo. "Take a look." He quickly typed into the Computing Contraption:

```
>> module APocketFullofMethods
>>    NUMBER_OF_METHODS = 42
>> end
=> nil

>> NUMBER_OF_METHODS
NameError: uninitialized constant NUMBER_OF_METHODS

>> APocketFullofMethods::NUMBER_OF_METHODS
=> 42
```

NOTE   *These examples will work if you try them out, so go ahead!*

"Here, I've defined a module called APocketFullofMethods," Haldo said. "Inside it, I've put a constant, NUMBER_OF_METHODS, which equals 42. You see that if I try to get to NUMBER_OF_METHODS from outside the module, I get a NameError, but if I type APocketFullofMethods::NUMBER_OF_METHODS, I get 42!"

"Wonderful!" said the King.

"But what are those two colons in a row for?" asked Scarlet.

"Ah, I've seen this before," said the Queen. "That's the *scope resolution operator*, right, Haldo?"

"Oh, yes," said Haldo, "but I find that name a bit confusing. Really, you can think of it as a way of looking things up: the four dots look like two little sets of eyes. It's how we specify which module to look in to find something we've created."

"That's cool!" said Ruben.

"Isn't it?" said Haldo, "Ruby modules are mostly good for two things. The first, as I showed you, is mixing new behavior into a Ruby class. The second is called *namespacing*. You can think of it as making individual spaces for the things you name—mostly methods and constants—to live in." He pushed his sunglasses up on his nose. "You see, if you define a method with a certain name, and then define it again, Ruby replaces the old version of the method with the new one. But if you put a method inside a module with the same name as a method or constant outside the module, you can use them both!"

"Modules must create a new scope!" said Ruben. "So having two methods with the same name and putting one in a module is like having two identical sodas, only one's in the fridge and the other's not. With methods, one's in the module (the fridge) and one isn't, so you know which one's which based on where it is."

"Exactly," said Haldo.

"And everything we just said about methods works for constants, too, right?" asked Scarlet.

"It does!" answered Haldo.

"What happens if you put one module inside another?" asked Ruben.

"You just need to keep using those :: dots," said Haldo. "For instance, if you had a module Pastel inside the Colorize module and you wanted to get to the NUMBER_OF_PASTEL_COLORS constant inside the Pastel module, you'd type Colorize::Pastel::NUMBER_OF_PASTEL_COLORS."

"If things inside a module are namespaced, like you said," Scarlet asked, "does that mean you can have two things with the same name, only one's inside the module and one's outside?"

"Absolutely!" Haldo said. He typed:

```
>> module Namespace
>>   GREETING = 'Hello from INSIDE the module!'
>> end
=> nil

>> GREETING = 'Hello from OUTSIDE the module!'
=> "Hello from OUTSIDE the module!"
```

"Here, I've defined two constants with the same name: GREETING. The first one is inside the Namespace module, and the other is in the main scope, outside any module. Here's how we tell Ruby which one to get." He typed some more:

```
>> GREETING
=> "Hello from OUTSIDE the module!"
>> Namespace::GREETING
=> "Hello from INSIDE the module!"
```

"I get it!" said Ruben. "The two colons tell Ruby which scope to use!" He thought for a moment. "Can we do all of this for class methods, too? I mean, if a module can contain methods created with def, can't it have methods that get added to the including class with self.def?"

Haldo nodded. "You *can* use the scope resolution operator to get class methods as well as constants, but in Ruby, we usually get class methods using the dot, and constants using the two colons. Since the method is a class method," he continued, "it's just like calling a method on a regular old object. Remember, classes are objects! Here's an example—we haven't defined any of these methods, so the code won't run, but it would look something like this:

```
MyClass.fancy_class_method
MyClass::CLASS_CONSTANT
```

"Whew!" said the King, sitting down on a bale of hay. "I think I've got all this—surprisingly." Scarlet and Ruben grinned at each other.

"What I *don't* understand," the King continued, "is how these scoundrels broke the Colorize module so quickly. They were only in the stables for a few seconds! How fast do they type?"

"I think I might have just found the answer," said the Queen, who had been inspecting the Panda Provisionator 3000. She reached around to the side of the machine and pulled out a small bit of scuffed metal.

"What's that?" asked Haldo.

"This," said the Queen, "is a Key-a-ma-Jigger. It's a little device you can preload code onto. Our mischief-makers must have known something about how the Provisionator works and preloaded some code onto this little machine to break it. They just had to plug it in and run!"

"Sweet corn muffins!" said the King. "We're up against professionals."

"I'll say," said Ruben, frowning. "How are we going to catch them? They've got to be a mile away by now."

The Queen had been studying the Key-a-ma-Jigger, and her mouth curled into a small smile. "I think I know that, too," she said. "Have a look! Key-a-ma-Jiggers are sold on little rings of five, and this one still has the ring on it. That means this was probably their last one!" She closed her fist around the tiny machine. "My guess is that they need more, and there's only one place in the whole kingdom that makes Key-a-ma-Jiggers."

"Where?" asked Scarlet, Ruben, and Haldo at the same time.

"Yes, dear, *where?*" asked the King.

"The Refactory!" replied the Queen.

"The Refactory!" said Haldo. "That's in the center of the kingdom. The Loop can take you there in just a few minutes!"

"Let's go!" said the King. "We'll take the express straight to the center of the kingdom. Let's catch these poisonous perpetrators purple-handed!"

"To the Loop!" said the Queen. She turned to Haldo. "Haldo, do you mind staying behind and fixing the Provisionator?"

"Not at all, Your Highness," he said. "It shouldn't take long."

"Thank you," said the Queen. She turned to the others and said, "Quickly, now!" And with that, they ran out of the stables toward the Loop platform on the hill next to the palace.

a horse of a different color

Now that you know how modules work, you can help Haldo fix up the Panda Provisionator and get all the pandas back to the right color! With any luck, you'll have them all fixed up in time for the Purple Panda-monium Parade.

Let's begin by making a new file called *colorize.rb* and typing the following code. We'll actually be making *two* files this time around: one for the module and one for the class that includes it.

colorize.rb

```
module Colorize
  def color
    :purple
  end
end
```

First, we set up the Colorize module and created a very simple color method that just returns the color we want (:purple).

In another file *in the same folder* on your computer, create the ***panda_food.rb*** file and type the following code into it. It might be a little weird writing two files instead of just one, but there's nothing here you don't already know how to do!

panda_food.rb

```
❶ require './colorize'

❷ class Food
     def serve
       puts 'Food is ready!'
     end
   end

❸ class PandaFood < Food
❹    include Colorize

     attr_accessor :calories

❺    CALORIES_PER_SERVING = 1000

     def initialize
       @calories = CALORIES_PER_SERVING
     end

     def serve
       puts 'One piping hot serving of panda food, coming up!'
     end

❻    def analyze
       puts "This food contains #{@calories} calories and is #{color}."
     end
   end

❼ hogarths_food = PandaFood.new
   puts hogarths_food.analyze
```

First, we require *colorize.rb* in our *panda_food.rb* file at ❶. Next, we define a very simple `Food` ❷ class that our `PandaFood` class inherits from ❸, and we include the `Colorize` module in our `PandaFood` class at ❹. We round it all out with a constant to tell us how many calories are in each serving ❺ and an analyze method to tell us about the food's calorie content and color ❻. (You can't be too careful when it comes to your food!) Finally, we create an instance of `PandaFood` and call the analyze method on it ❼.

As always, try running the code in your file by typing `ruby panda_food.rb` from the command line. Make sure you're in the same folder as your *panda_food.rb* file and type:

```
$ ruby panda_food.rb
```

You should see this:

```
This food contains 1000 calories and is purple.
```

Purple panda food! Our pandas are saved!

This should work for Haldo's purposes nicely, but you can make this code even better with a little elbow grease (which you can purchase directly from the Refactory for the low, low price of nine ninety-nine ninety-nine ninety-nine ninety-five). For example, our `Colorize` module has only one method, and all it does is return the color purple. How might we change the `color` method to set whatever color we wanted? What other methods might we want to add to `Colorize`?

We also don't do a whole lot with our `Food` class—`PandaFood` overrides the only method `Food` has! What else could we add to `Food` to make it even better? (Hint: The possibilities are endless!)

Finally, remember the code Haldo saw on page 211 that had been tampered with? It looked like this:

```ruby
module Colorize
  def color
    [:red, :blue, :green, :yellow].sample
  end
end
```

If you're feeling adventurous, try changing the code in your *colorize.rb* file to this code and then rerun `ruby panda_food.rb`. See how the color changes each time, just like our heroes saw?

you Know This!

I can tell you've got a great grasp on all this module business. (I'm an excellent judge of many a character.) Let's go over it one more time, though, just to make sure *I* know it. Haldo did a lot of explaining and I didn't do any, so I want to be sure this is all sealed up tight in my noggin.

First, we learned about modules and how they're basically just like classes, except you can't create instances of them with the new method. We saw that we could use modules as *namespaces*, which is just a fancy way of saying they let us organize our code nicely, like so:

```ruby
module Bucket
  MAX_BITS_AND_TRINKETS = 100

  def announcing_bits_and_trinkets
    puts 'Step right up! Bits and trinkets available now!'
  end
end
```

We also learned about *constants* (like `MAX_BITS_AND_TRINKETS`), which are just like Ruby variables, only their values aren't supposed to change. (You *can* change them, but Ruby will issue a stern warning.) Constants are always CAPITALIZED.

We saw that we could also use modules as *mixins* by using `include` or `extend`. When we use `include`, it adds all the methods in the module to instances of whatever class is doing the including; when we use extend, those module methods are added to the class itself:

```ruby
module Greetings
  def sailor
    puts 'Ahoy there!'
  end
```

```
  def pirate
    puts 'Avast, ye salty dog!'
  end

  def robot
    puts 'BEEP BOOP WHAT IS UP'
  end
end
```

There, we've just created a Greetings module with a few methods. Next, we'll create a Message class and include the Greetings module:

```
class Message
  include Greetings
end
```

Then we'll see that any instance of Message can use the methods defined in Greetings!

```
>> message = Message.new
=> #<Message:0x007fd6022c7948>

>> message.pirate
Avast, ye salty dog!
=> nil
```

If we extend Message with Greetings instead, then the Greetings methods can be used by the Message class itself:

```
>> class Message
>>   extend Greetings
>> end
=> nil

>> Message.robot
BEEP BOOP WHAT IS UP
=> nil
```

Remember, it's the `Message` class *itself* that now has the robot method, not an instance of `Message`! If we try to create an instance of `Message` and call the robot method on it, we'll get an error:

```
>> my_message = Message.new
=> #<Message:0x000001030cdf88>
>> my_message.robot
NoMethodError: undefined method `robot' for
#<Message:0x000001030cdf88>
```

But if a class *includes* Greetings, then instances of that class have the method instead:

```
>> class Message
>>   include Greetings
>> end

>> my_message = Message.new
=> #<Message:0x00000103108d18>
>> my_message.robot
BEEP BOOP WHAT IS UP
=> nil
```

By including modules into classes that already inherit from other classes, we can get all the benefits of inheriting from multiple classes with the simplicity of having just one superclass:

```
module Enchanted
  def speak
    puts 'Hello there!'
  end
end
```

There, we've got our `Enchanted` module again with its tried-and-true speak method.

```
class Animal
  def initialize(name)
    @name = name
  end
end
```

```
class Dog < Animal
  include Enchanted

  def bark
    puts 'Arf!'
  end
end
```

We've seen this before: we just define an Animal class and a Dog class that inherits from it. Dog has one method: bark.

```
>> bigelow = Dog.new('Bigelow')
=> #<Dog:0x000001049df148 @name="Bigelow">

>> bigelow.bark
Arf!
=> nil

>> bigelow.speak
Hello there!
=> nil
```

Finally, we see that Dog instances like bigelow can use bark (which it got from Dog) and speak (which it got from Enchanted)!

This is all fine and dandy when our modules and classes are in the same file, but what happens when they're not? That's right: we can use require! To pull a file we wrote into another file, we just use the require method and give it a string with the name of the file we want (no .rb file extension necessary). Remember, we need to use dots and slashes to tell Ruby where to look: ./ means "look in the current folder" and ../ means "go outside the current folder and look around." If we want to go *two* folders up, we'd use ../../; if we wanted to get at a file called *genius_idea_3.rb* in the current folder but nested inside the folders *fancy_things* and *genius_ideas*, we'd type ./fancy_things/genius_ideas/genius_idea_3.

So for example, if we had *colorize.rb* in the same folder as the following Ruby script, we'd write it like this:

```ruby
require './colorize'
class Food < PandaFood
  include Colorize
  # ...and so on and so forth
end
```

Finally, you saw that we could use the *scope resolution operator* to get at particular constants located in modules (even deeply nested ones!), and we can simply use the dot syntax we're used to for getting ahold of class methods:

```ruby
MyClass::AModuleInsideThat::YetAnotherModule::MY_CONSTANT
MyClass.some_method
```

With that, you now officially know everything there is to know about Ruby classes and modules! (Okay, okay, there's always more to learn, but you know all the stuff you'd use to write everyday Ruby programs.) You know so much Ruby, in fact, that we're going to take a short break from learning new stuff to focus on *rewriting* some of the code we already know. Rewriting your code so it still does the same thing but looks nicer or runs faster is called *refactoring*, and—as luck would have it!—that's exactly what the Refactory is all about.

11
Second Time's the Charm

Refactoring at the Refactory

The King, the Queen, Ruben, and Scarlet leapt from the Loop platform the moment it eased to a halt at the Center o' the Kingdom station and the doors *whoosh*ed open. They made a beeline for the gleaming red metal gates of the Refactory, which they could already see from the station exit.

"Right through here!" said the King. "Quickly now!" As they approached, the two guards manning the gates hastily pulled them open, trying to salute at the same time.

The four of them sped through the gates and down a long paved road. The Refactory loomed ahead: a huge red metal block of a building with a dozen chimneys puffing a pleasant-looking pink smoke.

They arrived at a large set of gleaming double doors that were propped open. A warm red light shone from within. Without hesitating, the King and Queen strode inside, and Ruben and Scarlet followed.

"My good man!" called the King, waving at a man in a hard hat holding a clipboard. "We've got an emergency! We need to speak to the Foreman, posthaste!"

The man looked up and nearly dropped his clipboard. "Your Majesty!" he said. "Of course, of course! Right away!" He dashed off into the recesses of the Refactory, clutching his helmet to his head with one hand and his clipboard with the other.

The King, the Queen, Ruben, and Scarlet stood in the entry-way, catching their breath. Scarlet looked around. "Where are we?" she asked.

"This is the main entrance to the Refactory," said the Queen. She nodded toward the glow coming from farther inside the building. "Over that way is the Refactory floor, where all the actual work takes place."

"That's where they make Key-a-ma-Jiggers?" asked Ruben.

The Queen nodded. "Among other things," she said.

Ruben opened his mouth to ask what else the Refactory made, but at that instant, the young man in the hard hat returned, followed by a much older man with twinkling eyes and a great big bushy beard.

"Your Majesty! Your Highness!" the older man said to the King and Queen, bowing to each in turn. "What can I do for you?"

"Seal the factory!" said the Queen. "We have reason to believe there are intruders in the Refactory, and they must be stopped!"

The bearded man nodded curtly and walked across the Refactory's narrow entryway to a bright red telephone. He picked up the receiver and dialed a single digit. When he spoke into the phone, his voice echoed throughout the entire Refactory:

SEAL ALL EXITS! THIS IS NOT A DRILL!
SEAL ALL EXITS! THIS IS NOT A DRILL!

The old man placed a hand over the phone's receiver. "What do these intruders look like?" he asked.

"We're not sure," said the Queen. "but there are four of them."

The man nodded again and got back on the phone:

BEGIN SECTOR-BY-SECTOR SEARCH FOR FOUR INTRUDERS! DETAIN ANY SUSPICIOUS PERSONS AND REPORT IMMEDIATELY!

With that, he hung up the phone and strode back to the rest of them, smiling.

"That should do the trick," he said. "If there are any intruders in the Refactory, my team will find them and call us at once."

"Thank you so much!" said Scarlet. "But, um, who exactly *are* you?"

"Why, I'm the Foreman, Rusty Fourman!" the man said, tipping his hard hat. "I'm in charge of all operations here at the Refactory." He gestured to the young man who had fetched him. "This is Marshall Fiveman, my right-hand man."

"Pleased to meet you," Marshall said.

"Pleased to meet you, too!" said Ruben.

"Rusty has been running the Refactory for as long as I can remember," said the King.

"How long is that?" asked Scarlet.

"Oh, I don't know," said the King. "At least several days."

"Years and years!" said Rusty, laughing. He tugged on his beard and suddenly became serious. "I imagine these intruders are what brought you out my way. I have no doubt we'll catch them soon, but do you know what they might be doing here?"

"Yes!" Scarlet said, fishing around in her pocket. "Do you make these?" she asked, holding out the Key-a-ma-Jigger.

Rusty peered at the small piece of metal in her hand. "Well, yes, we do make Key-a-ma-Jiggers here," he said. "And a few other things. Mostly, though, we're in the business of refactoring Ruby code."

"Refactoring?" said Ruben. "What's that?"

"It's basically when you rewrite your programs," Rusty said.

"Rewrite them?!" Ruben said. "But I spent so much time writing them the first time! Why would I do it again?"

"Because you can make your code faster, easier to read, or easier to update, and it still does the same work." Rusty said. He thought for a moment. "It might be easier if I show you. We can do a few of the more common Ruby refactorings, and I think you'll get the idea pretty quickly." He looked at his watch. "With the factory sealed tight, it's only a matter of time before my crew finds your culprits. In the meantime, let's refactor a little Ruby!"

The Foreman beckoned them closer and led them deeper into the Refactory, toward the warm glow that turned everything inside the building a deep red. He walked over to a long, arched railing overlooking a gently bubbling pool of what looked like molten red metal and opened up a familiar-looking machine—a Computing Contraption! The King, the Queen, Scarlet, and Ruben walked up to him as he began to type at the keyboard.

"Now then," said Rusty, scratching his nose with one hand and continuing to type with the other, "in all my years at the Refactory, I've seen a lot of Ruby. Over time, I've found patterns in the code that work very well, and patterns that don't work so well. Would you like to see a few of the good ones?" he asked.

"Absolutely!" answered the King.

Variable Assignment Tricks

"For example," Rusty said, "I often see code where the person who wrote it would like to set a variable to a particular value, but *only* if the value hasn't already been set. So I might write something like this that checks whether a particular variable is nil and, if so, sets it to a default value." And he typed:

```
>> rubens_number = nil
=> nil

>> if rubens_number.nil?
>>   rubens_number = 42
>> end
=> 42
```

"That looks perfectly all right to me," said the King.

"Oh, it's quite correct Ruby," said Rusty, "and it will do exactly what we think it will—because rubens_number is nil, Ruby sets it to 42. But there's a much clearer way to write it!" He typed some more:

```
>> rubens_number ||= 42
=> 42

>> rubens_number
=> 42
```

"You can think of ||= as being a combination of || for 'or' and = for variable assignment," said Rusty. "That combination

says: 'Set rubens_number to 42 if it doesn't already have a value.'
It's the same thing as typing this!" He typed some more:

```
>> rubens_number = nil
=> nil
>> rubens_number = rubens_number || 43
=> 43
```

"What if the variable *does* already have a value?" Scarlet
asked.

"Let's find out!" said Rusty. He typed some more:

```
>> scarlets_number = 700
=> 700
>> scarlets_number ||= 42
=> 700
>> scarlets_number
=> 700
```

"In this case," Rusty said, "scarlets_number already has a value
of 700, so ||= doesn't do anything. As I mentioned, || means 'or,'
and you've likely seen that = means 'assign this value to a variable.'" Scarlet and Ruben nodded.

"So," Rusty continued, "when we write ||=, we're telling
Ruby: 'Hey! You should *conditionally assign* this value to this
variable.' That's just a fancy way of saying we want Ruby to use
the value it already knows *or* use the new value if the variable
isn't set. For rubens_number, there was no value, so 42 was set; for
scarlets_number, we'd already set 700 as the value, so ||= 42 did
nothing."

"But couldn't we write this?" Scarlet asked, and typed:

```
>> rubens_number = 42 if rubens_number.nil?
=> 42
```

"Why, yes!" Rusty said, and his great bushy beard turned
upward as he smiled. "I wouldn't necessarily use that code in
this example, since I can just as easily use ||=, but it's a very
common refactoring to use inline ifs and unlesses in Ruby."

"What do you mean by *inline?*" asked Scarlet.

"I'll show you!" said the Foreman, and he typed more code into the Computing Contraption:

```
>> if !rubens_number.nil?
>>   puts 'Not nil!'
>> end
Not nil!
=> nil
```

"That'll get the job done," said Rusty, "but why use if and ! if we can just use unless?"

```
>> unless rubens_number.nil?
>>   puts 'Not nil!'
>> end
Not nil!
=> nil
```

"Now, that's a bit better," Rusty continued, "but it's still more lines of code than we need. If we've got an if or unless but no else, we can write the whole thing in one line, like this."

```
>> puts 'Not nil!' unless rubens_number.nil?
Not nil!
=> nil
```

"Now *this* is the best!" said Rusty. "Not only can we convert if !s to unlesses, but we can also write unless on a single line with the variable we're testing!"

"And we can do that with if, too?" asked Scarlet.

"You bet!" said Rusty, and he typed:

```
>> puts '42! My favorite number!' if rubens_number == 42
42! My favorite number!
=> nil
```

"Now, just as with if, we can use else with unless," said Rusty, "but while if/else makes a lot of sense to me, I find unless/else confusing."

Crystal-Clear Conditionals

"I agree," said the King, rubbing his head. "So we should convert if !s to unlesses, and we can make if or unless one line if there's no else?"

"Precisely," said Rusty. "This is confusing:

```
>> unless rubens_number.nil?
>>   puts 'Not nil!'
>> else
>>   puts 'Totally nil.'
>> end
Not nil!
=> nil
```

"But *this* is clear as day!"

```
>> if rubens_number.nil?
>>   puts 'Totally nil.'
>> else
>>   puts 'Not nil!'
>> end
Not nil!
=> nil
```

"In fact," Rusty continued, "we could write these as two one-line statements—one if and one unless. I don't think that's as easy to understand, but I'll show it to you in case you're curious."

```
>> puts 'Not nil!' unless rubens_number.nil?
Not nil!
=> nil
>> puts 'Totally nil.' if rubens_number.nil?
=> nil
```

"Remember," said Rusty, "puts returns nil, so that's why we see it after the =>. But since rubens_number is 42 and *not* nil, Ruby doesn't print 'Totally nil.'.".

"I think the if/else one is the easiest to understand," said Ruben, "but it's still a lot of extra lines. If there *is* an else, is there any simpler way to write it?"

"As it happens, there is," said Rusty. "We can use a *ternary operator*. It looks like this!"

```
>> puts 1 < 2 ? 'One is less than two!' : 'One is greater than two!'
One is less than two!
=> nil
```

"Sweet limbo of lost twist-ties!" cried the King. "What in our peaceful kingdom is that?"

"It's not nearly as scary as it looks. We'll just use a question mark followed by a colon in our code," said Rusty. "In this case, we want our code to print something out using puts. Next, we give Ruby an *expression*: something that will either turn out to be true or false. In this case, that's 1 < 2." Rusty scratched his beard. "Then we write a question mark, followed by what Ruby should do if the expression is true. Finally, we write a colon, followed by what Ruby should do if the expression is false. Since 1 *is* less than 2, Ruby prints out One is less than two!" He thought for a moment. "Really, you can think of it as writing an if/else, just all on one line. The ? is like a shorthand if, and the : is like a shorthand else."

"That's quite marvelous," said the Queen, "but don't you find it a bit hard to read?"

"Sometimes," admitted Rusty, "so I'll often stick to a regular if/else. But if it's a very short bit of code, I'll sometimes refactor an if/else into a ? :."

"What if the expression you want to check is a method with a question mark?" Ruben asked. "Will the ternary operator still work?"

"Oh, yes," said Rusty, and he quickly typed:

```
>> bill = nil
=> nil
>> puts bill.nil? ? "Bill's nil!" : "Bill's not nil at all."
Bill's nil!
=> nil
```

"That third line can look tricky with the two question marks so close together," said Rusty, "so you want to be a bit careful with them. Remember, `nil?` is a built-in Ruby method that returns true if the object it's called on is `nil` and `false` otherwise."

"It's also important to remember that `nil` gets returned because `puts` has no return value, not because it's returning bill!" said the Queen.

"Quite right, quite right," said Rusty.

"This looks pretty good," said Scarlet, squinting at the Computing Contraption screen, "but I feel like a whole bunch of ? : symbols in a row—or even if/elses!—would get hard to read. Is there a good way to write code when Ruby should do a lot of different things without our having to write ifs and elses all over the place?"

when you need a case statement

"You've got a keen eye for refactoring," said Rusty. "There *is* something we can use to replace ifs and elses in Ruby. And while I don't find myself using it a lot," he continued, "it *can* be much more readable than a long chain of `if`s, `elsif`s, and `else`s. It's called a case statement. Have a look!" He typed:

```
>> number = 1

>> case number
>> when 0
>>    puts "Zero!"
>> when 1
>>    puts "One is fun!"
>> when 2
>>    puts "Two. It's true!"
>> when 3
>>    puts "Three for me."
>> else
>>    puts "#{number}? I don't know that one."
>> end

One is fun!
=> nil
```

"We use the case keyword to tell Ruby which variable to pay attention to," Rusty explained. "Then we can use when to say: *when* this value is the case—that is, when this value is the variable we're looking at—do this thing!"

"And just like with if and unless, we use else to have Ruby do something when nothing matches," Ruben said.

"Exactly right," said Rusty.

"But is this all case statements can do?" Marshall piped up. "It seems to me it's not that interesting to just have them check whether a variable is a certain number."

"Oh my, no," said Rusty. "They can get mighty fancy!" He typed:

```
>> number = 7

>> case number
>> when 0
>>   puts "That's definitely zero."
>> when 1..10
>>   puts "It's a number between 1 and 10, all right."
>> when 42
>>   puts "Ah yes, 42. My favorite number!"
>> when String
>>   puts "What? That's a string!"
>> else
>>   puts "A #{number}? What in the world is a #{number}?"
>> end

It's a number between 1 and 10, all right.
=> nil
```

The code is annotated with markers: ❶ on the `when 0` line, ❷ on the `when 1..10` line, ❸ on the `when 42` line, and ❹ on the `when String` line.

"We can check whether a number is a certain value like 0 (❶) or 42 (❸), whether it falls in a range (❷), or even whether it's an instance of a particular class, like String (❹)," said Rusty. "case statements can quickly do a lot of work that if and else would take a long time to handle."

"That *is* quite fancy," said the King, "but if there's anything I've learned from Ruby, it's that the most delightful moments are when I can get something done without having to write out every last detail. Are there any refactorings like that?"

Simplifying Methods

"I thought you'd never ask," said the Foreman. "This is an old one, but a good one. Do you know about methods and return?"

They all nodded.

"Perfect," he said. "As you may or may not know, Ruby methods will automatically return the result of the last bit of code they evaluate. That means that if you want your method to return the last expression it evaluates, you can leave off the return keyword completely. Let's define a method that simply checks if the argument it gets is true."

```
>> def true?(idea_we_have)
>>   return idea_we_have == true
>> end
=> nil
```

"Now, that'll return true if idea_we_have is true and false if it isn't," Rusty said, "but it turns out that Ruby automatically returns the result of the last bit of code it runs. We don't need return at all!"

```
>> def true?(idea_we_have)
>>   idea_we_have == true
>> end
=> nil
```

"Ah, yes!" said the King. "I think we've seen this bit of Ruby wizardry before."

"All right," said Rusty, "but try *this* one on for size. If you have an expression that will give you back a Boolean—that is, it will end up being true or false—you don't have to compare it to true or false with ==. That's just an extra step! You can just return the variable that will be true or false *itself.*" He typed into the Computing Contraption:

```
>> def true?(idea_we_have)
>>   idea_we_have
>> end
=> nil
```

```
>> most_true_variable = true
=> true

>> true?(most_true_variable)
=> true
```

"most_true_variable is true, and since our method automatically returns whatever argument gets passed in, it returns true," the Foreman explained.

"Wonderful!" said the Queen. "I love how simple that method was. But will this work only for variables that are true or false?"

Rusty nodded. "Though there's another good refactoring that will let us determine whether a Ruby value is *truthy* or not."

"Truthy?" asked Ruben and Scarlet together.

"Truthy!" said Rusty. "When I say a Ruby value is *truthy*, what I mean is: this value is not false or nil. Remember how those two values work with if and unless?" he asked, and he typed:

```
>> my_variable = true
=> true

>> puts 'Truthy!' if my_variable
Truthy!
=> nil
```

"Because my_variable is true and true is a truthy value, the if statement code runs and Ruby prints out 'Truthy!'," Rusty said. "Now let's see what happens if we do the same thing with false."

```
>> my_variable = false
=> false
```

```
>> puts 'Truthy!' if my_variable
=> nil
```

"Nothing!" said the King.

"That's right," said the Foreman. "my_variable is false, so 'Truthy!' doesn't get printed out on the screen. The same thing happens with nil."

```
>> my_variable = nil
=> nil
>> puts 'Truthy!' if my_variable
=> nil
```

"Nothing was printed for false or nil because they're *falsey* values; every other value in Ruby is truthy," Rusty explained. "Have a look!" He typed some more:

```
>> my_variable  = 99
=> 99

>> puts 'Truthy!' if my_variable
Truthy!
=> nil
```

"You'll see, though, that nil and false aren't *exactly* the same, and 99 and true also aren't *exactly* the same." He typed again:

```
>> nil == false
=> false

>> 99 == true
=> false
```

"But!" he exclaimed, raising a single finger, "we can turn a *truthy* value into true and a *falsey* value into false with a simple !!. You see, the first ! makes Ruby return a Boolean, but since ! means 'not,' it's the opposite of what you want. The second ! fixes this by undoing the opposite you got from the first one!" The King, Scarlet, Ruben, and even the Queen looked puzzled. "Here, I'll show you," the Foreman offered, and he typed into the Computing Contraption:

```
>> truthy_value = 'A fancy string'
=> "A fancy string"

>> falsey_value = nil
=> nil

>> truthy_value
=> "A fancy string"

>> !truthy_value
=> false

>> !!truthy_value
=> true
```

"So truthy_value is a string," said Scarlet, "and since it's not false or nil, if you put it in an if statement, the code will run."

"Right," said Rusty.

"So," Scarlet said, "!truthy_value is false, and *not* !truthy_value—that is, !!truthy_value—is true!"

"You've got it!" said Rusty. "Now, here's how it works for falsey values."

```
>> falsey_value
=> nil

>> !falsey_value
=> true

>> !!falsey_value
=> false
```

"It's just the opposite!" said Ruben. "nil is falsey, so !nil is true and !!nil is false."

"Exactly," said the Foreman. "We could even write a method to see if something is truthy, like this."

```
>> def truthy?(thing)
>>    !!thing
>> end
=> nil

>> truthy?('A fancy string')
=> true

>> truthy?(nil)
=> false
```

"In this case, we've defined a truthy? method that takes a single argument, thing," said Rusty. "Then we call !!thing: the first ! returns false if thing is truthy and true if thing is falsey. Since this is the opposite of what we want, we use !! to make our method return true if thing is truthy and false if thing is falsey."

"That's amazing!" said Scarlet.

"Isn't it?" said Rusty. "Once we've defined truthy?, we can call it on 'A fancy string' to see that it's a truthy value, then on nil to see that nil is falsey."

"What else can we do to make our Ruby programs shorter and clearer?" Ruben asked.

"Well, this one might seem obvious," said Rusty, "but it's actually one of the hardest parts of programming—giving variables, methods, and constants good names!"

"What do you mean?" said Marshall, who was scribbling furiously on his clipboard.

"Well, let's use our truthy? method as an example," Rusty said. "Check out what would've happened if we'd picked a clumsier name." He quickly typed:

```
>> def is_this_a_truthy_thing_or_not?(thing)
>>    return !!thing
>> end
=> nil
```

"That looks terrible," said the King.

"Yes, it does," said Rusty. "Not only that, but it also has an extra return that we don't need. The simpler method is much nicer."

```
>> def truthy?(thing)
>>   !!thing
>> end
=> nil
```

"Aha! I see," said the King. "We want to give the Ruby objects we create simple, easy-to-remember names so we type less code and make fewer mistakes when we want to reference our code later."

"Bingo!" said Rusty. "Imagine if we had to type is_this_a_truthy_thing_or_not? every time we wanted to check if a value was truthy. It'd be pure madness!"

"How else can we cut down on rewriting code?" asked Marshall.

De-duplicating code

"Well, one nice way is to remove duplicated code whenever we can!" said Rusty. "It's much too easy to cut and paste code all through our programs, which then makes it very hard to change those programs if variable names or values change. Take a look at this," he said, typing:

```
>> def king?(dude)
>>   if dude == 'The King'
>>     puts 'Royal!'
>>   else
>>     puts 'Not royal.'
>>   end
>> end
=> nil

>> def queen?(lady)
>>   if lady == 'The Queen'
>>     puts 'Royal!'
```

```
>>    else
>>      puts 'Not royal.'
>>    end
>> end
=> nil
```

"I've defined two methods here," said Rusty. "The first one, king?, checks whether the argument passed in is 'The King'; if so, it puts 'Royal!', and otherwise it puts 'Not royal.'. I've also defined a second method, queen?, that checks whether the argument passed in is 'The Queen'. See how much of that code is repeated?" Rusty continued. "It was very boring to type, and what's more, if we want to change any of the messages that get printed out, we have to do it in two places! I'd much rather type this," he said, and so he did:

```
>> royal?(person)
>>    if person == 'The King' || person == 'The Queen'
>>      puts 'Royal!'
>>    else
>>      puts 'Not royal.'
>>    end
>> end
=> nil
```

"Now we've got one method that does the work of two," Rusty said.

```
>> royal?('The King')
Royal!
=> nil
>> royal?('The Queen')
Royal!
=> nil
>> royal?('The jester')
Not royal.
=> nil
```

"I like that a lot better," said Ruben. "And we could have written that with the ternary operator if we wanted, right?"

"Of course!" said Rusty. "We can get to that in a little while, if you like."

"Before we do," interrupted the King, "I worry that if we go *too* far down this road of combining methods, we might get methods that do *too much* work and are very hard to think about."

"Happens all the time!" said the Foreman. "While it's true that you often want to write the least amount of code you can, sometimes you end up writing very large, hard-to-think-about methods that really should be broken up into smaller pieces. Take a look at this method that came through the Refactory just the other day," he said, and he typed into the Computing Contraption:

```
>> list_of_numbers = [1, 2, 3, 4, 5]
=> [1, 2, 3, 4, 5]

>> def tally_odds_and_evens(numbers)
>>    evens = []
>>    odds = []
>>    numbers.each do |number|
>>      if number.even?
>>        puts 'Even!'
>>        evens.push(number)
>>      else
>>        puts 'Odd!'
>>        odds.push(number)
>>      end
>>    end

>>    puts "#{evens}"
>>    puts "#{odds}"
>> end
=> nil
```

"First, it sets up a few variables," Rusty said. "The evens array stores even numbers, the odds array stores odd numbers, and the list_of_numbers stores the numbers to check for evenness or oddness."

"Next, the tally_odds_and_evens method iterates over a list of numbers and checks to see whether each one is even or odd with Ruby's built-in even? and odd? methods. For each number, tally_odds_and_evens prints out whether it's even or odd, then adds it to the appropriate array."

```
>> tally_odds_and_evens(list_of_numbers)

Odd!
Even!
Odd!
Even!
Odd!
[2, 4]
[1, 3, 5]
=> nil
```

"As you can see," Rusty said, "it's pretty complicated."

"I'll say!" said the King. "I can hardly follow a word of it."

"It might be easier if we broke down this big method, tally_odds_and_evens, into a few smaller, well-named ones," said Rusty, and he typed:

```
>> list_of_numbers = [1, 2, 3, 4, 5]
=> [1, 2, 3, 4, 5]

>> def tally_odds_and_evens(numbers)
>>    evens = []
>>    odds = []
>>    numbers.each do |number|
>>      alert_odd_or_even(number)
>>      update_tally(number, evens, oddsna)
>>    end

>>    puts "#{evens}"
>>    puts "#{odds}"
>> end
=> nil
```

"First, we'll rewrite the tally_odds_and_evens method. We'll move the code that prints Odd! or Even! to its own method, alert_odd_or_even, and we'll move the code that updates the tally to its own method, `update_tally`. We'll write each method in just a minute," Rusty said.

"That makes sense," said the King.

"Next, we'll take out the part that writes `Odd!` or `Even!` on the screen and wrap it up in a method called `alert_odd_or_even`. In fact, we can use the ternary operator we learned about to make it a one-line method!"

```
>> def alert_odd_or_even(number)
>>   puts number.even? ? 'Even!' : 'Odd!'
>> end
=> nil
```

"After that," Rusty continued, "we'll put the code that updates the evens and odds arrays into its own method, `update_tally`."

```
>> def update_tally(number, evens, odd)
>>   if number.even?
>>     evens.push(number)
>>   else
>>     odds.push(number)
>>   end
>> end
=> nil
```

"That's the same code we had before, just wrapped up in its own method. It makes the overall `tally_odds_and_evens` method look much better, though, and it still works the same way," Rusty explained.

```
>> tally_odds_and_evens(list_of_numbers)

Odd!
Even!
Odd!
Even!
Odd!
[2, 4]
[1, 3, 5]
=> nil
```

"Overall, it's a bit more code," Rusty admitted, "but now it's clearer what's doing what, and we can change what gets printed out or how we update our lists of even and odd numbers independently from one another if we want to."

"Excellent!" said the King, beaming. "I like my Ruby methods to be just like me: short and simple!" The Queen, Ruben, and Scarlet stifled a laugh.

Rusty pushed his hard hat up on his head. "That's all the refactoring I can think of off the top of my head," he said. He looked at his watch again. "I'm surprised we haven't heard back from any of the search teams yet. What were you telling me these ne'er-do-wells were after?" He thought for a moment, then snapped his fingers. "Ah, yes! Your Key-a-ma-Jigger. That's why you're here in the first place, I take it?"

"Yes!" said Scarlet. "We found this plugged into the Panda Provisionator 3000 over at the Royal Stables, and we thought that it might be the last one our mysterious bad guys had, so they might have come back here for more." She held the small piece of metal out to the Foreman once more.

Rusty nodded. "Yes, that's one of ours," he said. "And if your troublemakers are looking for more, they'd almost certainly be trying to get into the Vault of Tricky Things and Trinkets!"

"My word!" said the Queen. "What's that?"

"It's where we keep a large number of items," said Rusty, "like Ruby code we've found particularly hard to refactor and various things and trinkets. It's also where we keep a lot of our inventory, including our Key-a-ma-Jiggers."

The King struck his palm with his fist. "If that's where the Key-a-ma-Jiggers are, I'm sure that's where we'll find our culprits!" he said. "Could you call down and have your teams head there right away?"

No sooner had the King asked than the Foreman's red telephone began ringing off the hook.

Rusty ran to the phone and picked it up. "Hello?" he said. He listened intently for a moment, then gasped. He covered the receiver with his hand. "One of my teams caught four intruders down by the Vault!" he said. He put the phone to his ear again, then sighed deeply. "All right," he said. "Send every available worker. And hurry!" He hung up.

"What was it?" asked the Queen. "Did your team catch them?"

"No," groaned the Foreman, "they've escaped!" The Queen's face fell; the King covered his face with his hands; Scarlet and Ruben turned to each other, mouths open.

"But!" Rusty said, holding up a single finger, "every one of my workers is in hot pursuit. Our four villains were seen heading straight for the Refactory's loading docks, and that's a one-way street! We'll have them surrounded faster than you can rename a Ruby method."

"Then what are we waiting for?" said the Queen. "Let's go see who we've been chasing all this time!" And with that, all five of them charged off to the loading docks in the depths of the Refactory.

Re-Refactoring

Practice makes perfect! Now that you've learned a whole bunch of ways to make your Ruby code even shorter and simpler to read, it's time to apply them to a couple of particularly gnarly methods. Not to worry, though: if you didn't have any trouble with the refactorings we saw earlier, these'll be a breeze! (Even if you stumbled here and there, you'll be a refactoring master by the time you're through with these examples.)

Let's begin by making a new file called *first_try.rb* and typing the following code. We'll actually be making *two* files this time: one for the initial code and one for the refactoring we'll do. *first_try.rb* defines a method, all_about_my_number, and sets the number to 42 if no number is passed in. After that, it prints some information about the number, including what the number is and whether it's positive, negative, or zero.

first_try.rb

```ruby
def all_about_my_number(number)
  if number.nil?
    number = 42
  end

  puts "My number is: #{number}"

  if number > 0 == true
    return 'Positive'
  elsif number < 0 == true
    return 'Negative'
  else
    return 'Zero'
  end
end
```

If this doesn't look like great code to you, don't worry! We're about to refactor it. In the same folder on your computer, create another file called *refactored.rb* and type the following code into it. This code will do exactly the same thing as the code in *first_try.rb*, but it will look much nicer.

refactored.rb

```ruby
def describe_number(number)
  number ||= 42

  puts "My number is: #{number}"

  sign(number)
end

def sign(number)
  case
  when number > 0
    'Positive'
  when number < 0
    'Negative'
```

```
  else
    'Zero'
  end
end
```

As always, you can run the code in your file by typing **ruby first_try.rb** and **ruby refactored.rb** from the command line. Since we made two files in the previous chapter and there's no new code here, there shouldn't be any big surprises! (Though there may be some small ones.)

The first difference you'll probably notice is in the case statement; earlier, we did something like this:

```
case number
when 0
  puts 'Zero!'
# ... and so on
```

And now we're doing this:

```
case
  when number > 0
# ... and so on
```

These are both 100 percent correct Ruby. If you have a variable and you just want to check whether it equals a certain value, is a certain class, or is in a certain range, you'd use the first syntax; if you want to do specific checks on a value (like number > 0), you'd use the second one.

You probably also saw that we skipped right over some refactorings. For instance, we removed the == check from lines like if number > 0 == true. Sometimes you'll start to refactor one way, then realize there's an even better way to do it! Other times there are a whole bunch of ways to refactor your code that are all equally good, and you just happen to pick one over another.

Finally, we managed to pull out a bunch of repetition (including some return statements that we can let Ruby handle implicitly!) and broke out the code that checks the sign of a number (positive, negative, or zero) into its own method.

How could we make this refactoring even more awesome? There are probably an unlimited number of ways, but here are a few to get your gears turning. For example, we refactored the nil? check into an ||=. This works okay, but is there something else we could do? (Hint: We learned about setting default arguments in Chapter 7.) Also, we have an if/else statement that we converted to a case, but would it have made sense to use a ternary operator somewhere instead? Why or why not? Explain your answer in 6,000 words or more. (Hint: Don't do that—it would be unbelievably boring.)

One more example to bake your noodle: we don't do any checking to make sure that the argument that gets passed to our method really *is* a number. What happens if we put in a Boolean? A string? What could we do to refactor our method so it would be okay with non-number inputs?

you know this!

Okay! It might have seemed at first that this chapter wouldn't have a whole lot to offer—after all, we're just rewriting the sort of code that we've been writing all along—but it turns out that *re*writing our Ruby code can be even more challenging than writing it the first time. Just to make sure you're up to those challenges (hint: you absolutely are), let's go over the refactorings we covered one more time.

First, you saw that we can set a value *conditionally* with ||=. In other words, we can tell Ruby to set a value for a variable if that variable doesn't already have one, but to use the existing value if it does:

```
>> my_variable ||= 'pink smoke'
=> "pink smoke"

>> my_variable
=> "pink smoke"
```

Here, `my_variable` isn't already set, so `||=` sets it to `'pink smoke'`. If the variable already has a value, though, `||=` won't change it. Check it out!

```
>> your_variable = 'blue smoke'
=> "blue smoke"

>> your_variable ||= 'pink smoke'
=> "blue smoke"

>> your_variable
=> "blue smoke"
```

You also saw that we can replace `if !` with unless:

```
>> if !my_variable.nil?
>>    puts 'Not nil!'
>> end
Not nil!
=> nil

>> unless my_variable.nil?
>>    puts 'Not nil!'
>> end
Not nil!
=> nil
```

And you saw that we can even put an `if` or `unless` *inline* if we don't need an else:

```
>> puts 'Not nil!' unless my_variable.nil?
Not nil!
=> nil
```

If an `else` is involved, it's usually better to stick to a regular if/else.

```
>> if true
>>    puts 'True!'
>> else
>>    puts 'False!'
>> end
```

```
True!
=> nil
```

However, for very short if/elses, sometimes it makes sense to use the *ternary operator*, like so:

```
>> puts true ? 'True!' : 'False!'
True!
=> nil
```

You learned that we can even use the ternary operator with methods that have question marks in them! Just be sure to use two question marks: one that's part of the method name and one that's part of the ternary statement:

```
>> jill = nil
>> puts jill.nil? ? "Jill's nil!" : "Jill's not nil at all."
>> Jill's nil!
=> nil
```

We also talked about replacing long chains of if/elsif/else with case statements. A case statement takes a variable and does different things depending on its value:

```
>> random_trinket = 'plastic cup'
=> "Plastic cup"

>> case random_trinket
>> when 'plastic cup'
>>   puts "Plastic cup's on the up and up!"
>> when 'pet ham'
>>   puts "A pet ham! What are you, an elf?"
>> when 'star monkey'
>>   puts "I've always wanted one of those!"
>> else
>>   puts "A #{random_trinket}, huh? Never heard of it!"
>> end
Plastic cup's on the up and up!
=> nil
```

Next up, we reminisced about Ruby's *implicit return*. Ruby methods automatically return the result of the last bit of code they evaluate, so these two methods do exactly the same thing:

```
>> def number_42?(number)
>>   return number == 42
>> end
=> nil

>> number_42?(42)
=> true

>> number_42?(43)
=> false

>> def number_42?(number)
>>    number == 42
>> end
=> nil

>> number_42?(42)
=> true

>> number_42?(43)
=> false
```

Next, you found out that when we're using variables that are Booleans (true or false), we can just return those variables directly instead of comparing them to true or false with ==. This works:

```
>> def thing_true?(thing)
>>    thing == true
>> end
=> nil
```

But this does the exact same thing and uses a little less code:

```
>> def thing_true?(thing)
>>    thing
>> end
=> nil
```

```
>> the_truest_thing_ever = true
=> true

>> thing_true?(the_truest_thing_ever)
=> true
```

In fact, we can get the *truthiness* of any Ruby value by using two "not" symbols (!) in front of the object. A *truthy* Ruby value will act like true in an if statement, and a *falsey* one will act like false. All Ruby values are truthy except for false and nil. Truthy values run the code in the if statement:

```
>> if true
>>   puts 'Woohoo!'
>> end

Woohoo!
=> nil
```

And falsey ones don't:

```
>> if false
>>   puts 'A waltz.'
>> end
=> nil
```

Nothing happens! Nothing happens with nil, either:

```
>> if nil
>>   puts 'A dill (pickle).'
>> end
=> nil
```

Since all values except false and nil are truthy, a regular string will be truthy in an if statement:

```
>> if 'fancy string'
>>   puts 'For a fancy king!'
>> end

For a fancy king!
=> nil
```

You can always check the truthiness of a value in Ruby with !!:

```
>> !!nil
=> false

>> !!'fancy string'
=> true
```

I also mentioned something you probably already knew in the back of your mind: giving good names to our constants, variables, and methods is important! See how much better the second method name is than the first?

```
>> def is_this_value_truthy?(value)
>>    !!value
>> end
=> nil

>> def truthy?(value)
>>    !!value
>> end
=> nil
```

Last but not least, you saw that removing duplicated code and breaking our programs apart into small methods that do very specific jobs can make our Ruby code easier to write, understand, and change. The more code you read, the more you'll see this is true, so don't hesitate to ask your local adult to help you find snippets of Ruby code on the Internet to read through!

Speaking of bits of code, we're about to see a fresh delivery of Ruby syntax when we follow the King, the Queen, Scarlet, Ruben, and Rusty down to the loading docks. The constant picking up and dropping off that occurs down there will be a perfect opportunity to explore Ruby *input* and *output*—also called *I/O*—and we just might catch our first glimpse of the evildoers who have been turning this peaceful kingdom completely upside down.

12
Reading, Writing,
and
Ruby Magic

File Input and Output

Ruben looked around him and sighed. "Why did we run all the way here if the freight elevator goes so *slow*?" he asked.

"You know," said the King, rubbing his beardy chin, "I really don't know. But I imagine it'll be here any minute!"

No sooner had the King spoken than the freight elevator arrived with a great *clang*. The doors slid open, revealing a huge metal elevator car.

"All aboard!" said Rusty, and they all climbed in. Rusty punched a round red button labeled LOADING DOCKS, and with another *clang*, the car began to slowly descend into the heart of the Refactory.

"We'll be there in a jiffy," Rusty said.

"A *slow* jiffy," Scarlet said. Ruben stifled a laugh.

"Not to worry," Rusty said. "Every worker in the Refactory is down there, so there's no chance those villains'll escape!"

The King paced around the elevator car. "I can't wait to question those scoundrels," he said. "All this trouble they've caused! I'll be keen to know what drove them to it."

"I'll bet they're evil ninja wizards!" said Ruben.

"More like evil robot pirates," said Scarlet.

"Whoever they are, they'll have a lot to answer for," said the Queen. "But we'll know soon enough. We're close—I can feel it!"

"That we are," said Rusty. "Next stop: loading docks!"

A moment later, the freight elevator doors groaned open, and the King, the Queen, Scarlet, Ruben, and Rusty stepped onto the immense, bustling floor of the Refactory loading docks.

"Foreman here!" Rusty yelled to the crowd of men and women in hard hats as he led the group up a metal walkway and onto a large platform in the center of the enormous room. "What've we got?"

"Sir!" said Marshall, climbing up the walkway, "I rushed down here ahead of you to try to assess the situation. It looks like we've got four intruders holed up in one of the loading docks."

"Which one?" Rusty asked.

Marshall shook his head. "We don't know! They hid before we could see where they went. All we know is that we had the docks surrounded when they disappeared, so they must still be in here somewhere."

Rusty nodded and stroked his beard for a moment. "Well," he said at last, "best get to finding them." He walked to the edge of the platform and stepped on a large round indentation with his boot. In a hiss of steam, a column rose out of the platform. On the side facing the Foreman shone the unmistakable glow of a Computing Contraption screen.

"Each dock is controlled by a Ruby program," Rusty said as the King, the Queen, Ruben, and Scarlet gathered around him. "Ruby treats each of them as a *file*. If we can open each file, we'll find our missing criminals!"

"A file? You mean, like a regular computer file?" Scarlet asked.

"The very same!" said Rusty. "Ruby can open just about any file you can think of: Ruby programs, text files, pictures, you name it!"

The Queen smiled. "I know all about files!" she said. "I'd be happy to lend a hand opening all these docks to find our culprits." She cracked her knuckles. "How many files are there?" she asked.

Rusty gestured to the far wall, which was covered in hundreds of heavy metal doors.

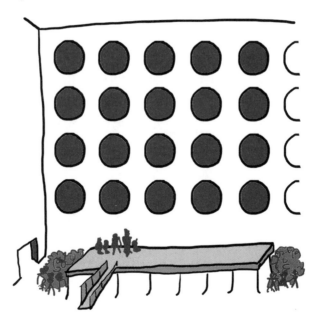

"Oh my," said the Queen. "Well, then! We'd better get started." She turned to Scarlet and Ruben. "To do this, we'll need to use Ruby's *file I/O* methods," she explained. "The I/O part stands for 'input/output.' *Input* is what you put into a file, and *output* is what comes out."

"Like when you write a text file or save a picture?" Scarlet asked.

"Very much like that," the Queen said. "Ruby can write input to a file, which is just like typing it with the keyboard and clicking Save. It can also read output from a file, which is just like double-clicking on the file and opening it!"

The Queen turned to Rusty. "Is there a test file I could use to show how it works?" she asked.

Rusty nodded. "Try *lunch.txt*," he said. "I think it just has the text ONE KAT-MAN-BLEU BURGER, PLEASE in it."

"What's a Kat-Man-Bleu burger?" asked Ruben.

"It's the Wednesday lunch special in the Refactory cafeteria!" Rusty said. "The food's not as good here as the food at the Hashery, but it does all right. That file just has the most recent lunch order in it."

Opening a File with Ruby

"Very good!" said the Queen. "Now, if you have a file called *lunch.txt* that contains only the text ONE KAT-MAN-BLEU BURGER, PLEASE, you can get to it like this!" She began typing:

```
>> file = File.open('lunch.txt', 'r')
=> #<File:lunch.txt>

>> file.read
=> "ONE KAT-MAN-BLEU BURGER, PLEASE\n"
```

"That's exactly the same as if you had double-clicked on *lunch.txt*, only we can read the file's text right inside Ruby! The \n at the end of PLEASE is Ruby's way of representing 'newline.' If you open the file, it'll just be the text ONE KAT-MAN-BLEU BURGER, PLEASE with a blank line under it."

The Queen thought for a moment. "Let me explain a bit more. `File.open` tells Ruby to create a file object based on a file called *lunch.txt*."

"What about the `'r'`?" Ruben asked.

"That's called a *mode*," said the Queen, "and it tells Ruby what *mode* it should open the file in. `'r'` means we're just reading the file for now, not changing it."

"Okay," said Scarlet, "so we've got a file object stored in `file`. What does calling the read method do?"

"Exactly what you'd think!" said the Queen. "It reads the contents of the file and shows them to us." She paused.

"Though usually, we open files with a block, like this." She typed some more:

```
>> File.open('lunch.txt', 'r') { |file| file.read }
=> "ONE KAT-MAN-BLEU BURGER, PLEASE"
```

"Once again, we've got `File.open`, and we pass in the name of the file we want to open as a string, followed by a second string that tells us what mode to open the file in. In this case, we've used `'r'` for 'read.'"

"With you so far," said the King.

"Instead of saving the file object to a `file` variable and calling read on it, like we did before," the Queen continued, "we pass `File.open` a block. We pass `file` to the block instead and call `file.read` inside the block!"

"Is there a difference between opening a file with a block and opening a file without one?" Scarlet asked.

"A very important difference!" said the Queen. "When you open a file with a block, the file is closed as soon as the block is finished. But if you open a file *without* a block, it won't automatically close. See?" She typed:

```
>> file = File.open('lunch.txt', 'r')
=> #<File:lunch.txt>
>> file.closed?
=> false
```

"How do you close a file if you *didn't* open it with a block?" Ruben asked.

"By using the close method, like this!" the Queen said, typing:

```
>> file = File.open('lunch.txt', 'r')
=> #<File:lunch.txt>

>> file.read
=> "ONE KAT-MAN-BLEU BURGER, PLEASE"

>> file.close
=> nil
```

"That seems easy enough," said the King, "but why do we need to close files in the first place?"

"Ruby keeps track of all the files we open, and the computer we're running Ruby on will only let us open a certain number of files at a time," the Queen explained. "If we try to open too many without closing them, we could make the computer crash!"

"Sweet kite-flying porcupines!" said the King. "We certainly wouldn't want *that*."

"Also, if you don't close a file," the Queen continued, "Ruby won't know you're done with it, and unexpected things can happen later if you try to use a file you haven't properly closed. You might even delete everything in it by accident!"

"Okay, we'll make sure to close any files we open," Ruben said. "It sounds like opening a file with a block is the easiest way to do that."

"What else can we pass into the open method besides 'r'?" asked the King, scratching under his tiny crown. "Can we do things besides just read files?"

WRITING AND ADDING TO FILES

"Of course, dear," the Queen said. "You see, Ruby does exactly what you tell it, which means you must be very exact when you tell it to do anything. When you open a file, the first argument you give the open method is the filename, and the second one tells Ruby what it should expect to do with the file. You can do a lot with open—for instance, open 'r' tells Ruby to open a file but *only* to read from it, starting from the beginning of the file."

"What are some of the other modes?" Scarlet asked.

"Well, you can use open 'w' to write to a file," the Queen said. "Using the 'w' mode will tell Ruby to create a new file with the name you give it, or it will completely overwrite any file that already has that name."

"Overwrite!" said Scarlet. "You mean it will replace everything in the existing file with whatever text you give it?"

"That's right," said the Queen.

"What if you want to *add* to an existing file?" asked Ruben.

"For that, you can use the 'a' mode," the Queen said. "That still tells Ruby to create a brand-new file with the name you give it if that file doesn't already exist, but if that file *does* exist, Ruby will start writing at the end of the file, so you won't lose anything that's already there."

"Reading, writing, and adding," said Scarlet. "I think that's everything we want to do. But what happens if you use a mode that tells Ruby you're going to do one thing, but then you try to do something else?" she asked.

"I'll show you!" said the Queen. She typed into the Computing Contraption:

```
>> file = File.open('lunch.txt', 'w')
=> #<File:lunch.txt>
>> file.read
IOError: not opened for reading
```

"An error!" said Ruben. "We'll have to be careful to use the right modes when we open files, then."

"Precisely," said the Queen. "Remember: Ruby does exactly what you tell it. If you use the 'w' mode to tell Ruby you're opening a file only for writing, then try to read from the file instead, Ruby will get confused and produce an error."

"What if you want to read *and* write to a file?" asked the King, who was busy inspecting a puff of pink lint he'd found stuck to his beard.

"Then we need to pass a slightly different mode to File.open," the Queen said. She turned to Rusty. "What's today's cafeteria special?" she asked.

"Grilled cheese!" said Rusty. The Queen nodded and typed into the Computing Contraption:

```
>> file = File.open('lunch.txt', 'w+')
=> #<File:lunch.txt>

>> file.puts('THE MELTIEST OF GRILLED CHEESES')
=> nil
```

"Wow, what was that?" said Ruben. "I didn't know you could use puts to write to a file!"

"Yes, you can," said the Queen. "The only difference between puts and write is that puts adds an extra blank line after whatever you type, which Ruby represents with an \n (remember, that stands for 'newline'). If you open the file, it'll just be the text THE MELTIEST OF GRILLED CHEESES with a blank line under it!"

"Now, we'll try to read the lunch text back," said the Queen, "but take a look at what happens the first time we try!"

```
>> file.read
=> ""

>> file.rewind
=> 0

>> file.read
=> "THE MELTIEST OF GRILLED CHEESES\n"
```

"Whoa!" said Scarlet. "We got nothing but an empty string the first time we called file.read, but after you called file.rewind, we could read the text in *lunch.txt*. What does rewind do?"

"Just like you can press REWIND on a remote control and send a movie back to the beginning, Ruby uses the rewind method to send you back to the beginning of a file. If you don't rewind and then you try to read right after you've written to the file, you'll just get an empty string!" replied the Queen.

"Like trying to press PLAY when you're already at the end of a movie!" said Ruben.

"Precisely," said the Queen.

"That all makes sense," said Scarlet, "but we used the `'w+'` mode, which means we overwrote the original *lunch.txt* file!"

"That we did," said the Queen. "Let's put it back! I'll show you a couple of new tricks while we do." She began typing:

```
>> file = File.open('lunch.txt', 'a+')
=> #<File:lunch.txt>

>> file.write('ONE KAT-MAN-BLEU BURGER, PLEASE')
=> 31

>> file.rewind
=> 0

>> file.readlines
=> ["THE MELTIEST OF GRILLED CHEESES\n", "ONE KAT-MAN-BLEU BURGER,
PLEASE"]
```

"First, we reopen *lunch.txt* for writing with `File.open`, using the `'a+'` mode," the Queen explained. "This tells Ruby we want to add our new text to the end of the file instead of replacing all the text that's already there. Next, we call `file.write` and pass in the new text we want to add to the end of *lunch.txt*."

"Why does Ruby return `31` when we call `file.write`?" Ruben asked.

"An excellent question!" said the Queen. "Ruby is telling us that it successfully added 31 characters to the end of *lunch.txt*."

"I see," said Ruben. "So the `'a+'` mode must mean that we add to the file—so we don't get rid of what's already there—and the + part means we can add to *and* read the file!"

"Correct!" said the Queen. "You'll also see that since adding the text puts us all the way at the end of the file, we call file.rewind to 'rewind' our position to the very beginning. That's why file.rewind returns 0: we're at the very start of the file!"

"But what does that readlines method do?" Ruben asked. "Does it just give us back an array of lines of text from the file?"

"Right again," said the Queen. "Because I used puts to add the first line, ONE KAT-MAN-BLEU BURGER, PLEASE was added on its own line. The readlines method just goes through and creates an array from the file, where each item in the array is a single line of text. So we have an array with two elements here."

"Astounding!" said the King, peering over his wife's shoulder.

"Isn't it?" she asked. "There's also a readline method, which just gives us back one line at a time. See?" She typed some more:

```
>> file.rewind
=> 0

>> file.readline
=> "THE MELTIEST OF GRILLED CHEESES\n"

>> file.readline
=> "ONE KAT-MAN-BLEU BURGER, PLEASE"
```

"We can even use readlines with each to print out all the lines at once!" the Queen said, typing even more quickly:

```
>> file.rewind
=> 0

>> file.readlines.each { |line| puts line }

THE MELTIEST OF GRILLED CHEESES
ONE KAT-MAN-BLEU BURGER, PLEASE
=> ["THE MELTIEST OF GRILLED CHEESES\n", "ONE KAT-MAN-BLEU BURGER,
PLEASE"]
```

"That's amazing!" said Ruben.

Avoiding Errors While Working with Files

"I think I'm starting to understand file input and output now. But what happens if I try to use a file that doesn't exist?" Ruben asked as he reached over to the Computing Contraption's keyboard and typed:

```
>> File.open('imaginary.txt', 'r')
Errno::ENOENT: No such file or directory - imaginary.txt
```

"An error!" Scarlet said. "That makes sense. Is there any way to find out if a file exists *before* we try to use it?"

"Good question!" said the Queen. "If we're not sure whether a file exists, we can use Ruby's built-in `File.exist?` method to check." She typed:

```
>> File.exist? 'lunch.txt'
=> true

>> File.exist? 'imaginary.txt'
=> false
```

"Wonderful, wonderful!" said the King, clapping his hands together. "With all these magnificent Ruby tools, I have no doubt we can capture these crooks quite quickly."

"You're right!" said the Queen. She turned to Rusty. "Is there anything in the Ruby program that represents all the loading docks?" she asked.

Rusty nodded. "There's an array, `loading_docks`, which is an array of files. Each file represents a loading dock door, so if you open and read all the files, all the doors should open!"

The Queen thought for a moment, her fingers hovering above the keyboard. Then she typed into the Computing Contraption:

```
loading_docks.each do |dock|
  current_dock = File.open(dock, 'r')
  puts current_dock.read
  current_dock.close
end
```

One by one, the doors to each loading dock rolled open, hung ajar for a moment, then slid shut. Descriptions of each dock's contents began to fill the Computing Contraption's screen.

"Ruby code . . . Ruby code . . . shipment of Key-a-ma-Jiggers . . . *there!*" shouted Rusty, pointing to a door in the center of the far wall.

Four shadowy figures leapt from the loading dock near the lower-left corner of the wall just as the doors began to slide shut again.

"Freeze!" shouted the King. "We've got you surrounded!"

The four figures moved with surprising speed, knocking over several Refactory workers as they tried to make their way to the nearest exit.

"Stop them!" Rusty yelled as the five of them ran down the metal walkway to the loading dock floor.

Several Refactory workers struggled with the intruders, but they were too fast and too slippery. In just a few seconds, they'd made it all the way to the exit!

"Make way, make way!" cried the Queen, and the five of them reached the Refactory exit just as the shadowy villains escaped through the door. Without breaking stride, the King, the Queen, Ruby, Scarlet, and Rusty barreled through the doorway and into the narrow corridor leading back the way they'd come in.

"Are they headed for the freight elevator?" Ruben panted as they ran.

"Much worse!" Rusty said. "They're headed straight for the WEBrick road!"

The King and Queen gasped together. "The WEBrick road!" said the Queen. "That leads straight out of the kingdom! If they get out through the kingdom gates, we'll *never* catch them!"

"Then we'll just have to be sure that doesn't happen," Rusty said. He turned and called over his shoulder: "Everyone, after them!" And with that, every single person in the Refactory ran toward the small bright exit sign, with the King, the Queen, Scarlet, Ruben, and Rusty leading the pack.

all Loading docks, Report for duty!

We've nearly caught our crooks red-handed! Oh man, the suspense is killing me. Who *are* they? Will the King, the Queen, Ruben, Scarlet, and Rusty catch them in time? What's on the Refactory cafeteria lunch menu for tomorrow? Questions worth pondering until the end of time, for sure—or at least, until the end of this chapter. In the meantime, let's get in just a bit more practice reading from and writing to a file.

Let's start out by making a new file called *loading_docks.rb* and typing the following code. This is a simple little program that will create a text file for each of our loading docks, write some text into it, and then read it back to us.

loading_docks.rb

```
def create_loading_docks(❸docks=3)
❶  loading_docks = []

❷  (1..docks).each do |number|
❹    file_name = "dock_#{number}.txt"
      loading_docks << file_name
```

```
❺      file = File.open(file_name, 'w+')
       file.write("Loading dock no. #{number}, reporting for duty!")
       file.close
    end

    loading_docks
  end

❻ def open_loading_docks(docks)
❼   docks.each do |dock|
      file = File.open(dock, 'r')
      puts file.read
      file.close
    end
  end

❽ all_docks = create_loading_docks(5)
❾ open_loading_docks(all_docks)
```

While there are a few bits of code that are making appearances from earlier chapters, there's nothing brand-new here for you to worry about. Let's walk through the code line by line.

First, we set up an empty array called loading_docks ❶, which we'll use to store the names of all the loading dock files we'll create (so we can read them later). Next, we use the (1..docks) range to create as many loading docks as the create_loading_docks method requires ❷ (it defaults to 3 if no number is passed in ❸).

For each number in the range, we call a block that creates a file with that number (such as *dock_1.txt*) and adds that filename to the loading_docks array ❹. We then open the file, write a string of text into it, and close it ❺.

Finally, in the open_loading_docks method ❻, we simply take our array of loading dock names (it looks something like ["dock_1.txt", "dock_2.txt"...], and so on), and for each filename, we open the file for reading, read its contents, and close it ❼. So when we run this script with all_docks = create_loading_docks(5) ❽ and open_loading_docks(all_docks) ❾ at the bottom, we end up creating *dock_1.txt* through *dock_5.txt*, each of which has its individual number and the "reporting for duty!" string in it.

Pretty great, right?

As always, you can run the finished script by typing `ruby loading_docks.rb` at the command line. When you run it, you'll see this:

```
Loading dock no. 1, reporting for duty!
Loading dock no. 2, reporting for duty!
Loading dock no. 3, reporting for duty!
Loading dock no. 4, reporting for duty!
Loading dock no. 5, reporting for duty!
```

If you look in the directory where you ran *loading_docks.rb*, you'll also see a *.txt* file for each dock, containing the very text our script printed out!

But I'm sure your head is already spinning with ways to improve this humble little script. For instance, we could change the number of files we create from 5 to 1, 3, 10, or any other number we choose! Just be careful—creating too many files will not only fill up your folder, but it could even crash your computer. (That's why we defaulted to 3 and only did 5 in the example.)

You probably noticed that we wrote to the files with the `'w+'` mode, meaning that if we run the script again, it will overwrite the files with the new content. What if we want to add to the file instead, though? (Hint: The `'a+'` mode might be involved.)

For that matter, what if we want to write something fancier than just a plain old text file? What if we want to write a file that writes *another Ruby file*? This is not only possible, but it's a big part of what professional programmers do every day. Try to write a file with a small bit of Ruby in it—something as simple as `puts 'Written by Ruby!'`. (Make sure you write the file with *.rb* at the end instead of *.txt* so Ruby can run it.)

Finally, how might you work in some of the file methods we saw, like exist?, rewind, or puts? Are there other file methods in the Ruby documentation at *http://ruby-doc.org/core-1.9.3/File.html* that might be cool to use? Remember to ask your local adult before going online!

You Know This!

You can read! You can write! Well, okay, you already knew how to do those things, but now you know how to do them *with Ruby*. I don't doubt that you're a full-fledged Ruby sorcerer by now, but just to make sure there's nothing unclear about this new Ruby wizardry we've covered, let's take a second to review it.

You saw that Ruby can create, read, write, and understand *files*, which are exactly like the computer files you already know about: text documents, pictures, Ruby scripts, and more. Ruby can open a file that already exists with the open method:

```
>> file = File.open('alien_greeting.txt', 'r')
=> #<File:alien_greeting.txt>
```

It can read a file with the read method:

```
>> file.read
=> "GREETINGS HUMAN!"
```

And when we're finished using a file, we should close it using the close method:

```
>> file.close
=> nil
```

It turns out we can accidentally crash our computer by keeping too many files open at once, so it's always a good idea to close any file we've opened. Luckily, if we open a file with a block, Ruby automatically closes the file for us:

```
>> File.open('alien_greeting.txt', 'r') { |file| file.read }
=> "GREETINGS HUMAN!"
```

Ruby is pretty picky about being told what to do, so we have to use different *modes* to tell Ruby which input and output *mode* it should use. When we use 'r', we tell Ruby that we expect it only to read files, and when we use 'w', we tell it we expect it only to write files. To tell Ruby it should both read *and* write a file, we can give it the 'w+' mode:

```
>> new_file = File.new('brand_new.txt', 'w+')
=> #<File:brand_new.txt>

>> new_file.write("I'm a brand-new file!")
=> 21

>> new_file.close
=> nil

>> File.open('brand_new.txt', 'r') { |file| file.read }
=> "I'm a brand-new file!"
```

You found out that 'w+' will overwrite a file—that is, it will replace *everything* in the existing file with whatever string we tell Ruby to put in there. If we just want to *add* to a file instead of replacing it completely, we can use the 'a' mode ('a+' if we want to add to the file *and* read from it):

```
>> file = File.open('breakfast.txt', 'a+')
=> #<File:breakfast.txt>

>> file.write('Chunky ')
=> 7

>> file.write('bacon!')
=> 6

>> file.rewind
=> 0

>> file.read
=> "Chunky bacon!"
```

Speaking of our friend rewind, you saw we could use it to back up to the start of the file and read the whole file:

```
>> file = File.open('dinner.txt', 'a+')
=> #<File:dinner.txt>

>> file.write('A festive ham!')
=> 14

>> file.read
=> ""

>> file.rewind
=> 0

>> file.read
=> "A festive ham!"
```

In that first file.read, the string is empty because we're at the end of the file. After we rewind, though, we go back to the start, and when we file.read again, our text is there.

You discovered that if we want to add a blank line after a line of text, we can use a file's puts method instead of write. When we read the file back, Ruby shows us the blank line as a backslash and the letter *n* (\n):

```
>> file.puts('A sprig of fresh parsley!')
=> nil

>> file.rewind
=> 0

>> file.read
=> "A festive ham!A sprig of fresh parsley!\n"
```

In fact, you saw that we could use the readline and readlines methods to read out lines of a file one by one. readline reads one line from the file at a time, and calling it a bunch of times reads each line, one after another:

```
>> file = File.new('dessert.txt', 'a+')
=> #<File:dessert.txt>

>> file.puts('A gooseberry pie')
=> nil

>> file.puts('A small sack of muffins')
=> nil

>> file.rewind
=> 0

>> file.readline
=> "A gooseberry pie\n"

>> file.readline
=> "A small sack of muffins\n"
```

If we want to read the lines of our file all at once, we can use file.readlines with a call to the each method and a block:

```
>> file.rewind
=> 0

>> file.readlines.each { |line| puts line }
A gooseberry pie
A small sack of muffins
=> ["A gooseberry pie\n", "A small sack of muffins\n"]
```

Finally, you saw that we could check whether a file exists by using the exist? method:

```
>> File.exist? 'breakfast.txt'
=> true

>> File.exist? 'fancy_snack.txt'
=> false
```

Files and file input/output probably don't seem like a big deal to you now (especially since you know a lot about how they work), but they're a major part of how computers get work done. Don't hesitate to mess around with creating and changing your files on your computer, and—with permission—hunt around the Internet for more information on files, how they work, and any interesting bits of Ruby code you can run to improve your understanding. But enough out of me: our heroes are hot on the tails of the tricksters who have been mucking things up in the kingdom all day, and we're about to find out who they are, what they want, and whether the King, the Queen, Ruben, Scarlet, and the crew of the Refactory can stop them once and for all!

13
Follow the WEBRick Road

Ruby and the Internet

The King and Queen burst through the Refactory exit and into the bright late-afternoon sunshine, Ruben and Scarlet following hot on their heels. Ahead of them, the WEBrick road stretched far away, its dark red bricks glowing softly. In the distance, they could make out the hunched shapes of the four mysterious villains retreating, and farther still, the wall that marked the outer edge of the kingdom.

"They're so fast!" Ruben gasped, his hands on his knees. "We'll never be able to catch them!"

"Never say never," Rusty said, jogging up behind them. "There *must* be something we can do."

The Queen turned to him. "Is there any way to shut down the WEBrick road?" she asked.

Rusty thought for a moment. "I'm not sure," he said, "but I have an idea." He flipped up all the pages of his clipboard and pulled out a thin piece of metal with a familiar-looking screen. "This is my portable Computing Contraption," he said. "My workers and I will go on ahead and try to catch these snakes. In the meantime, if there's anything you can do to shut down the road and keep them from escaping, you can do it on this little computer."

"Right!" said Scarlet, taking the hand-held computer from the Foreman. Rusty gave her a wink, then motioned to the men and women of the Refactory who were rapidly pouring out of the exit. "This way, everyone! Let's try to head these villains off! Move, move, move!"

As the Refactory workers ran down the deep red road, the King, the Queen, Scarlet, and Ruben huddled around the Foreman's portable Computing Contraption.

"Okay, first things first," said Scarlet. "How can we shut down the road?"

The King tugged on his fluffy white beard. "It seems to me," he said, "that we should first check to be sure the road is working properly! If it's already off for some reason, we can join Rusty's team up ahead and apprehend these goons."

Scarlet and Ruben looked at each other. "That's . . . actually a great idea," Ruben said. "How do we test to see if the road is open?"

"Well," said the King, "the WEBrick road, like all things in the kingdom, runs on Ruby, and it's the main connection between the kingdom and the rest of the world. If we can use Ruby to check whether we can get information from outside the kingdom, we'll know if the road is working."

"That's it!" said Ruben. "If we can connect to the Internet with Ruby, then we'll know the road is open!"

"But how do we do that?" said Scarlet. "I feel like I know Ruby pretty well now, but I don't even know where to begin with connecting to the Internet."

"I think I know a way," said the Queen. "You see, connecting to the Internet is just like connecting to a file—you just have to tell Ruby the right way to do it! May I?" she asked. Scarlet nodded and handed the Queen the portable Computing Contraption. The Queen began to type.

"Remember how we could write our code in separate Ruby files, then use require to pull one script's code into another?" the Queen asked. Scarlet and Ruben nodded. "Well," the Queen continued, "it turns out there are little bundles of files that come with Ruby that we can require, too!"

"There are?" asked the King, incredulous.

"Absolutely!" said the Queen. "You can think of these bundles of files as tiny libraries of code that we can use in our own projects. They're called *gems*."

"That's right! I think I've heard of Ruby gems before," Ruben said. "Is there a gem for connecting to the Internet?"

Using the open-uri Ruby Gem

The Queen nodded. "The open-uri gem," she said. "It lets your Ruby code open Internet sites the same way it can open files!

Once we require it in our IRB session, we'll be able to do all sorts of wonderful things." She typed into the Computing Contraption:

```
>> require 'open-uri'
=> true
```

She handed the little machine back to Scarlet. "Loaded up and ready to go!" she said.

Scarlet looked at the screen. "Don't I need './open-uri', not just 'open-uri'?" she asked.

"Not for gems!" said the Queen. "That's true for files you create, but if you're requiring a gem, you can just type the name as a string. One of the many things Ruby does for you is keep track of where gems are installed on your computer. Since it already knows where to find them, you don't need to look in the current directory with ./. Just type the name of the gem, and Ruby does the rest."

"Perfect!" said Scarlet. "Now we just need a website to test whether the WEBrick road is working."

"Aha!" said the King, raising a finger in the air. "We can test it with my favorite website!"

"Which one is that?" asked Scarlet, poised to type into the keyboard.

"*Example.com!*" the King said, beaming. The Queen rolled her eyes.

"It's as good as any," Scarlet admitted, and she typed into the tiny Computing Contraption.

NOTE   *You'll need to be connected to the Internet for this code to work! Go ahead and grab your local adult if you need help connecting to the Internet.*

```
>> site = open('http://www.example.com')
=> #<StringIO:0x000001032de2f0>
```

"First," Scarlet said, "we've used the open method to tell Ruby to create an object based on the website of the URL we entered. Then we can just use the .read method as we did on a regular text file, and that will give us the contents of the site at *www.example.com!*"

```
>> site.read
=> "<!doctype html>...
```

The screen quickly filled with code from the *example.com* website.

"It's working!" Scarlet said. "The WEBrick road must be turned on. Now we just need to find a way to shut it down!"

Ruben thought for a moment. "Hey, wait," he said, "does the kingdom request *and* send information through the WEBrick road?"

"It does," said the King.

"Does that mean there's some kind of *web server* running?" Ruben asked.

The Queen snapped her fingers. "Ruben, you're a genius!" she said. Ruben blushed slightly. The Queen turned to Scarlet. "Not only is there a web server running, but it's a *WEBrick web server.*" She began talking quickly and gesturing excitedly. "The WEBrick server is a special piece of Ruby code that sends information out of the kingdom. You see, when you visit a website, you're asking a web server—that is, a computer somewhere on the Internet—for information. Well, when people on the Internet want information about our kingdom, our very own WEBrick web server sends it!"

NOTE *The WEBrick server isn't something that exists only in the kingdom—that's the real name of the Ruby web server you're using right on your own computer!*

"And if that web server is turned off . . . " Ruben began.

" . . . then nothing and no one can get out of the kingdom!" Scarlet finished.

"Now we just need to figure out how to find the server to shut it down," Ruben said.

"Well," said the King, kicking at a bit of dust, "I actually might be able to help with that. You see, I lose things so frequently that I've gotten to know the Computing Contraption's search function very well."

"Perfect!" said Scarlet. "What do we think the file is called?"

Investigating the Kingdom's Web Server

"Well, you might want to search for *WEBrick* or *server*," the King said. "That's what I'd do, at any rate."

Scarlet nodded and pressed a few keys, searching for the file. She squinted, shook her head, typed, sighed, thought, and typed some more.

"I think I've got it!" she finally said. "I found a file called *server.rb*."

"Open it, open it!" said Ruben, standing on tiptoe to see the screen better.

Scarlet opened the *server.rb* file, and this is what they saw:

```ruby
require 'webrick'
include WEBrick

server = HTTPServer.new(
  :Port => 3000,
  :DocumentRoot => Dir.pwd
)
trap('INT') { server.shutdown }

server.start
```

"Let's see," said Scarlet. "It looks like the first two lines require the webrick gem and include the WEBrick module."

"That looks right to me," said Ruben. "Then it looks like the next few lines create a new WEBrick server. I'm not sure what the port is for, but it's set to the number 3000. What does the Dir.pwd part mean?"

"I think I know," said the Queen. "Just like Ruby uses the File class for methods that work on files, it uses the Dir class for methods that work on *directories*, which is just a fancy way of saying *folders*." The Queen pointed to the screen. "The pwd method returns the *present working directory*, so Dir.pwd is just Ruby's way of saying 'this folder right here.' The web server is running, and it's sending information out of this folder!"

"Okay!" said Scarlet. "We've just got to shut it down, and I think I see a clue. The `trap('INT') { server.shutdown }` line—what does that do?"

The Queen studied the screen for a minute. "If I remember correctly, that's Ruby's way of saying that when it gets an *interrupt signal*, it will shut down the server!"

"An interrupt signal?" Ruben asked. "Does that mean we have to tell the server to quit running?"

"Exactly," said the Queen. "But how?"

"Hold down the CTRL key and the C key at the same time!" the King suddenly. Everyone turned to look at him. "Just do it!" he urged, waving his hands in the air. "We haven't a moment to lose!" Scarlet nodded and immediately pressed the keys, and this is what she saw:

```
INFO  going to shutdown ...
INFO  WEBrick::HTTPServer#start done.
```

"We did it! We did it!" Scarlet and Ruben jumped up and down and hugged each other.

The Queen turned to the King, smiling. "How on *Earth* did you know how to do that?" she asked him.

The King smiled sheepishly. "Well, I manage to break my Computing Contraption so often, I've learned to use CTRL-C to stop programs!" They all burst into laughter.

"Now that the server is shut down," Scarlet said, "nothing and no one can get out of the kingdom! Quick, let's get down the WEBrick road and see if we stopped the bad guys in time!"

The four of them hurried down the bright red path, hoping against hope that they'd closed the WEBrick road in time. In the distance, they could see the huge group of Refactory workers milling around. As they got closer, they could start to pick out individual workers, then faces. Soon they were close enough to see that Rusty was frantically waving them over, and just beyond him in the center of the group were the four hooded hooligans!

"Great coats! Sweet breakfast gravy! Glorious corn muffins! We've got them!" cried the King, nearly weeping with joy.

As they ran up to the group, the Foreman turned to them, beaming. "Your Majesty! Your Highness!" he said, addressing the King and Queen in turn. "I don't know how you did it, but you shut down the WEBrick road long enough for us to catch these villains! They were pulling on the gates to the kingdom wall, trying to escape, when we cornered them here." He crossed his arms and smiled, his entire big bushy beard rising on his face. "I'm pleased to formally hand them over to you."

"Thank you, Rusty," said the Queen. The King and Queen moved into the center of the group, where two Refactory workers each held one of the four mysterious figures. Ruben and Scarlet followed close behind.

"You scoundrels have been creating utter pandemonium in our kingdom!" the King said.

"And depriving all the citizens in the kingdom of their Purple Panda-monium Parade," the Queen said, frowning.

"Yes, precisely," said the King. "And we've had enough of it! It's time for you to reveal who you *really* are." The King nodded to the Refactory workers. Each placed a hand on either side of each prankster's hood.

"On my count. One . . . two . . . two and a half . . . *three*!" cried the King, and the workers yanked back the hoods. The crowd gasped. Standing before them, flicking their tongues and hissing, were four enormous snakes!

"Literal snakes!" said Rusty. "How about that?"

"Pythonssss, actually," hissed the snake nearest to Rusty.

"Sweet hibbeldy-jibbeldy! A talking snake!" said the King, hiding behind a particularly brawny Refactory worker.

"The name issss Terry," the snake said. "Terry One, actually." She gestured with her head to the snake next to her. "That's John," she said. "Then Terry Two, then Graham."

"Pleassssed to meet you," said John.

"Well, we're certainly not pleased to meet *you*," said the King, recovering his courage. "What in the name of the Carmine Pines did you think you all were *doing*, causing such trouble?" He started counting on his fingers. "Stealing my string! Clogging the Mysterious Pipe! Looping up the Loop! Crashing the Hashery's Computing Contraption! Hacking into the Queen's machine! De-purpling the pandas! The list goes on and on!"

Graham looked around uneasily. "Your ssssstring? We didn't steal your ssstring!" he said.

The King threw up his hands. "Okay, fine, maybe that was me," he said, "but the rest was all your doing. I demand an explanation!"

Terry Two lowered her head; Ruben and Scarlet couldn't tell if she was angry or sad. "It's becaussse everyone was all about Ruby, Ruby, Ruby!" she said. "No one wanted to use Python anymore."

"Python?" asked Ruben.

"You ssssee?" said Terry Two, nodding her head at Ruben. "The boy's never even heard of Python!"

"What is it?" Ruben asked, inching forward.

Terry Two sighed. "A programming language, very much like Ruby," she said.

"But better," John piped up.

"Oh, much better," Terry One chimed in.

"But no one in the kingdom uses it," Terry Two continued. "We thought if we got people thinking that sssssomething was wrong with Ruby, they might make the sssswitch."

Scarlet stepped closer to the pythons, angry. "You should have tried to show how good a language Python is, not try to make people think there's something wrong with Ruby!" she scolded.

John shook his head sadly. "No one would lisssssssten," he said, "so we thought our besssst chance would be to attract attention, even if it had to be negative." No one could be quite sure, but it looked like the enormous snake had tears in his eyes.

The King's expression softened a bit. "You all know Python?" he asked.

The pythons looked at each other, clearly confused. They slowly nodded.

"Tell me about it," said the King.

"It's quite a wonderful language," said Graham. "It has sssstrings and numbers and Booleans."

"Arrays, too!" added Terry One.

"Objects and methods and classsses," said John, "and you can write programs that do anything you like."

The King nodded, walking in a small circle. "It seems to me," he said, "that Ruby and Python aren't all that different, then."

The pythons were silent for a moment. "Perhapssss not," John said, finally. "But if that'ssss so, why not use Python instead of Ruby?"

"I suppose my question," the King said, "is why do you need to choose? Why not write whichever you prefer?" Terry One opened her mouth to speak, but the King continued. "In fact," he said, "what if I told you that it's possible to write Ruby that *turns into Python?*"

There was total silence. Ruben, Scarlet, and the Queen shot one another amazed looks.

"You see," said the King, "I've never been a very good programmer. Programming has never come easily to me. So I spend much of my time practicing and reading articles and sample code, trying to become better." He reached into his robe and pulled out a small scroll. "During my research, I discovered a truly amazing bit of code that can transform Ruby code into instructions that Python can understand. You can write Ruby, and Python programs will come out! Isn't that amazing?" he asked, becoming excited. "You can write *any language* you want *any way* you want, and you can still tell stories to a computer that will make it do anything you like. That's the beauty of programming!"

The pythons didn't say anything for a moment. Finally, Terry One spoke up. "I . . . hadn't thought of it that way before," she said.

"I suppose what I'm trying to say," said the King, "is that all curiosity, all honest desire to learn, all sharing and teaching, is *always* welcome in this kingdom. Yes, we happen to use Ruby to run our day-to-day lives. Yes, it's the language that many of our citizens know and prefer and even *think* in. But that doesn't make it the only way, and it certainly doesn't mean we think there's nothing to learn from Python!"

Rusty cupped his hands around his mouth. "Hear, hear!" he said, and the entire crowd burst into applause.

"What do you say?" the King asked gently, approaching the four pythons. "Would you like to help us learn a bit about Python, and we can teach you some Ruby?"

The pythons exchanged glances, then began to nod.

"We're ssssso terribly ssssorry," Graham said. "We were just ssssad and frusssstrated, and we didn't know how to tell everyone how we felt."

"We hope we didn't wreck anything too badly," Terry Two said.

"We'll help repair anything we broke," Terry One added.

"I tried the hash at Hank'ssss Hashery," John said. "It was the mosssst amazing food I've ever tasted. I'd help fix a hundred Ruby programs if I could eat there again!"

"Then it's settled!" the King said. He looked at the Queen, who smiled and nodded. He returned his gaze to the four pythons. "By the power vested in me by the many citizens of my kingdom, you are hereby officially pardoned of all wrongdoing!" He leaned forward slightly. "And if you'd like to come back to the palace for some cake and tea, that would be fine, too."

The pythons nodded eagerly, overjoyed.

"That would be ssssssplendid," said Terry One. "Thank you sssso much!"

The King held his arms over his head. "Everyone back to the Royal Palace!" he cried. "Cake and tea for everyone!"

A massive cheer went up in the crowd. The Refactory workers who had been holding the pythons released them, and the
group swept the King, the Queen, Scarlet, and Ruben up onto
their shoulders.

"You really saved the day, Your Kingliness!" Scarlet said to
the King. He dismissed the compliment with a wave of his hand.

"You kids did all the
saving!" he said. "Without you,
we'd never have solved this
mystery and brought peace
and prosperity back to the
kingdom."

"Let's say we *all* had a piece
of the pie," said the Queen.
"And speaking of! Let's add a
little pie to this cake-and-tea
party."

"Let's!" said the King, who
had been patting the pockets
of his robe for the last several
seconds. "Oh, turnips," he
said. "Now where did I put
my string?"

Beyond the Kingdom Walls

Holy cannoli! Pythons! I wouldn't have seen that coming 42 miles
away. I've still got so many questions! How did they sneak into
the kingdom? What cool Python tricks do they know that a Ruby
programmer like me could learn? And how did they manage to
work a Key-a-ma-Jigger with no hands?

While I ponder these and other great mysteries, feel free to
get in a little more practice with the WEBrick web server. Go
ahead and create a new file called *web_server.rb* and type in
the following code.

web_server.rb

```ruby
require 'webrick'
include WEBrick

server = HTTPServer.new(Port: 3000)

server.mount_proc '/' do |request, response|
  response.body = 'Your Ruby adventure is just beginning!'
end

trap('INT') { server.shutdown }

server.start
```

This code's a bit different from the last version you saw, but there's nothing here you haven't seen! The only tricky bit is the mount_proc method, which is built into WEBrick. This tells the server how to respond to certain requests; in this case, if you go to the / URL on your computer, you should see the message assigned to response.body. Your computer's built-in website is *http://localhost/*.

As usual, you can run your finished script by typing **ruby web_server.rb** in the terminal. Once you've started your script, you should see some numbers and text, like this:

```
INFO  WEBrick 1.3.1
INFO  WEBrick::HTTPServer#start: pid=78115 port=3000
```

(Your numbers will be slightly different, but the words should be pretty similar.) When you see the text appear, your web server is up and running! Open your favorite web browser (such as Chrome, Firefox, Internet Explorer, or Safari) and go to *http://localhost:3000/*. If everything's working right, you should see Your Ruby adventure is just beginning! in the browser window. Crazy, right? Your first website has just been born! (I'm gonna name her Marigold.) When you're done using your server, hold down CTRL-C in the terminal where WEBrick is running to shut it down.

This web server is a pretty simple affair, and if I know you, you're already thinking of ways to make it better. Well, don't hold back! Feel free to play with the code in the *web_server.rb* file. (You'll need to use CTRL-C to shut down the server and restart it each time you make changes in order to see them.) For example, you could start just by changing the `response.body` string, then move on to playing with the port number or adding more `mount_procs`.

Here's a hint: What if you add the following code to your *web_server.rb* file, then go to *http://localhost:3000/favorite_vegetable*?

```
server.mount_proc '/favorite_vegetable' do |request, response|
  response.body = 'Certainly not yams!'
end
```

If you want to see the gems that people all over the world have made available, you can visit the RubyGems website at *http://rubygems.org/*. For just about any task, someone has probably created a gem to do it, so you should always stop by RubyGems. Take your time to read through the information on the site, and you'll be able to download other people's gems and use them in no time!

Speaking of sharing code, that magical little program that can convert Ruby to Python really does exist! It was written by a programmer named *why the lucky stiff* and can be found on *GitHub*, a website where people share the code they write with people all across the planet. You can find the GitHub website at *https://github.com/* and the Ruby-to-Python project—called *unholy*—at *https://github.com/whymirror/unholy/*. (The code is very advanced, but if you keep at it, I think you'll start to get it. I've yet to meet a brighter bulb!)

you Know this!

We took some of the code and concepts you already knew a few steps further in this chapter, so let's take a second to make sure it all made sense.

You learned that we can use Ruby to get information about websites on the Internet by using the open-uri gem:

```
>> require 'open-uri'
=> true

>> site = open('http://www.example.com')
=> #<StringIO:0x000001032de2f0>

>> site.read
=> "<!doctype html>..."
```

A *gem* is just a set of files that someone else created to make writing your Ruby programs easier. We can require gems into our programs just as we can require files we wrote ourselves, only we need to put a ./ before our filenames, and for gems, we can just write the name as a string after the require method call.

Feel free to try this code with other websites! Just be sure to get permission first, and be careful—some websites send back a *lot* of code, and it may fill up your terminal window.

You also saw that we don't have to settle for just *requesting* information; we can *serve* it to visitors using *web servers* like WEBrick:

```
require 'webrick'
include WEBrick

server = HTTPServer.new(:Port => 3000)

server.mount_proc '/' do |request, response|
  response.body = 'WEBrick is online and running fine!'
end

trap('INT') { server.shutdown }

server.start
```

You learned that we can modify web server code to write simple messages, that we can see the changes in our code by stopping and restarting the server, and that CTRL-C will let us stop our server (once we get it running) by typing ruby `server_file_name.rb` or calling `load 'server_file_name.rb'` from inside IRB.

Finally, we talked a little bit about using gems written by other people by visiting the RubyGems website (*http://rubygems .org/*) and reading and sharing code all over the world through the GitHub site (*https://github.com/*). If you want to set up accounts on these sites, grab your nearest adult and ask!

Our story may be over, gentle reader, but that doesn't mean I'm quite done blabbering yet. We covered a *lot* of Ruby magic in the last several hundred pages, and I'd be a terrible teacher, writer, and programmer if I just said, "Welp, see ya!" and left it at that. Take a deep breath, turn the page, and let's spend just a few more sentences going over all the crazy, amazing, wonderful stuff we've learned.

14
WHERE
TO GO
NEXT

The Big Picture: What You Know

Man, what a story. What intrigue! What suspense! It was so astounding, I barely talked at all toward the end there. You probably noticed that. I pop in and out a lot.

It may seem like we haven't come all that far, but if you remember back to when you first picked up this book, you didn't know anything about Ruby at all. You'd probably never heard of Senior Apprentices to Royal Plumbers, Hasheries, or Dagrons, let alone strings, object IDs, or methods. Now you know about all those things and more!

We've covered so much, I feel it's only right to do one last quick review. For my own sake. Just to keep everything straight in my scattered mind. Don't worry—it'll be real quick; if you need a more in-depth refresher, thumb back to the earlier chapters and reread the "You Know This!"

sections (because you totally do, even if you don't always remember every last detail).

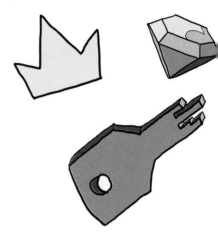

We started out by learning how to install and set up Ruby. No small feat! We got Ruby up and running on our computer, learned how to run snippets of Ruby code with IRB, and discovered how to write files, called *scripts*, that let us collect a bunch of lines of code and run them all at once.

Once we figured out how to run code, the next step involved writing something that was interesting to run. Remember back when you only knew how to print strings and add numbers? When the thrill of programming was all about putsing phrases and multiplying things together? Those were the days! But once you start learning to write stories that you can make happen in real life—that is, programs—you want to write bigger and better ones as quickly as you can. So we moved on to control flow (using if, elsif, else, and unless) and Booleans (true and false), and in no time flat, we were controlling the way information moved through our programs, repairing the Mysterious Pipe, and guiding Haldo through an underground maze.

Then we were really off to the races! We started talking about Ruby loops and iterators, using methods like each to print out all the values in an array (which is like a list of items: [1, 2, 3]), update a hash (which is like a short dictionary of items and values: { name: Lou, fancy: true }), and help Hank and Squeaky Jim fix the Hashery computer. We learned about ranges, which are just a series of numbers or letters (like (0..5) or ('a'..'z')), and symbols, which are simply names or labels we use in Ruby. For instance, we saw them used as hash keys, as in { hamburgers: 'delicious' }.

That's when things started getting interesting! Scarlet found a python scale on the Hashery floor, leading the group on a voyage to the Carmine Pines. We met the Off-White Knight, who showed us how to create our very own methods using the def keyword. We also saw how to do all kinds of fancy method tricks, like setting default arguments, using splat parameters, and writing methods that can take blocks by using the yield keyword.

We went on to meet the Dagron, who explained Ruby objects and classes (which are just objects that create other objects). We learned about where in a program our variables could be seen and used, covering global, class, instance, and local variables. We even learned about a special Ruby value, self, that refers to the current object! As we dove deeper into Ruby class syntax, we covered attr_reader, attr_writer, and attr_accessor, which are shortcuts we can use so we don't have to write methods to get and set instance variables every time we want to update them from outside our class.

We also discovered (courtesy of the Queen) that some classes can *inherit* from others—that is, they take on some of the properties and abilities of other classes—and that classes can let us reuse code through inheritance. We saw that classes that inherit from other classes can *override* methods from their superclass—for example, a GuardDog that inherits from Dog can have its own version of a bark method that does something different from what Dog's bark method does—and that we can always "reach up" to the superclass and call one of its methods using super.

The Queen also taught us about *modules*, which are just like Ruby classes except we don't create instances of them! They're for mixing in behavior by using include or extend, which allow us to reuse code from lots of sources while still using only one superclass. Modules are also for *namespacing*, or organizing our code so that we don't have to cram all of it into one file.

By using modules, we can easily control where all our variables, constants, and methods are available in our Ruby programs, and we can create classes with one superclass that inherit behavior from a whole range of sources.

Then we voyaged on to the Refactory, where we learned how to rewrite our code to make it clearer without changing the way it behaves. We saw a bunch of cool tricks for improving our Ruby, including breaking up big methods into smaller ones and removing duplicate code so that each method did one thing and did it well. We also learned about file input/output at the Refactory, including how to open, read, and write files with Ruby.

Finally, we covered Ruby and the Internet, learning about Ruby gems, and web servers like WEBrick, and useful websites like the RubyGems site and GitHub. We saw the King, the Queen, Scarlet, and Ruben use their Ruby knowledge to catch the pythons and ultimately show them that Ruby and Python are both excellent programming languages, and you used your Ruby knowledge to arrive here, at the end of this book, chock-full of wisdom. I couldn't be prouder! That's the honest-to-gravy truth.

additional Resources and Further Reading

While there's a lot of Ruby magic in these pages, we didn't cover *everything* there is to know about Ruby. There is a huge number of amazing books and websites that will help you learn even more about Ruby and programming, and I've listed a bunch here! Don't feel pressured to read all (or any) of these books or sites—they're just new places to keep learning Ruby now that you've finished this book.

Beginner Books

These books are great for beginners.

Beginning Ruby, 2nd Edition, by Peter Cooper (Apress, 2009). This is just what it sounds like! A fantastic introduction to Ruby

Programming Ruby, 4th Edition, by Dave Thomas, Andy Hunt, and Chad Fowler (The Pragmatic Bookshelf, 2013). This is sometimes called the "pickaxe book," because it has a huge picture of a pickaxe on the cover. Lots of Ruby programmers say this is their go-to Ruby book, and I can promise there's not a single question about Ruby you might have that isn't covered in here.

The Ruby Programming Language by David Flanagan and Yukihiro Matsumoto (O'Reilly Media, 2008). Yukihiro "Matz" Matsumoto is the creator of the Ruby language, so he's got lots of great insights into what Ruby can do and what makes it great. This is another awesome introductory Ruby book.

Why's (Poignant) Guide to Ruby by why the lucky stiff (*http:// en.wikipedia.org/wiki/Why's_(poignant)_Guide_to_Ruby*). This is the Ruby book I first learned from, and if you read it carefully, you'll see I snuck a few of why's tricks and jokes into this very book. why's guide is a magical, manic, illustrated guide to Ruby. When you're done with this book, pick up that one! I promise you'll be glad you did.

Intermediate Books

These books are a bit more advanced.

Design Patterns in Ruby by Russ Olsen (Addison-Wesley Professional, 2007). This book is about good patterns for writing your Ruby code. You'll learn from the pros!

Eloquent Ruby by Russ Olsen (Addison-Wesley Professional, 2011). Want to learn to write code like a native Rubyist? Read this book!

The Well-Grounded Rubyist by David Black (Manning Publications, 2009). Imagine a book just like this one, only with fewer magical creatures and more stuff about fancy Ruby topics like threads and error handling. All imagined? Congratulations! You've imagined *The Well-Grounded Rubyist*. (Imagine that!)

Wicked Cool Ruby Scripts by Steve Pugh (No Starch Press, 2008). If you're looking for a fanciful cookbook, a veritable cornucopia of Ruby script recipes for everything from games to web servers, pluck this book off your nearest store shelf (or ask your folks to order it off the Internet).

Advanced Books

These books are the most complex of all!

Metaprogramming Ruby 2 by Paolo Perrotta (The Pragmatic Bookshelf, 2014). This book explores the deep, dark secrets of how Ruby can read its own code and change it while it runs! Not for the faint of heart.

Practical Object-Oriented Design in Ruby by Sandi Metz (Addison-Wesley Professional, 2012). If you want to write Ruby like a pro, you can't do better than this book. Your objects will sparkle and your classes will gleam when you're done!

Ruby Under a Microscope by Pat Shaughnessy (No Starch Press, 2013). This book goes straight to the core of what makes Ruby . . . well, Ruby! It covers all the details of how all those little bits and bytes, zeros and ones, turn into Ruby code. If you read this book and understand every bit of it, please call me up and explain it.

Online and Multimedia

Railscasts (*http://railscasts.com/*)   Ruby on Rails is a popular framework, or set of tools, that Ruby programmers use to make web applications. These screencasts by Ryan Bates show you how Ruby code powers Rails applications, and Ryan's instructions make it easy to follow along at home. As with Ruby Tapas, not all these screencasts are free, so you'll need your local adult's help to sign up if you want to be able to watch them all.

Ruby5 podcast (*http://ruby5.envylabs.com/*)   This is more Ruby news, but in podcast form! If you like listening more than reading, this one's for you.

Ruby Rogues (*http://rubyrogues.com/*)   This is another podcast, though I think this one is more like listening to blog posts than it is like listening to the news. If you're interested in hearing more about the ins and outs of Ruby, its gems, and its tools, give the Ruby Rogues a listen.

Ruby Tapas (*http://www.rubytapas.com/*)   For those of you who like to watch videos instead of read or listen, these screencasts by Avdi Grimm give you short introductions to different parts of Ruby that you might not know about. Only a few of the screencasts are free, though, so if you want to watch them all, you'll need your local adult's help.

Ruby Weekly (*http://rubyweekly.com/*)   Curated by the very same Peter Cooper who wrote *Beginning Ruby*, this once-a-week email is packed with helpful Ruby articles, tutorials, and videos. It's pretty advanced stuff, but after you've been writing Ruby for a while, it'll be the first place you look for Ruby news.

Interactive Resources

Codecademy (*http://www.codecademy.com/tracks/ruby/*) If you ever want to practice running Ruby in the comfort of your own web browser, you can do the Ruby lessons over at Codecademy. Fun fact: I wrote all these courses, so they should seem pretty familiar! The only downside is that they cover a lot of the same information you've learned here, so they might be a little *too* familiar. If you want to practice writing code and reviewing what you've learned, though, head on over and start typing— it's free! (You must be 13 or older to create an account.)

Code School (*https://www.codeschool.com/paths/ruby/*) Code School is another great website for learning Ruby. Like Codecademy, it requires that you be 13 or older to create an account, and unlike Codecademy, it isn't free. It's got lots of good videos, though, so if you learn best by watching someone else work, this might be the site for you.

Ruby Koans (*http://rubykoans.com/*)   Imagine if you took all the knowledge of this book and divided it up into a bajillion wise little sayings in the form of Ruby programs. Those are the Ruby koans! If you're looking for more practice and love to learn by doing, go ahead and download the koans and start programming. They also do a great job of teaching you about testing, since each koan is like a failing test that you have to fix to get it to pass; the more lines of code you repair, the greater your Ruby enlightenment.

Ruby Monk (*https://rubymonk.com/*)   This is sort of like a mix between Codecademy's courses and the Ruby Koans. The more exercises you complete, the further along the path to Ruby mastery you'll progress!

additional topics

We talked about tons and tons of Ruby goodness, but there are a few bits and trinkets of the language we didn't get to—mostly because they're not quite as much fun as what we covered, plus these topics are a bit on the trickier side. If you're curious and want to learn more about them, though, I've dashed off a quick list here.

The `Enumerable` module   You might have wondered during our adventures how both arrays *and* hashes know how to use the each method. It's because they both mix in the `Enumerable` module, which you can use directly in your own classes to simplify your code! It includes all kinds of handy methods like `all?`, `any?`, `include?`, and `find`. You can read all about it in the official docs: *http://ruby-doc.org/core-2.0.0/Enumerable.html*.

Regular expressions   Regular expressions are like a mini-language inside Ruby that lets you match patterns in words or phrases. For example, you could use them to find strings that contain only uppercase letters or check whether a string is a valid email address. Regular expressions exist in many languages, but you can find some Ruby-specific information at *http://www.regular-expressions.info/ruby.html*. You can also use a free tool called Rubular at *http://rubular.com/*. Rubular lets you test out your regular expressions in real time, so you can see what your patterns match and what they don't.

Procs and lambdas   These are not quite blocks and they're not quite methods—they're somewhere in between! You can think of them either as methods without names or as "saved" blocks you can run over and over. You can learn more about them in the Ruby Monk exercises (see "Interactive Resources" on page 307).

Information hiding   You can keep information in your Ruby classes more secure by using the private and protected methods. These come in handy when you're writing Ruby as part of a group or team, and while they don't completely prevent other programmers from using methods they shouldn't, they can help your teammates understand which methods they can rely on and which ones are still "under construction." You can read more about the public and protected methods in the Ruby docs: *http://www.ruby-doc.org/core-2.0.0/Module.html#method-i-private*.

Handling exceptions   Every now and then, we saw our Ruby code throw an error. Usually I explained why it happened and we went on our merry way, but if you think about it, that's not always the best way to do things. Sometimes when an error (also called an *exception*) happens, we want to do something about it, like set a default value or print a message to the screen. Handling exceptions in Ruby is called—you guessed it—*exception handling*, and if you want to learn more about it, you can read Avdi Grimm's *Exceptional Ruby* (*http://exceptionalruby.com/*).

Reflection/metaprogramming   Remember when we talked about file I/O, we saw it was possible to write Ruby code that writes Ruby code? This means that Ruby has the ability to look at its own code and change it! The inward-looking part is called *reflection*, and the ability for Ruby to change its own programming is called *metaprogramming*. This is some of the hardest Ruby code to write, but if you're feeling up to it, you can learn all about it from Paolo Perrotta's book *Metaprogramming Ruby*.

Debugging   We talked a little bit about fixing errors in our code, but we didn't talk about writing tests for it or *debugging* (that is, fixing) it in a systematic way. Writing tests to prove your code is correct and becoming good at debugging it are very important skills for any programmer to have. If you're interested in learning more about both, you can read about the built-in Ruby testing library, MiniTest, in the Ruby documentation at *http://ruby-doc.org/stdlib-1.9.3/libdoc/minitest/spec/rdoc/ MiniTest/Spec.html*. If you're feeling particularly adventurous, you can read about my favorite testing library, RSpec, at *http:// rspec.info/*.

Threads and processes   In all our Ruby programs, we really only did one thing at time: we'd set a variable and then use it, or maybe we'd iterate over an array and print each item to the screen. We never really did two things at *exactly* the same time. With Ruby threads and processes, it's possible to do two things at once! As you might imagine, juggling multiple things at once is many times harder than handling just one process at a time, so learning to use Ruby threads and processes takes some practice. If you want to learn more, you can read Jesse Storimer's *Working with Ruby Threads* (*http://www.jstorimer .com/products/working-with-ruby-threads/*). Careful—this one's really advanced!

Creating websites   Finally, while we did talk about Ruby web servers like WEBrick, we didn't talk much about creating entire websites with Ruby. You may have heard of Ruby on Rails (I mentioned it when describing Railscasts on page 306), which is a big library of code made up of many gems that helps make writing websites with Ruby easier. It's a good way to build web-sites and very popular, but sometimes newer Ruby programmers have trouble understanding all the things it does and decisions that went into making it. If you want to make websites with Ruby, you might want to start with a smaller, simpler program (and one of my favorites) called *Sinatra*. You can find it online at *http://www.sinatrarb.com/*.

I admit it: I've been dragging my feet. I don't want the book to end! But alas, I've dispensed all my Ruby wisdom. Now you know everything I know, plus you've got all the smarts and experience of the King, the Queen, Ruben, Scarlet, and all of their friends combined. I knew you could do it! I believed in you from the start. So even if the book has to end, at least it ends with me being right!

When you close this book, I want you to do one thing: fire up your own personal Computing Contraption and write yourself a Ruby program. It can do anything you want, big or small, silly or serious. Don't worry if it breaks! The only way we learn is by writing programs and breaking them and fixing them and making them better, so it's perfectly okay if your program breaks or doesn't do what you want at first. You're writing stories and poems for a machine, and the biggest part of the adventure isn't having a finished, perfectly working program—it's all the crazy things that happen along the way.

So go! Go write the best program you can, and have *fun*. I'll be seeing you.

Installing Ruby on Mac and Linux

Installing on Mac

New Macs ship with Ruby 2.0 already installed, so if you're here, you're likely using an older Mac that has Ruby 1.8.7. Not to worry! We'll get you upgraded in a jiffy.

Open up your terminal and type the following code. (The $ just shows you where to start typing—don't type the $!) This will install a tool called RVM (Ruby Version Manager) as well as Ruby 2.0.

```
$ \curl -L https://get.rvm.io | bash -s stable --ruby=2.0.0
--auto-dotfiles
```

Once you do this, you'll see a whole bunch of text pop up to tell you that your computer is downloading Ruby. When it's all done, close your terminal, reopen it, and enter `ruby -v`. You should see your computer print a response with `ruby 2.0.0` in it!

If your Ruby version still isn't Ruby 2.0, you can try install-
ing it using the Homebrew package manager. First, install
Homebrew:

```
$ ruby -e "$(curl -fsSL https://raw.github.com/Homebrew/homebrew/go/
install)"
```

Once that command completes successfully, you can simply
type this:

```
$ brew install ruby
```

At the time of this writing, Homebrew automatically installs
Ruby 2.1.3. This is just a slightly newer version than Ruby 2.0,
and it will work with the code examples in this book.

Installing on Linux

Open up your terminal and type the following code. (The $ just
shows you where to start typing—don't type the $!) This will
install a tool called RVM (Ruby Version Manager) as well as
Ruby 2.0.

```
$ \curl -L https://get.rvm.io | bash -s stable --ruby=2.0.0 --auto-
dotfiles
```

Once you do this, you'll see a whole bunch of text pop up to
tell you that your computer is downloading Ruby. When it's
all done, close your terminal, reopen it, and enter ruby -v. You
should see your computer print a response with ruby 2.0.0 in it!

If you get an error or your computer tells you that Ruby isn't
installed, grab your trusty adult and check out the Ruby installation page at *https://www.ruby-lang.org/en/installation/*. There
may be a recent package designed especially for your version of
Linux, and it may be easier to use that package to install Ruby,
rather than using RVM. You can also ask your adult to go on
IRC and get help from the folks in the #ruby channel.

B

TROUBLE-shooting

When running your Ruby scripts or using IRB, you may run into some common errors. I've listed a few of them here, along with tips for fixing them!

ERRORS RUNNING RUBY SCRIPTS

There are two common errors that you might see when running Ruby scripts from the command line: "command not found" and "no such file or directory." Here are some suggestions for how to resolve them.

Command Not Found

If you're running a Ruby script and you get some output that looks like this:

```
$: command not found
```

it probably means you accidentally typed a $ before your `ruby` command. I use the $ symbol to show you that you're running a Ruby script from the command line with a filename (like `ruby my_fancy_script.rb`); you shouldn't type the $ itself!

No Such File or Directory

If you get an error that looks like this:

```
No such file or directory -- some_filename.rb (LoadError)
```

it means you tried to run `ruby some_filename.rb`, but that file didn't exist in the folder you're currently in.

To fix this, first make sure you're in the folder where you saved your Ruby script. You can change from one folder to another using the `cd` command (for "change directory"). See "Creating Your First Script" on page 12 for help using the `cd` command.

If you're in the correct folder and your command still gives you an error, double-check the spelling of your file! (I mistype the names of Ruby files all the time.)

ERRORS Using IRB

There are a few common errors that you might see when using IRB. Here's how to fix them, along with some other handy tips for fixing typos and mistakes.

Undefined Local Variable or Method

If you try to call a method in IRB and get something like this:

```
NameError: undefined local variable or method `some_method_name' for
main:Object
```

it means you tried to use a method that Ruby doesn't know about. When you exit and restart IRB, Ruby forgets everything you were previously doing—so if you defined a method, exited IRB, and started it again, you'll need to redefine that method to keep using it. (See "Defining Your Own Methods" on page 114 if you need a refresher on how to define methods.) If your method is from a file, make sure you load that file using the command load 'your_file.rb', and if all else fails, double-check that you've spelled your method name correctly.

Syntax Error

If you get an error that looks like this:

```
SyntaxError: (irb):1: syntax error, unexpected 'something_here'
```

it means you wrote Ruby code that's not quite right, and IRB doesn't know what to do with it. Double-check your code for tiny errors, like typos, missing commas between elements in arrays, or missing hash rockets (=>) or colons in hashes.

Can't Convert nil into String

If you get an error like this:

```
TypeError: can't convert nil into String
```

it means you tried to do something with one Ruby type (like a string, integer, or nil), but Ruby expected a different type. This often happens when something is nil and you don't know it; if you see this error, try putsing out the values of all your variables to make sure each one is the type of thing (string, integer, array, and so on) that you expect! (See "Getting to Know IRB" on page 10 for help with the puts command and "A Bit More About Variables" on page 22 for a refresher on the types of variables.)

you weRe Saying . . . ?

From time to time, you might see Ruby print something like this:

```
...?
```

This means that Ruby expects you to "finish your thought." Usually it means you pressed ENTER without closing a string, or maybe the last thing you typed was a + or - sign. All you need to do is finish that thought—complete the expression you started to type, close the string or array you opened, or whatever it is Ruby is waiting for—and you'll be all set. For example:

```
>> 1 +
...? 2
=> 3
```

If you have no idea what Ruby is waiting for, or you simply mistyped and want to start over, you can press CTRL-C to tell IRB not to wait for you. You'll get your regular IRB prompt back and can continue from there. (For more about CTRL-C, see "Investigating the Kingdom's Web Server" on page 290.)

cleaR the ScReen

Sometimes you'll type a whole bunch in IRB and will want to clear the screen. You can do this in several ways, depending on which operating system you're using. On a Mac, you can press ⌘-K or CTRL-L, or you can type system 'clear' into IRB and then press ENTER. If you're using Linux, typing CTRL-L or entering system 'clear' should work. If you're using Windows, typing CTRL-L or entering system 'cls' (not 'clear'!) should do the trick.

Go Back to a Previous Command

If at any point you want to go back to a previous command you typed into IRB, just hit the up arrow on your keyboard! This is great if you just cleared the screen and then realize you need to retype a command, or if you mistyped a command and want to try again without retyping everything you just did.

Look It Up!

Finally, if you ever see an error that you don't know how to handle, go ahead and search for it on the Internet (after you get your local adult's permission!). Everyone gets errors, so it's likely that someone else has already figured out how to handle any error you might run into. Even the best programmers look up things they don't know on a daily basis. The more comfortable you get hunting for answers when you're stuck, the happier and more productive you'll be when writing Ruby.

Index

Ruby Wizardry is set in Century Schoolbook, TheSansMono Condensed, Unearthed BB, and Housearama Kingpin. The book was printed and bound by Edwards Brothers Malloy in Ann Arbor, Michigan. The paper is 60# Husky Opaque, which is certified by the Sustainable Forestry Initiative (SFI).

The book uses a RepKover binding, in which the pages are bound together with a cold-set, flexible glue and the first and last pages of the resulting book block are attached to the cover with tape. The cover is not actually glued to the book's spine, and when open, the book lies flat and the spine doesn't crack.

UPDATES

Visit *http://nostarch.com/rubywizardry/* for updates, errata, and other information.

MORE SMART BOOKS FOR CURIOUS KIDS!

JAVASCRIPT FOR KIDS
A Playful Introduction to Programming
by NICK MORGAN
DECEMBER 2014, 336 PP., $34.95
ISBN 978-1-59327-408-5
full color

LAUREN IPSUM
A Story About Computer Science and Other Improbable Things
by CARLOS BUENO
DECEMBER 2014, 192 PP., $16.95
ISBN 978-1-59327-574-7
full color

PYTHON FOR KIDS
A Playful Introduction to Programming
by JASON BRIGGS
DECEMBER 2012, 344 PP., $34.95
ISBN 978-1-59327-407-8
full color

LEARN TO PROGRAM WITH SCRATCH
A Visual Introduction to Programming with Games, Art, Science, and Math
by MAJED MARJI
FEBRUARY 2014, 288 PP., $34.95
ISBN 978-1-59327-543-3
full color

RAILS CRASH COURSE
A No-Nonsense Guide to Rails Development
by ANTHONY LEWIS
OCTOBER 2014, 296 PP., $34.95
ISBN 978-1-59327-572-3

THE MANGA GUIDE™ TO DATABASES
by MANA TAKAHASHI, SHOKO AZUMA, *and* TREND-PRO CO., LTD.
JANUARY 2009, 224 PP., $19.95
ISBN 978-1-59327-190-9

800.420.7240 or 415.863.9900 | sales@nostarch.com | www.nostarch.com

TOMARE!

止まれ
[STOP!]

You're going the wrong way!

Manga is a completely different type of reading experience.

To start at the beginning, go to the end!

That's right! Authentic manga is read the traditional Japanese way—from right to left, exactly the opposite of how American books are read. It's easy to follow: Just go to the other end of the book and read each page—and each panel—from right side to left side, starting at the top right. Now you're experiencing manga as it was meant to be!

CONTENTS

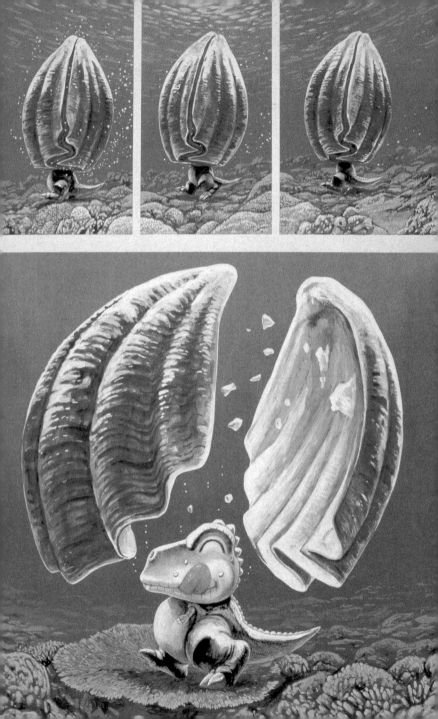

Chapter 5
Gon Plays with a Giant Shark.

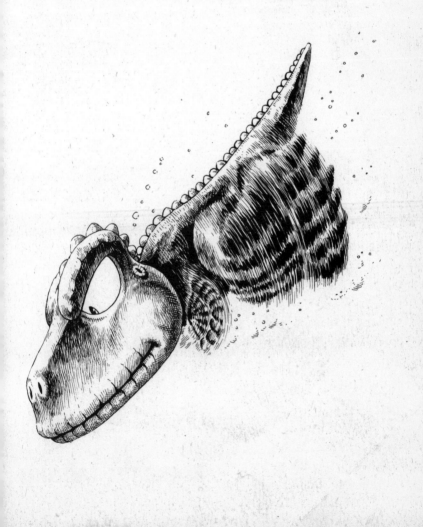

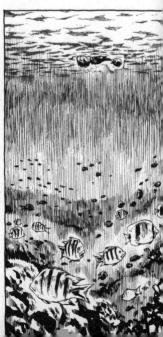

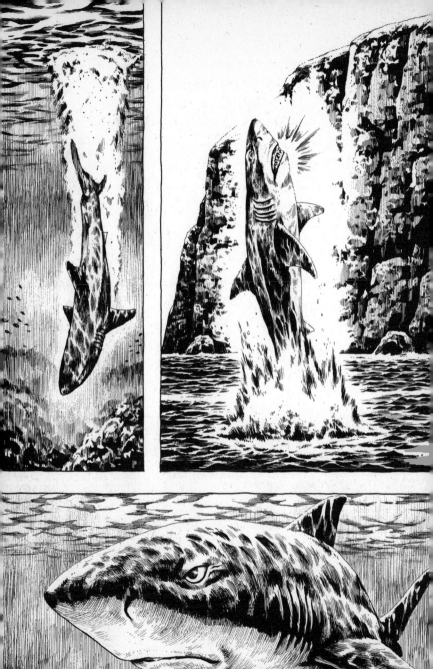

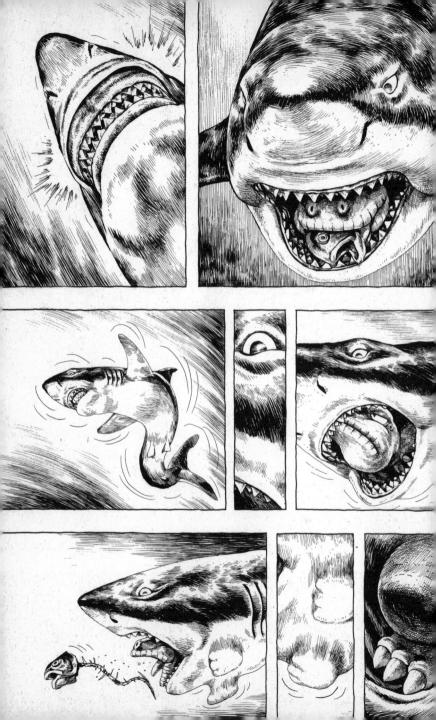

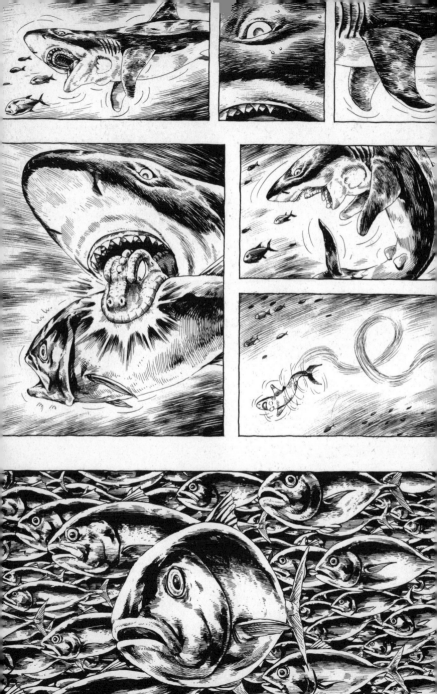

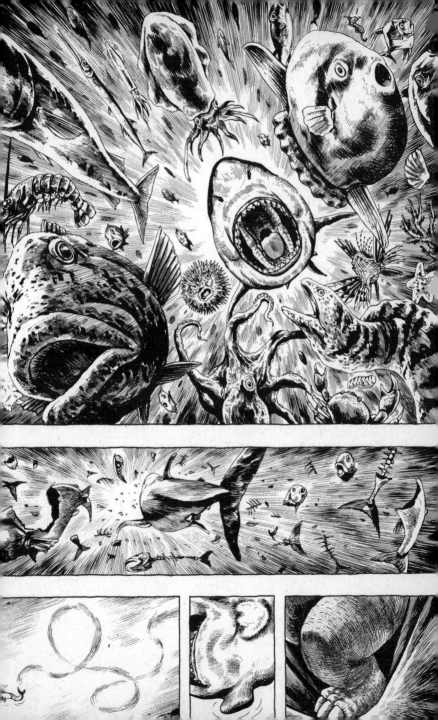

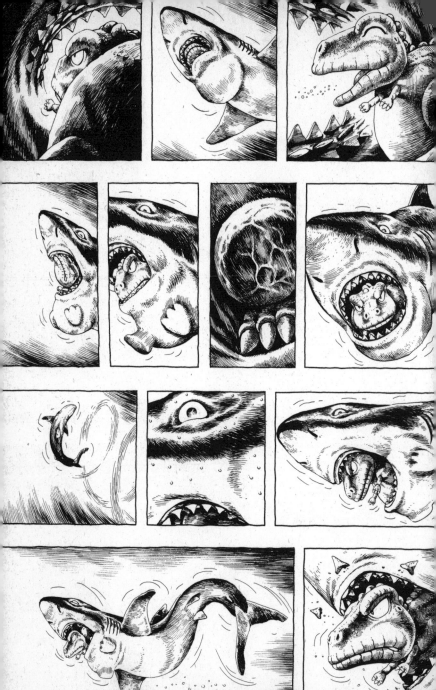

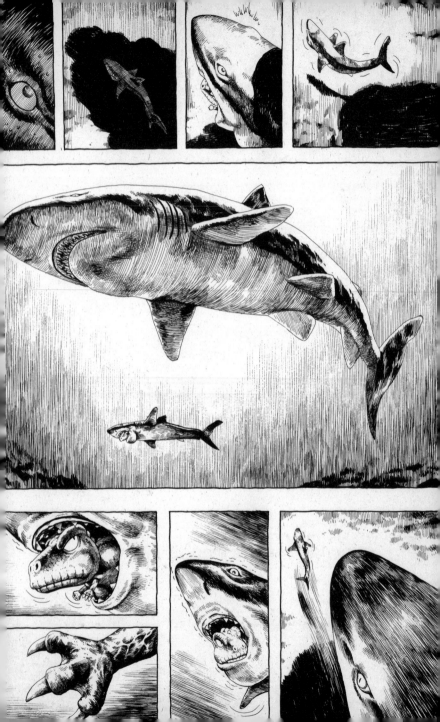

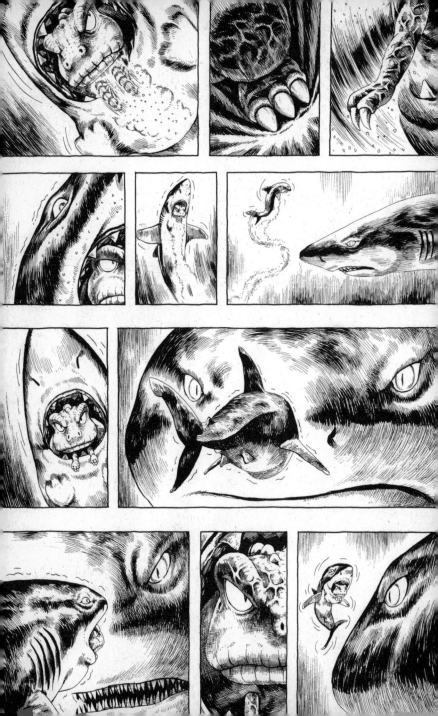

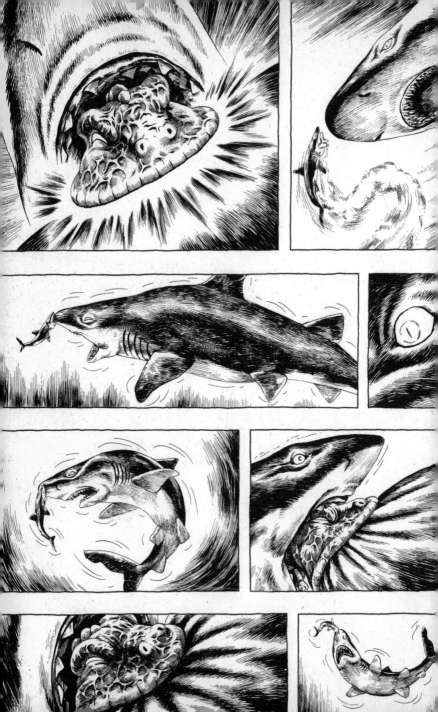

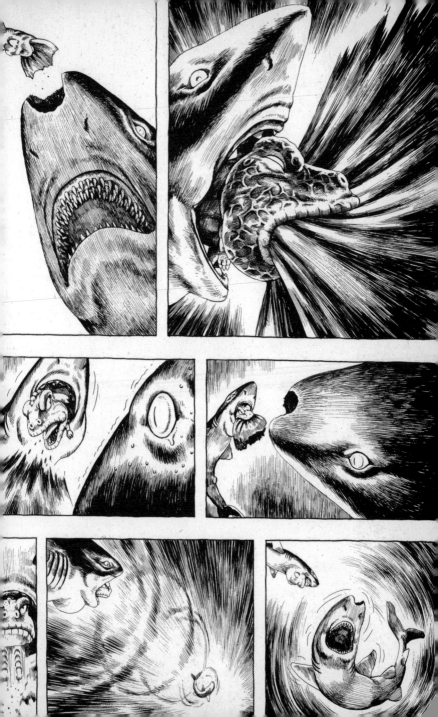

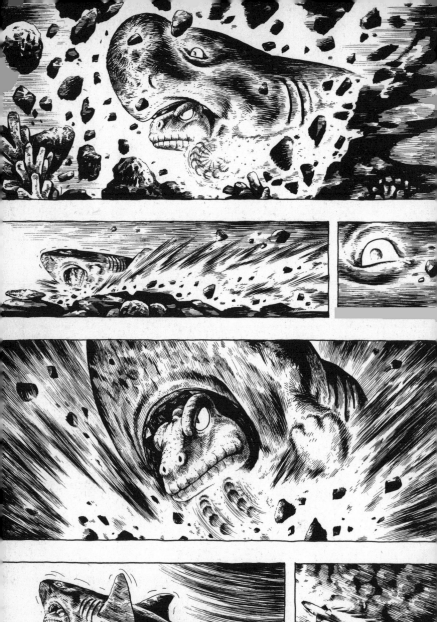

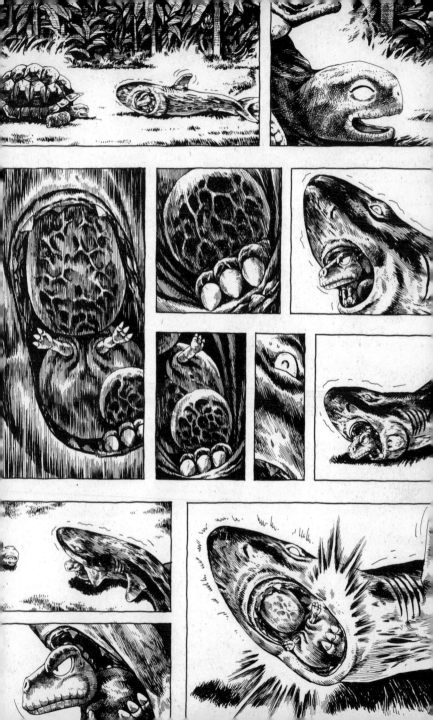

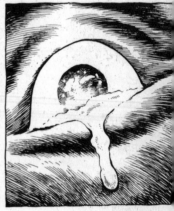

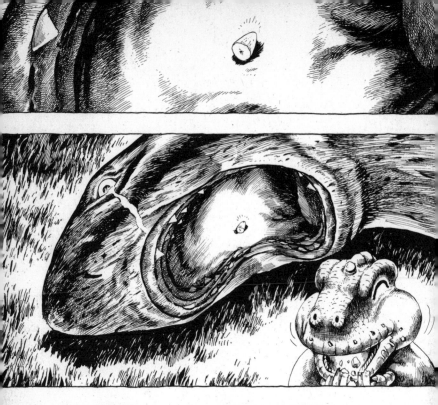

Giant Tortoise

Sand Giant Tiger Shark

Chapter 6
Gon Struggles Against a Tick.

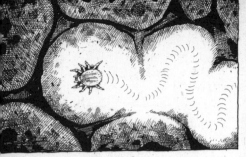

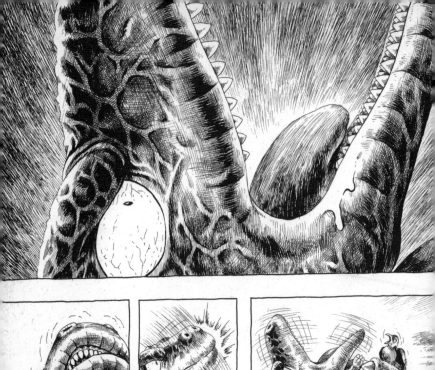

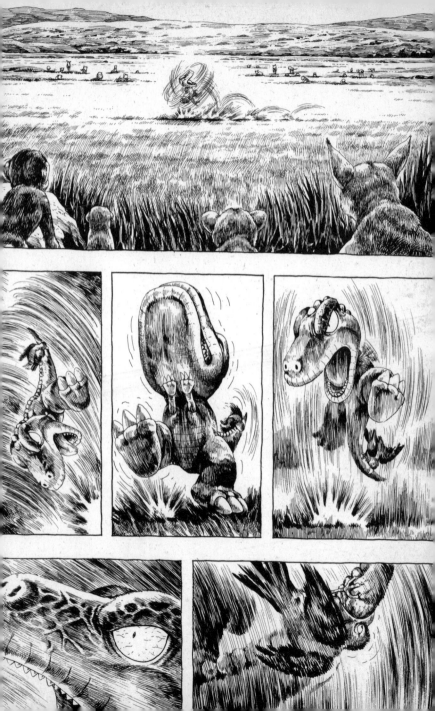

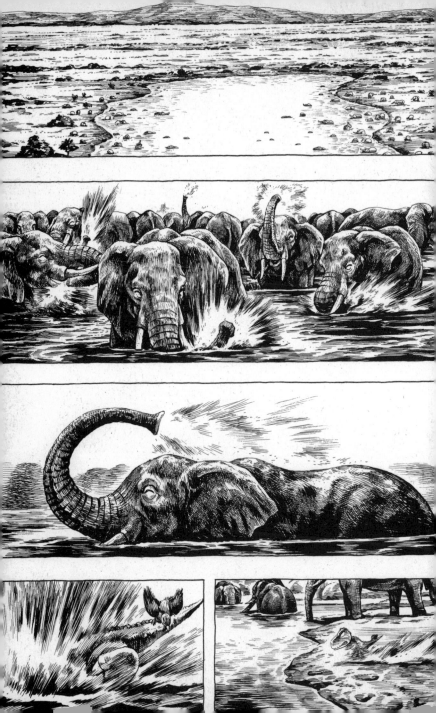

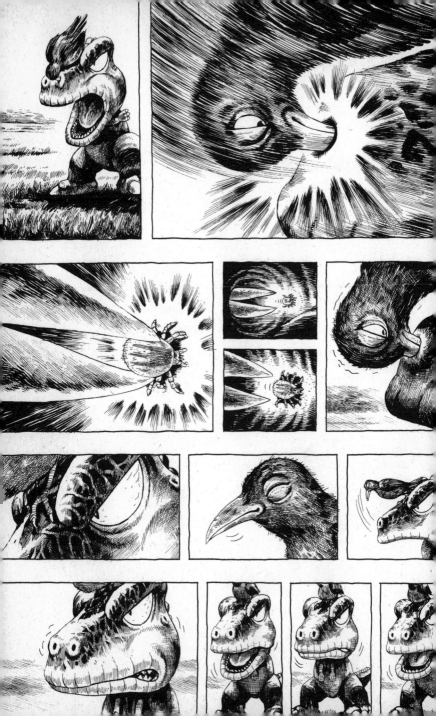

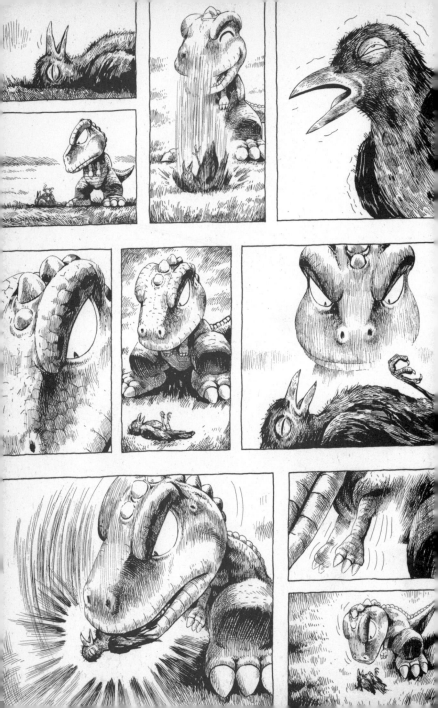

African Buffalo

Hard Tick

Warthog

Savanna Baboon

African Elephant

South African Hedgehog

Chapter 7
Gon Gets Angry at the Forest.

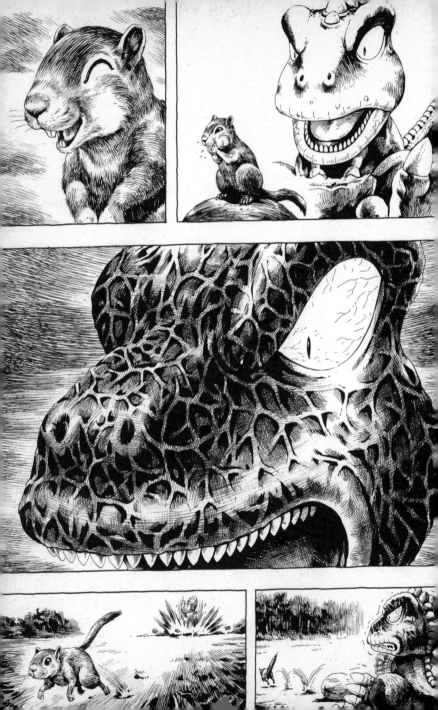

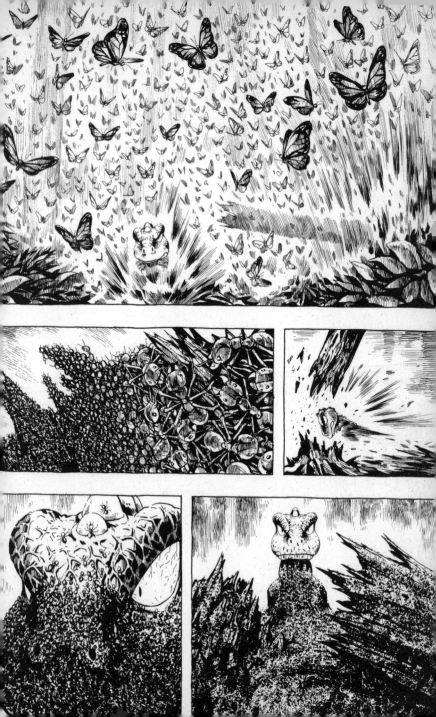

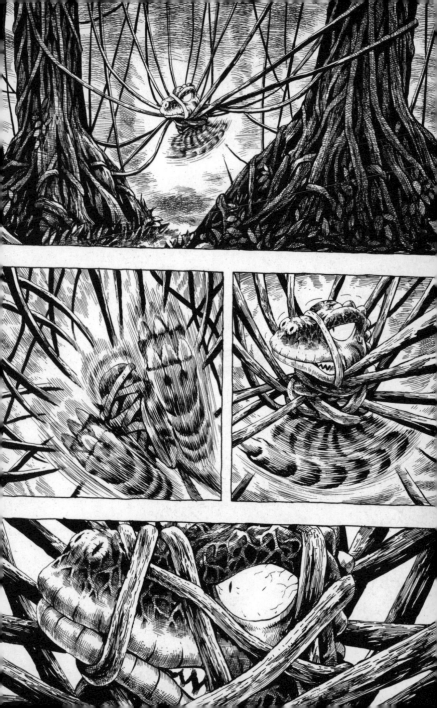

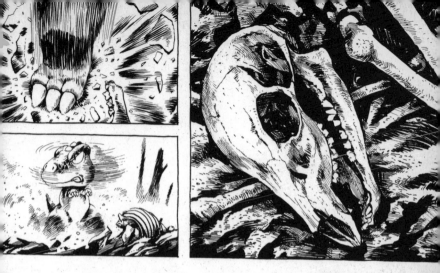

Squirrel Monkey

Tamandua

Tarantula

Ocelot

Green Anaconda

Three-toed Sloth

Chapter 8
Gon Lives with Penguins.

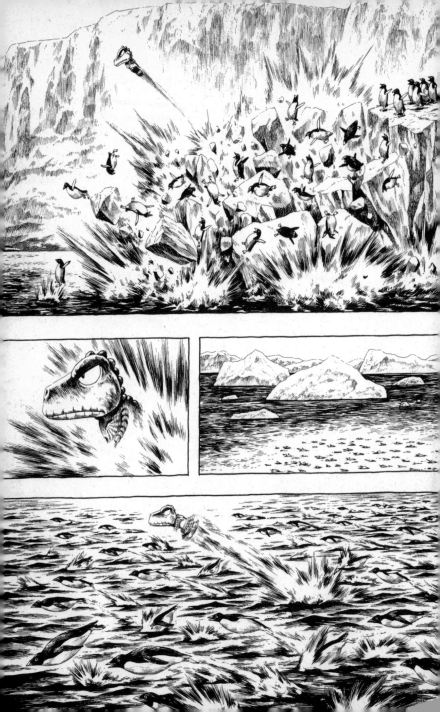

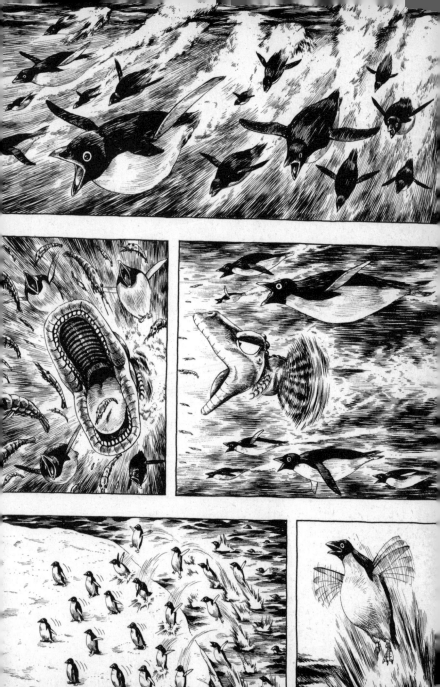

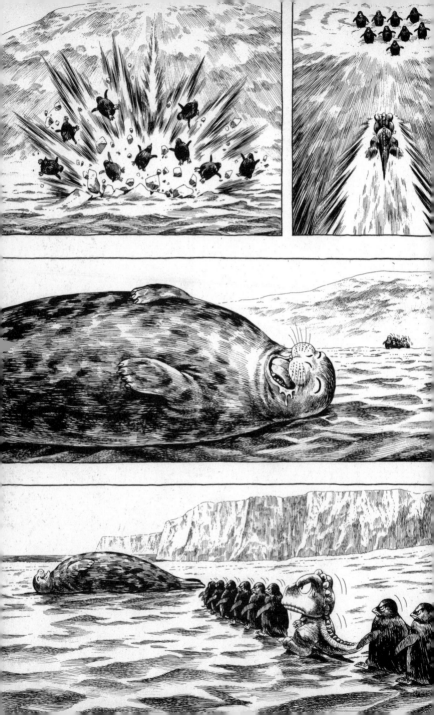

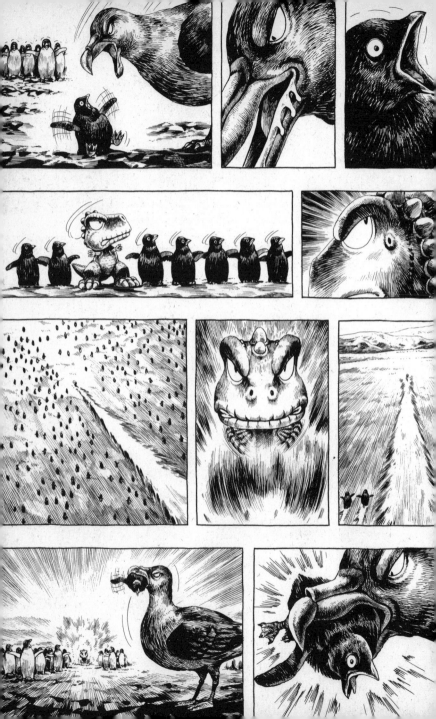

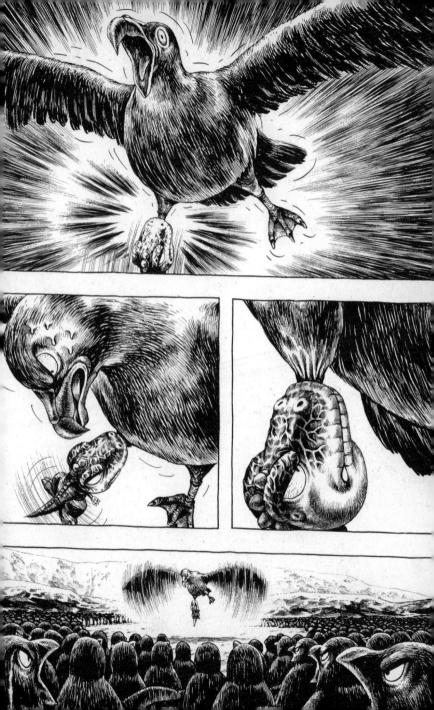

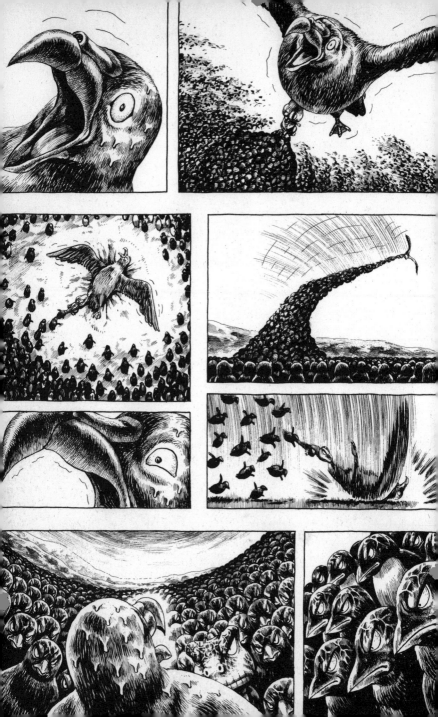

Southern Giant Petrel

Weddell Seal

To Be Continued!

White Shark

Yellow-billed Oxpecker

Pygmy Squirrel

Adelie Penguin

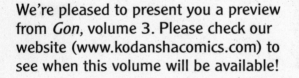

We're pleased to present you a preview from *Gon*, volume 3. Please check our website (www.kodanshacomics.com) to see when this volume will be available!

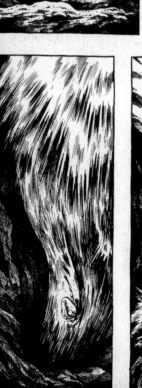